RELIGIONS OF MAN

Dr Whiting is the author of a number of books, research papers, slide sets and simulation games—he may be contacted through the publishers.

RELIGIONS OF MAN

J R S Whiting
MA DLitt FRHistS Dip Educ
King's School, Gloucester

STANLEY THORNES (PUBLISHERS) LTD

First published 1983
Reprinted 1983 with minor corrections
Reprinted 1984

British Library Cataloguing in Publication Data
Whiting, J. R. S.
  Religions of man.
  1. Religions
  I. Title
  200   BL80.2
  ISBN 0-85950-398-4

Typeset by Quadraset Ltd, Combe End, Radstock, Bath, Avon BA3 3AN
Printed and bound in Great Britain at The Pitman Press, Bath

RELIGIONS OF MAN

CONTENTS

FOREWORD

by
Professor John Bowker, University of Lancaster

It's hard to imagine any subject more important to study and understand than Religion. More important than Maths? or French? or Physics? or Engineering? Well, let's at least say that it is equally important, though maybe for different reasons.

There are three main reasons why it is so essential to understand and appreciate what religions are, and why they matter so much. The first is that religions are extremely dangerous. Think of all the evil and vicious things which have been done in the name of Religion: people have been tortured and burned alive; holy wars and crusades have been fought; whole groups of people have been kept in subordination and subjection—outcastes, slaves, women in relation to men. And think also of the many difficult and apparently insoluble problems in the world at the present time which have a religious part to them: Northern Ireland, the Middle East, the apartheid system in South Africa, the division between communist countries and others. It is not the case that religion *alone* creates those problems, but it is certainly true that religion has a part to play in them. If we want to live in a more peaceful world, it is important that we understand what there is about Religion which makes believers so passionate in their commitments and in their divisions from each other.

But there is a second reason why it is wise to study and understand Religion: religious belief has been the inspiration, not only of great violence and hatred, but also of almost all of mankind's greatest achievements, in art, poetry, music, architecture, spiritual exploration and discovery. The creative power of Religion is enormous in all parts of the world. And this is still true. To take just one example, we have just lived through one of the greatest ages of Christian poetry that has occurred in the whole history of Christianity. Of course, we are so close to it that it is hard to see it; but it is in fact the case that the last hundred years have seen an almost miraculous flowering of Christian vision, and also of Christians grappling with the reality of evil. So Religion is not disappearing or fading away. It is changing its forms of appearance and expression, but it remains a vital and creative force in many lives. Indeed, it is still the case that the majority of people alive on the planet today are committed to some form of religious belief.

And that leads to a third reason why it is so important to study and understand Religion. Religions are concerned with what may ultimately and in the end—and for ever—be the case. If it *is* the case that your life can find its rest in God and can abide in Him/Her for ever, it is obvious that the issues which religions set before us are a great deal more important than a choice between cornflakes and porridge for breakfast. Of course, it may be that what religions claim is false—it may be that there is no reality correctly described as God in whom we can find our eternal life. But we can scarcely know whether that is so before we make some exploration ourselves.

And that is the key note of this book—exploration. Dr Whiting is not attempting to persuade us into one particular path, but is, rather, helping us to understand some of the important paths of exploration which others have pioneered before us. What is certain is that the exploration *matters*, because the real question that is being asked is, not which religion is true, but what is true *about you*. By virtue of the fact that we are born, we know that we have many capabilities: we know that we are capable of eating, walking, talking, drinking; we know that we are capable of experiencing chemical and electrical activity in the brain which we can identify as love, hate, hope, envy, compassion, hatred; we know also that we are capable of entering into even further states of experience which transcend even such emotions as love—and religions describe what those states are and the ways in which you can enter into them; and it is equally widely reported (by those who have lived before us and who are living now) that we are also capable of entering into a union with God. We do not have to take up these possibilities if we do not wish to do so; but religions remind us that they are there. And they remind us also that the exploration of what we are, and of what we are capable of being and becoming, may take us into discoveries which endure even through and beyond the circumstance of death.

So this book is not asking of you, or even expecting, that you should be committed to one religion or another; but rather that you should be alive to the whole possibility of what it may mean to be human. The important thing to remember, as you follow or join in this exploration, is that these issues and possibilities *matter*: they matter greatly to those who have embarked on them and have made important and significant discoveries. Dr Whiting holds out the hope, in his conclusion, that perhaps all religions are different roads leading to the same truth. That may be so, but we cannot be sure of it. All roads do not necessarily lead to London simply because they are roads. Some lead to more exciting destinations like Wolverhampton, Newcastle and Timbuctoo. What this means is that religions are not necessarily or automatically true, simply because they are religions. If it *is* possible to be religiously right, it must also be possible to be religiously wrong. This means that there *are* issues of truth and choice in the religious exploration. And that in itself is a reason why religions matter so much to those who believe them.

So the study of Religion will take you into strange and sometimes astonishing new worlds. You will find this book a good guide, not least because it asks you sharp and clear questions on the way. It is only the beginning of the journey—buying the ticket at the ticket office and looking at the timetable before setting out on the journey yourself, if you wish to do so. But if you want to understand the complicated and dangerous world in which you are living, then you have shown great sense and wisdom in deciding to include Religion in the subjects that you study.

PREFACE

Religion is a vast topic and no one book can cover all its many aspects. This particular book has been written with GCE and CSE very much in mind. I hope, however, that it will prove useful beyond the requirements of the present examinations. In particular, I have included Eastern religions which are not normally covered in textbooks (Shintoism, Taoism and Buddhism) but which have many millions of adherents, some of whom live in Britain. Obviously it has not been possible to include all religions, so Zoroastrianism and Jainism, for example, have been left out (not to mention many modern cults such as Jehovah's Witnesses and Rastafarianism). Inevitably, too, some aspects of religion have been passed over briefly—the monastic tradition of Christianity, for example.

What I have tried to do is present eight religions objectively and sympathetically. Although the book contains a number of questions for examinees, there are many more questions inviting readers to get inside the shoes of other people with different beliefs. With a society that is increasingly multiracial there is a need for better understanding all round.

The structure of the book by topics is designed to produce a closer comparison of the religions concerned than would be possible if they were dealt with separately. However, the chapters have been subdivided religion by religion so that the reader can follow the study of one religion from beginning to end without difficulty, if so desired.

Three possible ways of using the book are suggested:

(a) By topics, as arranged chapter by chapter.

(b) By religions, taking religions in turn, chapter by chapter.

(c) By a combination of religions and topics, starting with Chapter 1, and then by religions for Chapters 2 and 3, ending with the remaining chapters by topics. This might be found to be a better way of ensuring that the basics of each religion were clear at the outset.

The index is also a glossary for quick reference to technical terms. It also indicates which religions are referred to in each case.

Numerous quotations from religious books have been given, as it is often difficult to get such books in translation form. Some biblical quotations have simply been given by chapter and verse to save space, as there should be no difficulty in obtaining a Bible. For students not used to reading the Bible, the Living Bible version may prove to be the easiest to follow, and many quotations are taken from that version.

Although the book has been written primarily for schools and colleges I hope that it may also prove beneficial to those outside, whether studying in groups or as individuals.

My thanks are due to the following who kindly supplied me with material, answered queries or checked the typescript or helped in other ways: Salvation Army Information Services; Hindu Centre, London; London Buddhist Centre; R El-Droubie, Minaret House, Croydon; Sikh Missionary Society; Sikh Cultural Society of Great Britain; J H Pennington; Bish Chaudhuri; Rev J B P J Hadfield; Rev J R Harwood; P Leung Kwong Ha; Clive Lawton of the Board of Deputies of British Jews; Salvation Army Gloucester Corps; Society of Friends, Gloucester; Rev R J Stephens; Stanley Rosenthal (British School of Ordinary Taoist Zen); Professor John Bowker and Dr Stewart McFarlane, Department of Religious Studies, Lancaster University. Special thanks are also due to Professor Bowker for his foreword.

Any writer of a textbook will be indebted to other writers, too numerous to recall. However, I must mention the help received from reading *Death and Eternal Life* by John Hick and *The Religious Experience of Mankind* by Ninian Smart. A lecture by Bishop Kenneth Cragg in Cheltenham elucidated the relationship between Christianity and Islam. Without the help of all these good people the book would have remained uncompleted.

J R S Whiting

Note on the first reprint

Many thanks are due to those who have pointed out errors in the text. Everything has been done to correct these.

JRSW

1.
WHAT IS RELIGION?

You, like everyone else, have needs which crave to be fulfilled. Hunger and thirst are your two most basic needs. But you also long for the love and care your parents and friends can give you. If your needs are very great, you, and your friends and relatives, may be hard-pressed to find the answers or supply the help you are looking for. Life can produce great sorrows—incurable diseases or deformities; loneliness; poverty. Overwhelming forces, such as war, famine or homelessness, may afflict you. The death of a loved one can bring grief to you.

Why is life so unfair? When will suffering end? How can I feel loved? How can I cope with fear or loneliness? What can I do if I have done something wrong? Do I really matter in such a big universe? What will make me really happy?

Too often life seems to be pointless. Of course it is not always so —it can be exciting, varied and fulfilling. Then arises the question of whom ought you to thank for health, love, happiness and success?

1. *Select three of the questions listed in the second paragraph which you think are the most important and say why you have chosen them. Why is it difficult to answer them? Can you think of any more questions?*

Your human needs and reactions are also religious ones. If the doctor cannot cure your illness, you can seek the help of some greater power we call God. Lonely, you can turn to God for comfort. Afflicted by some disaster you can look to Him for protection, help and guidance.

When we are perplexed about what we should do—about a career step or how far to go in a relationship with a close friend—we seek assurance by looking for the *truth*. Rules of behaviour for the good of all are laid down by all religions. Upset at death, we turn in our grief to the hope that God has arranged another life beyond this one. If a further life exists, it will help us to understand that our present life will be resolved and rewarded later on.

No matter where or when Man has lived, his religious needs have always been the same:

- Strength, to bear life's sorrows
- Protection, to survive
- Assurance, in time of doubt
- Faith, to soothe his conscience
- Conviction, to face life's dangers
- Sustaining courage, to cope with fear and loneliness.

But he also needs to know the very purpose of his existence on earth. Whichever way you look at it, the existence of anything is a mystery. Why on earth does anything exist? Indeed, why in the universe does anything exist? Why does the universe itself exist? Is there some purpose behind it?

All of these are hard questions. Science can help us to understand the causes of things such as diseases or how to reach the moon, but when we ask *why* anything exists at all we may well feel baffled.

Some people believe that only the material (atoms, etc.) in the universe exists. According to them, if we explain how this works we have explained all there is to explain. Even emotions of love and hate could be explained in terms of physics if we could work out all the equations. 'Life' is a complicated system but animals are just rather special machines. Man is an animal, which is just an extra-special machine.

2.   *In what ways are you like a machine?*

3.   *Are people really robots?*

People who hold these views are often called materialists. Some of them would call themselves atheists. The word 'atheist' means 'one who does not believe God is real'. An agnostic is someone who says we cannot tell whether God is real or not. Some people who reject the idea of God call themselves humanists. They say that humans have no need to worship and that Man is self-sufficient. In contrast to atheists and humanists, many people have had a *religious* view of the world.

The great religions of the world have grown up (or been revealed to mankind by God) over many centuries. Not only do they seek to supply answers and aids for us, but they also show us how to give thanks and praise for all that we have and enjoy. At different times in our lives we all need help, or want to express our joy and thanks, or want to try and solve the mystery of existence. It is worthwhile learning from the experience of millions of others by studying these religions.

When you were small and were learning to walk you often needed urgent assistance. Quickly you reached out for your parents' hands. This was because you had faith, or belief, in their ability to help you. Without this belief you would not have made the effort to grab their hands, for it would have been a pointless gesture.

We all have beliefs, or faith, in something, or somebody. It is natural to do so. We could not cope with life if we did not.

Belief in the ability of someone to help you may make all the difference. If you are seriously ill and you have faith in your doctor, your morale will improve and this will aid his skill. If you are to look to a greater power, God, then you will have to be prepared to make an effort to believe in Him to start with, just as you did in your doctor.

People's beliefs change as their knowledge increases. Twentieth-century Man believed that travel to the moon was possible and he got there, whereas nineteenth-century Man did not have that belief. Twentieth-century Man believes in germs, whereas early nineteenth-century Man did not. Before Charles Darwin explained his theory of evolution, people believed that the story of Adam and Eve was literally true. People's beliefs in superhuman power have changed too.

Primitive Man was being sensible when he believed there were unseen 'spirit' powers at work causing earthquakes or floods. Seeing an unusual object or some display of the powers of nature, he tended to be fascinated and overwhelmed. This made him worship the object or powerful force so long as it impressed him. In this way he 'created' gods in his mind for a while—'momentary gods'. He used his imagination to make up poetic stories about these spirits and why they behaved as they did. These myths served to make them even more real to him. He concluded that it would be wise to please them, for clearly a volcano's explosion or a drought showed they could get angry. Surrounded and often threatened by forces which he seldom understood, Man tried to penetrate the mystery of life.

Some came to believe that there were gods controlling specific parts of nature—for example, the rain, crops, thunder and so on. These can be thought of as 'nature gods'. Because primitive Man was so dependent on nature which could often be hostile, he devised ways to keep these gods happy.

Medicine men (shamans) developed charms, rituals and sacrifices to satisfy them in the hopes that the tribe would be protected and get the rain its crops needed. Today we have come to know so much more about the earth that these beliefs seem very primitive. But if you stand on top of a mountain and survey the view or look at the raging of the sea or the setting sun on a peaceful scene, you can still grasp that sense of awe at the wonders of nature which primitive Man felt. We can stand in awe too when the scientists explain to us the gigantic scope of the universe or the microscopic atoms that compose the simple things around us. A sense of awe is still part of our life. Who made all this? Who could have designed it all on such a gigantic and such a minute scale and built in an evolutionary pattern of such complexity? Why was it all made? Will it go on for ever? What is the meaning of life? What is Man's place in the universe?

We get the idea of 'the holy' or holiness—that extra-special something, a kind of covering or atmosphere, which is above and beyond mere worldly things and ways: 'Holy, holy, Lord God Almighty . . .'. 'God' is a word people use to describe the Being or creative energy who created the universe. It is said that such a Being must know everything and have unlimited power. In comparison we seem minute and unimportant. It would be surprising if we could know all about God. But we can have some ideas about Him. We might find our ideas agree with those of someone living on the other side of the world or we might not. If we pool our ideas and experiences we are bound to learn something. That is the purpose of this book.

Questions to bear in mind as you read on are: Who am I? What am I? Is there a God? What is God like? What is real? What is reality? Is there a purpose in living? Is there an after life? What is evil? What causes things to happen the way they do? What is the good life? What is true happiness? Is there such a thing as bad luck? Where did the world come from and where is it going?

4. *Select three questions from those listed above which you think are important, and say why you have chosen them.*

5. *What characteristics have these questions in common?*

Obviously the knowledge we acquire over the centuries makes us re-think our beliefs. Modern medical knowledge makes the medicine man's magic unnecessary and the contraceptive pill has challenged the traditional codes of sexual behaviour. Earthquakes can now be scientifically explained, whereas John Wesley in the eighteenth century saw them as God punishing the wicked. The Russian Communist astronaut Yuri Gagarin reported that he could not see God anywhere in outer space in 1961. Perhaps he thought Christians believed in an aged man on a throne surrounded by angels and the souls of the dead. If that is your idea of God, then you will soon find you must think again.

In spite of modern knowledge, we humans are still superstitious. You may take a lucky charm into the exam room, just as country folk in Hong Kong cross the road at the last minute so that evil spirits following them can be killed by the traffic, or Maltese bus drivers leave the driver's seat to St Christopher (the patron saint of travellers) and lean over to drive from the next seat.

Religions have to cater for all kinds of human needs and skills. They must answer the queries and challenges of the brainy and yet guide the simple-minded at the same time. They must supply encouragement and comfort. They usually provide a means by which believers can understand something of the Supreme Being and help them to make contact with the Being through prayer, ritual and service. They may devise a form of worship so that the worshippers feel they are doing the right thing and succeeding in conveying their thanks and praise to the Being. Many religions are a sophisticated communication system between earthly man and the Supreme Being. But religions also need to give behaviour rules for their followers if they are to live in fellowship.

6. *What challenges might a brainy person make to belief in God?*

7. *What comforts would someone look for in a religion?*

8. *Do you know of any religious rituals which could be described as sophisticated attempts to communicate with God?*

9. *What behaviour rules are essential for any religion?*

Religions inspire people with a creative urge. Music, pictures, sculpture, buildings and dances have been produced as a result of religious inspiration. Religions have dominated history—kings, politicians and soldiers have claimed that God supported their policies and actions. The sociologist and the psychologist can point to the important influence of religion in the lives of communities and individuals.

10. *List under these headings anything with religious inspiration behind it: (a) music, (b) pictures, (c) sculpture, (d) buildings, (e) dances.*

11. *Briefly describe incidents in history where (a) kings, (b) politicians, (c) soldiers have claimed God supported them in their policies or actions.*

So what are the basic ingredients of a religion? Consider this list.

(1) They look for the 'something else' or 'somebody' beyond the world of senses and scientific measurement. This 'something' or 'somebody' controls all.

(2) They have great figures, men of vision who seem to perceive the 'something else' more than other people.

(3) They all express themselves in the written word trying to encapsulate what they believe in.

(4) Each religion gives to its own people advice on how to behave and what to do to draw close to the 'something else' or 'somebody'.

(5) Religions are often practised by people coming together in common worship at special places.

(6) Religions often bring people together at special times for particular celebrations.

(7) All religions hold special funeral ceremonies and grapple with the problem of whether there is life after death.

In this book we shall be looking at each of these themes. Our journey will take us all round the world and we shall see how fascinating Man's response to the 'something else' actually is. We shall see too how important that response is to Man. For a religious person it is all-demanding. A person who believes in God feels called to serve and honour Him, often to the point of death.

2.
MEN, GODS AND HISTORY

Religions must begin in some way, at some time, but how and when? You will find that the answers will vary from religion to religion. The origins of Hinduism and Shintoism are now lost in the dim past, while Taoism was started by a legendary, mysterious figure called Lao-Tse. Judaism began with a well-off farmer called Abraham uprooting himself, while a rich prince started Buddhism by running away from home. Christianity and Islam were revealed through two men of humble origins, Jesus and Muhammad. The former is seen by his followers as the Son of God, while the latter claimed to be the bearer of God's word in the Koran. Sikhism was founded by the son of an army officer, Guru Nanak, who turned his back on his planned career. The time over which these eight religions began is approximately three thousand years: 1500 BC—AD 1500.

Although the racial, economic and social backgrounds of these holy men are different, they must have all possessed an inquiring mind and an ability to see to the heart of the great mysteries of life. They could see the truth and make sense of the meaning of life and could also do something else. They were able to explain and communicate what they had found to others. Those others would be able to see the truth for themselves, through prayers or ritual.

From then on it was up to their followers to organize their members into groups with rules, customs and buildings, together with systems for governing and money-raising. This development often led to arguments so that splinter groups were formed. Thus today a religion may have different sections in it.

What had these holy men discovered which they felt compelled to tell others about? Some were convinced that a multitude of gods and goddesses must exist. Obviously they would live something like human lives, even to the extent of showing human passions and squabbling amongst each other. To believe in many gods is called polytheism. Each god or goddess is in charge of running some part or aspect of the universe. Gods of rain, sun, battle and fortune are but a few of them.

Others argue there is only one God who controls everything. This belief is called monotheism. In this case the God must be all-powerful, all-knowing and absolutely perfect if He is to create and control the whole universe. He is likely to be just and possibly fierce, or He may be loving and caring. Not only will He rule the universe but He will lay down rules of behaviour for those who would serve Him. Although invisible, He will have some kind of personality which humans can understand and make contact with.

Buddhism is an exception to most religions because it argues that there is *no* God. Nevertheless, a way of life exists which one ought to follow if one wishes to find that truth.

It is now time to start on our world-wide journey to try to solve the mysteries of life and see if we can find the truth.

HINDUISM

Background. Hinduism dates back to 1500 BC in India and it has no single founder. The word 'Hindu' comes from the R. Indus, which in Sanskrit is Sindhu. The ancient Persians pronounced this as Hindu, and so all the people in that area were called 'Hindus'. This means that the word is really a geographical term and not a religious one. It would be better to call the religion 'Vedantism', meaning the 'knowledge of God'. It has also been called Sanātana Dharma ('eternal truth'). Today's 406 million (400 000 in Britain) Hindus recognize 330 million gods and goddesses behind whom is Brahman (pronounced BRAH-muhn).

Brahman. Hindus see God in the impersonal, neuter, form which they call Brahman, as well as in the personalities of all their gods and goddesses. We are all part of the impersonal form and eventually we will return to Brahman (see pp. 208 and 212). Brahman is described as the 'ultimate, holy power', the one great spirit God, the supreme soul of the universe. Brahman is present everywhere and is like a powerhouse 'lighting up' all the other gods and goddesses. Thus the gods reflect or illuminate the greatness of Brahman for us. Brahman is not a person and should be referred to as It. A man's atman (soul) is part of Brahman and it will eventually return to It. Here is an attempt to describe Brahman:

Brahma, the creator god

Shiva, the destroyer god

Why has Brahma got four heads? Why has Shiva got three eyes and four arms?

'infinite in the east . . . in the south . . . in the west . . . in the north, above and below, and everywhere infinite . . . unlimited, unborn . . . not to be conceived'. (Upanishads)

Because Brahman is so mysterious and impersonal It has made Itself manifest (clear to people on earth) in the forms of different gods and goddesses in a much more personal way. Because Hindus believe that God is always creating, they conclude that whatever is created eventually fades away or is destroyed and new creations are necessary. So there are three gods (Triad, group of three) responsible for this cycle of events. They are Brahma (pronounced brah-MUH), Shiva and Vishnu.

Brahma is the creator god with four heads which he needed to search for his daughter who hid from him when he wanted to seduce her. The other gods punished him for this wickedness, so he is not honoured today.

Shiva, the destroyer god, lurks on battlefields and cremation grounds and wears a garland of skulls. His hair, representing the Himalayan foothills, supports the R. Ganges as it falls from heaven. He has three eyes to see the past, present and future. He has four hands. Two hold the balance between construction (holding the drum of creation) and destruction; and two offer people salvation and protection. The one pointing to his toe (the soul's refuge) indicates there is no need to fear. Round his body is a serpent for the endless cycle of recurring years. He dances on the back of a demon (Ignorance) which must be destroyed if souls are to be saved. Shiva's dance keeps the universe alive with its energy. He is sometimes shown in the middle of a flaming circle standing for the universe. He destroys time and things which are old and worn out, so allowing new things to be born. Thus he is also the god of fertility. The crescent moon is his forehead and his neck is dark blue from swallowing poison at the churning of the ocean to save the earth. His wife, Kāli, or Durga, a fierce goddess, is popular today. To support Shiva is known as Shaivism, while the support of his wives or consorts (Shakti) is called Shaktism.

Vishnu as the tortoise god

Vishnu, the preserver god, has appeared in nine forms (avatars) already and is expected to appear in a tenth one. He comes periodically to encourage people to worship more readily. The world passes through cycles connected with his life. 360 days is a 'year of Brahma'; a life of Vishnu is 100 'Brahma years'. We are now in Kali yuga, which began in 3102 BC and will last 432 000 'Brahma years'.

Vishnu as the fish god

Vishnu as the boar god

Vishnu's nine avatars are as follows:

(1) *Maysya, the fish god.* He came to save Manu (primeval Man), who, like Noah, was caught by a world-wide flood. His fish horn pulled the cable of Manu's boat to save it.

(2) *Kurma, the tortoise god.* He recovered the valuables lost in the flood.

(3) *Varāha, the boar god.* He is the symbol of strength who delivered the world from the power of a demon who had carried it down to the depths of the ocean.

(4) *Nara-Sinha, the man-lion god.* He saved the world from demons.

(5) *Vāmana, the dwarf god.* He too saved the world from demons.

(6) *Rama, son of Brahman.* He used an axe to stop the tyranny of the warrior class over the priestly class of Brahmins.

(7) *Rama-candra, the perfect man.* He rescued his wife, Sita, from the tyrant king of Sri Lanka (see p. 48).

(8) *Krishna, the hero god.* As a boy he played naughty tricks before growing up to be a cowherd, when he chased all the gopis (milkmaids, see p. 11). Later he appeared as Buddha (see (9) below).

(9) *Buddha, the founder of Buddhism.* He came to point out the need to love animals and to stop sacrifices.

At the end of the Kali yuga Vishnu will come again as the world will be depraved and need reforming. It is said he will come on a white horse, with drawn sword to destroy the wicked and save the good. Rama and Krishna are by far the most popular of these avatars of Vishnu. To support Vishnu is known as Vaishnavism.

Other gods. Ganesha, god of fortune and wisdom, is a pink or yellow elephant. His father, Shiva, cut off his original head and put an elephant's one on him in anger. Hanuman, the monkey god, is the son of Pavana, the Wind, and so is able to fly. He came to help Rama-candra defeat the king of Sri Lanka because he could jump from India to the island. His monkey army formed a bridge for Rama and Sita to return to India (see p. 48). Among the other gods and goddesses now of less importance are: Agni (Fire); Varuna (Space); Pochama (Smallpox); Indra (Rain); Rudra (Storm); Indri (War). A Hindu believes personal devotion (bhakti) to a god will enable him to reach out to Brahman.

Ganesha, the god of fortune and wisdom

Krishna and the gopis. What trick did he play on them?

Rāmakrishna, a Brahmin priest of Kālī's temple at Calcutta, made Hinduism a more missionary religion by preaching that Krishna, Buddha, Jesus and Allah were all names for the same energy or reality. His chief disciple started the Rāmakrishna Mission in 1897 at Belur, Calcutta, with a temple devoted to a mixture of Hinduism, Islam, Buddhism and Christianity. This revitalized Vedantism and led to a lot of social and educational work, in America as well as India, in a way Hinduism had not known before.

1. *Draw pictures of some of the gods.*

2. *Put the word Brahman in the middle of a page and then draw spokes outwards and on the end of each spoke put the names of different gods. This should help you to see Brahman's relationship to the gods.*

3. *List four words which could be used to try to describe Brahman.*

Hanuman rescues Rama and Sita. Who is he trampling on?

SHINTOISM

Kami. Shintoism is a Japanese religion meaning 'The Way (*to*) of the Gods (*Shin*)'. It began about 650 BC, but had no particular founder. Shintoists worship some 8 million kami—i.e. gods, spirits or sacred objects. It is claimed that gods, people and the whole of nature are related in that they all have a kami-nature, the same divine 'blood'

11

in them. 'Kami' has a whole range of meanings, such as 'someone who possesses superior power', 'is pure like a clear mirror', 'mysterious', 'marvellous', 'reverence', 'an invisible power', 'soul' and so on. All people can become kami spirits in the end. So Shintoists do not have to worship God as Christians do, as they believe there is no definite line dividing them from kami spirits. However, they must show respect to kami.

To some extent it is possible to list different kinds of kami, according to what they do:

(1) Invisible powers—spirits of creativity, fertility, productivity.

(2) Natural phenomena—wind, thunder, rain.

(3) Natural objects—sun, mountains, rivers.

(4) Certain animals—fox, dog.

(5) Ancestral spirits—spirits of the dead.

In fact a kami can be anything which makes a person feel awe or reverence. The kami can work in one of two ways:

(1) Local area control—80 000 Ujigami (family) kami each protect particular areas of Japan. Originally they were the ancestors of leading families in these areas.

(2) Special protection provided by kami responsible for particular things such as help in exams, protection of insects.

Story of creation. Shintoism is not just a primitive nature worship religion for it sees all creation as one. This can be understood by following its story of creation. Originally the world was divided into two parts; the pure top part (heaven) and the impure lower part (earth). Izanagi (a male spirit) and Izanami (a female spirit) stirred the impure part with a spear and made an island and landed there to get married. They peopled the island with kami of trees, herbs, winds and so on. When Izanami died and began to rot in Hades (the place of the dead), Izanagi followed her, but she was so upset that he had seen her in a decayed state that she divorced him. In disgust at Hades, Izanagi washed himself in the sea and from his right eye came the moon goddess, and from his left eye, the sun goddess, Amaterasu, and from his nose the storm god, Susanoo.

Amaterasu, known as the 'Great-Sky-Shiner', was insulted by Susanoo, who had destroyed her ricefields, so that she went into the Cave of Heaven and the world became dark. Other kami enticed her out with a mirror hung on a sakaki tree. Thus day and night came into existence. She sent her grandson, Ninigi-no-Mikoto, to rule Japan and his great grandson became the first emperor. The emperors were regarded as divine until AD 1945. The Isé temple (see p. 129) houses the mirror given to Ninigi by Amaterasu.

Thus there is a firm link between this world and the Age of the Kami and we shall see why this is important in the next chapter. It is a religion without a creed—you do not have to hold certain beliefs. You can be a Shintoist without having to understand its teachings. You simply live them in your daily life. You are free to think almost entirely as you wish, and there is an unlimited variety of rituals to perform. Shintoism is hale and hearty because it is so adaptable and tolerant.

Recent history. With a divine emperor ruling Japan the religion was called State (Kokka) Shintoism. In World War II the term 'kamikaze' was used to describe pilots who attacked their foes in a suicidal way in the service of their emperor. But in AD 1945 the USA Commander-in-Chief who occupied Japan issued an order which said the Japanese government was no longer to support Shintoism in any way. No tax money was to be used. Shinto teaching was to stop in schools; god-shelves (kamidana, see p. 77) in offices, schools, etc. were to be removed; priestly training and all Shinto ceremonies were to be stopped. This deeply shocked the Japanese, and although it led to a partial collapse in standards of behaviour, the main result was renewed interest in Shintoism and sympathy for its priests. Today there is Jinja (Sanctuary) Shintoism with its jinjas (temples) and Kyōha (Sectarian) Shintoism with its kyokai (churches). The thirteen Kyōha sects specialize in rites and beliefs they have taken up, sometimes due to links with Buddhism and Confucianism. Today the voluntary National Association of Shinto Shrines looks after 100 000 shrines. There are now 35 million Shintoists, of whom 17 million belong to Kyōha sects.

4. *Draw a series of pictures to tell the story of creation and the lives of the kami gods down to the first emperor.*

5. *Draw six things the Shintoists thought kami controlled.*

6. *Why do you think the Japanese emperor gave up calling himself divine in 1946? What event had occurred that year in Japanese history? What effect was this likely to have on Shinto believers?*

7. *How do you think this primitive approach to religion managed to last so long as the state religion of Japan? Is its future likely to rest almost entirely on tradition now? Why?*

TAOISM

Lao-Tse. The legendary figure of Lao-Tse, or Lao-Tzu, is said to have founded Taoism (pronounced 'Dowism') in China. Born about 604 BC, he is said to have lived for 160 years. His name means 'Old Master' because it is claimed that he was born aged 60 years with white hair after being conceived by a shooting star and carried in his mother's womb for 82 years. He lived in central China and looked after the emperor's documents.

Some people say he was a recluse, a hide-away, while others claim he was sociable. In the end he decided to leave China. At the Hankao Pass the gatekeeper persuaded him to write down his beliefs before he left. In three days it is claimed he produced his 5000 characters (words) known as the Tao Te Ching (The Way and its Power, see p. 51). Then off he rode and was not seen again. He never preached to anyone or organized a religious group, so that Taoism rose from his book alone.

Tao and Te. Taoism has developed in two distinct ways, and we must follow its early history to understand this. Tao Te Ching is about the Way (Tao) and the Power (Te) that enables one to follow it. 'The Way' has three meanings:

(1) It is the mystery of mysteries behind everything in the universe. It is so overwhelming that we cannot grasp what it is by using our normal senses. We can only grasp it through mystical insight, and even then it is impossible to put into words what we have seen. Nevertheless, Tao is the reality behind all existence, what other religions would call God.

(2) Tao is also the way the universe works: the driving force which makes nature work; the Way which brings order and sense to all life, so preventing chaos. How it operates is explained in the Book of Chuang Tzu (see p. 52), which was partially written by Chuang Tzu (369–286 BC). The system is called Yin-Yang (it will be explained in Chapter 4).

(3) It is the Way we should order our lives so as to gear them to the way the universe works. Then life will go smoothly for us, for we will not be struggling against its flow. To do this we must use the Power (Te) at our disposal.

The two types of Taoism are:

(1) *Tao Chia*, Philosophical Taoism, involving the use of the Power (Te) which enters our lives when we gear ourselves to the Yin-Yang Way (Tao) the universe works (see pp. 78–81).

(2) *Tao Chiao* (Teachings of the Way), Religious Taoism, involving the use of priestly rituals with magical powers. These were proclaimed by Chang Tao Ling (AD 34–156) and can be found in *Tao Tsang,* the Taoism Canon, AD 1436 (see p. 52).

Gods and spirits. Chang Tao Ling was the first Heavenly Master of the Heavenly Master Sect who lived in Szechuan and belonged to the Five Pecks of Rice Sect. It is said he achieved immortality by mastery over hundreds of spirits by identifying their names and functions which he put into his Auspicious Alliance Canon Register. The leading spirits were the Three Pure Ones (San Ch'ing), the Lords of Heaven, Earth and Man, namely:

(1) The Jade Emperor (Yu-Huang, or Yah-husang Shang-ti). He is called Jade as jade is the symbol of purity. He rules a heavenly court with government ministries run by gods. These are ministries of thunder (Lei Pu), healing (T'ien I Yuan), fire (Huo Pu). Among other gods there is the kitchen god (Tzau Wang) who rules everyone's domestic life. He reports to the Jade Emperor each year on everyone's behaviour (see pp. 162–3). Kuan Yin, goddess of mercy, is very popular in Taiwan. She is pictured caring for a child as the protectoress of women and children. Also popular is Matzu, or Ma-Chu, nicknamed 'Granny'. She originally was a girl who set fire to her seaside home as a beacon for fishermen caught in a storm.

(2) Tao Chun, the Lord of the Earth, who is in charge of Yin-Yang.

(3) Lao-Tse, Lord of Man, who founded Taoism.

In some senses these gods are traditional Chinese ones rather than being specifically Tao Chiao ones. T'u Ti Kung is the name for the earth god who rules a small area, while Lu-pan is the god of carpentry, Mua-t'o, the god of doctors and Shou Hsing, the god of long life. Tao Chiao has split into many sects. The majority of Taiwan's 1300 priests are 'Red-headed' Taoists as they belong to the Spirit Cloud Sect and use mediums. They look after 2745 temples and 3 million Taoists. The more orthodox who do not use mediums are the 'Black-headed' Taoists.

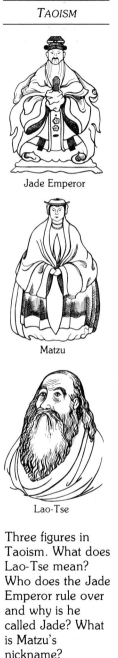

Jade Emperor

Matzu

Lao-Tse

Three figures in Taoism. What does Lao-Tse mean? Who does the Jade Emperor rule over and why is he called Jade? What is Matzu's nickname?

15

Recent history. In Communist China many temples were adapted for secular use or demolished. But in 1957 a Communist-controlled China Taoist Association was founded and some temples were repaired. In 1978 the Chinese People's Congress guaranteed religious freedom and the Political Consultative Conference now contains 16 representatives of various religions who serve as a department of religion to advise the government on how to follow a policy of religious freedom. It is difficult to tell how many Taoists there are, but there may be 30 million.

8. *(a) List under the headings (i) Tao Chia, (ii) Tao Chiao the books and the names of the people connected with their starting. (b) Name the Three Pure Ones.*

BUDDHISM

Siddhartha Gautama, the Buddha (563–483 BC), was the son of an Indian prince. The princedom was in the Himalayan foothills, 100 miles (160 km) north of Benares. Legends of signs in the sky, earthquakes, flowers appearing out of season and miraculous healings surround his birth. It is said that as soon as he was born he took seven steps and said in a lion's voice, 'I am the chief in the world. This is my last birth.' This refers to the fact that the Hindus saw him as the ninth incarnation of Vishnu (see p. 10).

His father had been warned not to let him see anything of pain, sickness and death, so he made sure that his son was kept within the palace grounds. Siddhartha grew up to be a great athlete. When he was 29 years old he managed to elude his father's guards on a number of occasions and so he saw the four signs (The Four Passing Sights) his father feared; namely, an old man, a sick man, a corpse and a monk. Now he knew that the world contained suffering, old age, death and the peace which could come from living as a monk.

He decided to leave his wife, son and 40 000 dancing girls and set out to find the causes of suffering and how to cure them. His escape is known as his Great Going Forth. For six years he wandered around seeing Hindu teachers and trying Raja Yoga (see pp. 72–3), but got nowhere. He fasted until he collapsed, and this led him to conclude that this was not the way. Clearly one's body could not escape disease, old age and death.

Now aged 35, he reached the town of Gaya on a tributary of the R. Ganges and sat down under a Bo-tree or Bodhi, which means tree

Siddhartha Gautama, the Buddha. His hands are in the teaching position and on top of his head is the 'growth' of Enlightenment.

16

of enlightenment. He decided to stay there at this 'Immovable Spot' until he understood all. The evil spirit Māra, King of Passions, tempted him with three voluptuous daughters, Gaiety, Caprice and Wantonness, who said, 'For you are in the prime of youth and vigour. Turn now your thoughts to love and take your pleasure. Look upon us, behold our cheeks and see how perfect are our forms . . .' Then Māra sent an animal army with weapons but they had no effect either. When these failed, he showed him death amidst hurricanes, rain and boiling mud. After this experience the 'Great Awakening' occurred, when Siddhartha realized the meaning of life. Now he took the name of Buddha, the Enlightened One, the 'Ideal Man'. Earthquakes are said to have taken place for a week at this point. He sat there for 49 days in rapture for now he knew the cause of suffering or dissatisfaction and how to cure it.

He believed there are two types of people:

(1) Ordinary or unenlightened people.

(2) Enlightened people, a new species or category of Man.

Everyone has an embryo of enlightenment in him. If properly nurtured, this embryo will develop and enable one to become an

The dying Buddha with Burmese monks discussing their faith. What did Buddha die of?

enlightened, ideal person. Such a person has supreme knowledge, love, compassion and energy. So you must have faith in your ability to enlighten yourself. His Four Noble Truths and Eightfold Path for life will be explained later (see pp. 85–90).

Buddha preached his first sermon in the deer park at Sarnath to the five holy men who had earlier deserted him. Then for more than 40 years after this he travelled as a missionary for nine months of each year and stayed in a monastery for the three rainy months. When he was over 80 years he died after eating some poisonous mushrooms. Because he died lying on his side, many statues show him in that position. He spoke in a popular way, easy for people to understand, unlike the Hindu brahmin priests. He used stories and parables to illustrate his points.

9. (a) *Compare Māra's temptations of Buddha with the devil's of Jesus (Matt. 4:1–11; Luke 4:1–13).*
    (b) *At what stage in their lives do these temptations take place?*
    (c) *What effect do they have on them?*
    (d) *Are there any other aspects of Buddha's life, or methods, which seem similar to those of Jesus?*

Buddha has been described as one of the greatest personalities of all times. He had a warm and patient heart for people but faced problems in a cool, careful way. He made things seem very simple. His teaching was about how to solve the problems of this life until you could eventually reach the truth after a series of lives on earth.

He said the Hindus were wrong in thinking there were *immortal* gods, and so there was no need for sacrifices, rituals and prayers to them. So there was also no need for priests. Man had no immortal soul; instead his personality consisted of ever-changing components that would die with him (see p. 219). Thus he challenged much of what the Hindus taught.

10. *Briefly recount what the following events mean in Gautama's life:*
    (a) *Four Passing Sights*
    (b) *Great Going Forth*
    (c) *Immovable Spot*
    (d) *Great Awakening.*

Buddhism came to be divided into two sections: Theravāda and Mahāyāna.

Theravāda (The Way of the Elders), also called Southern Buddhism, was established in Burma, Sri Lanka and Thailand. It taught that Buddha was simply a human who had pioneered the way to nirvana (see pp. 90 and 219) so showing others how it could be done. As he got there entirely on his own achievement, others must do likewise. Individuals must work their way across the sea of life on a 'small raft' (Hīnayāna) and achieve nirvana for themselves aided only by Buddha's teachings. The word Hīnayāna was first applied to the Theravāda Buddhists as a term of abuse by the breakaway section called Mahāyāna ('big raft') or Northern Buddhists.

Mahāyāna Buddhists covered China, Japan, Tibet and Korea with their idea of the big raft capable of holding many people who had put their trust in the eternal Buddha who had come to earth to help them find the way across the sea of life. This implies that Buddha can be worshipped as a god because he is eternal and comes down to earth. Northern Buddhists want to help others find nirvana rather than gain it for themselves. They classify god-like people into three kinds (the three-body doctrine):

Manushi Buddhas (man buddhas) once lived on earth but have now reached enlightenment through meditation. They live in nirvana beyond the reach of anyone's prayers. Gautama is the most famous Manushi.

Bodhisattvas (enlightened persons) have reached nirvana by meditation but have not yet entered it as they want to show others how to get there. They are prepared to share all the merit of goodness they have collected from their countless lives of self-sacrifice with other people so as to help them. Consequently they are regarded as saint-gods to whom one can pray. A popular Bodhisattva is the goddess of mercy (Kuan-Yin in Chinese, Kwannon in Japanese). She is pictured as a gracious lady standing on either a lotus flower, a cloud or a wave, and holding a baby. Women wanting babies pray to her. Japanese homes always have images or pictures of her. It is said that when people die she carries them to the Western Paradise (see p. 94). P'u-hsien, the laughing Buddha, is a popular Chinese Bodhisattva. His fat-bellied image is found in temple courtyards, and people carry small images of him for luck.

Dhyani Buddhas (meditation buddhas) are beings who have never been on earth. They live in nirvana but will share their happiness and help anyone who prays to them. They are pictured as monks with calm, kindly faces. Amida, Lord of the Western Paradise, is a dhyani buddha. He is worshipped by the Chinese and Japanese as it is believed he will take them to paradise by-passing the effects of people's earthly failings if they call on his name (see pp. 94 and 220).

Zen. Some Northern Buddhists are called Zen Buddhists. They believe you should concentrate on living life rather than reading and thinking about it. 'Zen' is a Japanese word for meditation (see pp. 93–4).

Recent history. Today there are 250 million Northern Buddhists. (Taiwan alone has 7½ million, served by 7750 priests in 2520 temples) and 50 million Southern ones. Buddhism suffered in Communist China, but in 1953 the Association of Chinese Buddhists was set up. In 1966–76 the Cultural Revolution led to the sacking of some monasteries, but Buddhism survived and many monasteries and relics were protected on State Council orders. In 1978 the People's Congress allowed freedom of religious belief, and in 1980 the Chinese Buddhist Theological Institute was reopened (it had been closed in 1966). Forty monks, aged 18–31, began a two-year course there before returning to their own temples. Buddhism is still surviving in China but under severe restrictions.

Buddhism began as a missionary religion and spread southwards from northern India to Sri Lanka, Burma, Thailand and Indo-China, and northwards to the Himalayan kingdoms and Tibet, and on to China, Vietnam, Korea and Japan. Nowadays it is increasing in Europe, America and the Pacific Islands. It is likely to become more of a challenge to Christianity in the West. A Buddhist Society was founded in England in 1907 and the London Buddhist Society started in 1924.

11. *Under the headings Southern and Northern Buddhism, list the countries following those forms of Buddhism and the 'raft' sizes and names.*

JUDAISM

Abraham. Judaism is the religion of the Jews. The word comes from the name of their original Middle Eastern kingdom of Judah or Judea. They believe that God made a Covenant (contract) with a farmer called Abraham in about 1800 BC (Gen. 17:1–8). As a result he uprooted his family, workmen and flocks and left Ur near the Persian Gulf for Hara, 500 miles (805 km) to the north-west. He then felt that God directed him to Canaan (Holy Land) and here God made it plain to him that he would protect his people.

This was how a small obscure people began their great history. They ignored the worship of many gods going on around them and came to grasp the point that there was only one God, who judged people fairly yet firmly. He was far more than a nature god (see pp. 22–3). Nature god worshippers simply took care to please their gods to ensure they themselves stayed alive contentedly. But God was prepared to direct the course of events, the course of history, in order to care for them, provided they would serve Him. Life for the Jews is not an illusion as Hindus believe earthly life to be, but the arena in which God works out His plans.

Moses. The Jews were not always fortunate. They became slaves of the Pharaoh of Egypt until Moses rescued them, around 1300 BC. When Pharaoh had ordered the death of all Jewish baby boys, Moses' mother had hidden him in such a way that Pharaoh's daughter found him and adopted him. But when Moses was a young man he killed an Egyptian slave-master and had to flee across the

1. Moses in the bulrushes.
2. Moses before the burning bush.
3. Moses crossing the Red Sea.
4. Moses with the Ten Commandments.

Four stages in the life of Moses.

Red Sea. Here God spoke to him and told him to return and rescue the Jews. God sent plague after plague on Egypt but Pharaoh refused to give in, even when He threatened to kill all the first-born children in the land. Moses alerted the Jews to kill lambs and smear the blood on their front doorposts so that when the slaughter occurred it would be assumed that their houses had been visited. After the slaughter Pharaoh told the slaves to go. Then he changed his mind and sent his army after them but they got across the Red Sea which was parted by God. The Egyptian army perished as the waters returned.

En route for the Promised Land the Jews camped near Mount Sinai. Moses climbed up to talk to God and returned with the Ten Commandments on stone tablets (Exod. 19:20, see p. 95). These and other rules he pressed on them to make them worship their God, and none other, and behave themselves.

Kings and prophets. After 40 years of nomadic life the Jews crossed the R. Jordan into the Promised Land. To help them settle down after a stormy tribal period, kings were appointed starting with Saul (1020–1005 BC). Under King Solomon (965–925 BC), their kingdom started its golden age. They saw God in those days as one who was slow to anger, but kind and forgiving while still prepared to punish. On Solomon's death, the twelve tribes split into two kingdoms, Israel in the north and Judah in the south. The Jews were ruled by good and bad kings. Some of the bad ones allowed idol worship, but men aware of God (prophets) called the people back to the true God. One of these was Elijah who lived in the ninth century BC. He showed God's power by calling down fire from heaven against idol worshippers.

In 722 BC Assyria overran and deported the inhabitants of Israel and in 586 BC the Babylonians deported those in Judea. During this long period they were inspired by prophets or wise men, who revealed more of God's nature to them so that they would know how He regarded them.

Amos (active 760–746 BC) was a herdsman. He preached that Israel would cease to be God's Chosen People because their behaviour was a sin against Him. God expected people to behave in a good moral way or He would judge them; sacrifices would be of no use. Another prophet, Hosea (active 750–735 BC) proclaimed that God forgave sinners if they repented; He was the God of Love. Before then it was believed that suffering was not connected with a person's sin; God sent good or bad regardless of a person's

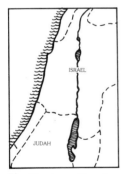

The Kingdom of Israel and Judah about 850 BC

character. Gradually there came the idea that a person suffered for his or his ancestors' sins. Isaiah (active 735–701 BC) claimed that God used the Assyrians to punish and purify the Jews and that the purified 'remnant' would survive. He forecast the coming of a human Messiah-King who would rule strongly, yet gently, and so deliver them. His arrival would change people's characters.

Jeremiah (active 627–580 BC) stressed that God dealt closely with individuals as they were precious to him. A person's sin would separate him from God. During the Exile (587–539 BC) while the Temple was out of reach, synagogues were started as religious and community centres. Ezekiel (active 593–571 BC) saw these setbacks as God's fair judgement on a sinful people, for He was a worldwide God who controlled kings. Ezekiel encouraged the Jews to appreciate that each individual was responsible for his own fate and was not affected by any bad behaviour of his ancestors. The Exile was due to the present nation's sins, not those of an 'earlier generation', so there was hope for the future. There could be no hope if an age was doomed by an earlier age's sin. Ezekiel saved Judaism from being abandoned by the Jews.

A Second Isaiah (about 550 BC) said that God's judgement was over with the end of the Exile. God was not only magnificently great but gentle too; He was a Shepherd to His flock. This Isaiah produced a new solution to the mystery of suffering when he said that someone could suffer for another's sins. When he said 'He was wounded for our transgressions [sins]', Isaiah introduced the idea of a Servant of the Lord who would extend God's Covenant to all nations. Much later on came the idea that there would be a period of rule by the Messiah, which means 'Anointed One', 'Saviour'. After this would come the 'End' when all would be judged. Some thought the Messiah would be a human being, others a superhuman, but none thought He would be divine. Most Jews of Jesus' time did not expect the Messiah to suffer, which explains why Jesus' disciples could not understand the idea that his Messiahship would involve his suffering. Certain Jews called Zealots expected the Messiah to lead a military movement against the occupying Roman army. In the opinion of Jews today the Messiah has still not come. This marks them off decisively from the Christians, who see Jesus as the Messiah, although a different type of Messiah from the one the Jews expect.

The Jews realized God was not a nature god in any way as He created everything. The sun, moon, mountains and rivers have no gods in them as they are all part of God's creation. His existence does not need proving to Jews; they take it for granted. He has not come down to earth as a person as Christians claim. People are created in His image, however, and so must demonstrate His justice and mercy by treating others similarly. The world is God's gift to people and they must treat it as such. People are free to choose whether they will respond or not. Jews do not reject the world and live as monks as they believe God meant them to enjoy His world. This world is not essentially evil and is not to be rejected.

Recent history. In the last hundred years many Jews have reconsidered their beliefs and there are now a number of different sects. Before looking at them, two vital factors must be dealt with:

(1) First there was the Holocaust in the 1940s when Hitler exterminated 6 million Jews in concentration camps in order to 'purify' the German race. This destroyed the largest concentration of Jews in the world; one-third of all Jews died. Of the 11–12 million Jews left in 1945, about 5 million lived in the USA, while 250 000 were in Displaced Persons Camps in Europe. In all, 1½ million needed a new haven. 150 000 went to the USA, many stayed in Europe, and by 1958, 850 000 survivors had joined the new state of Israel.

(2) The start of the state of Israel in 1948 in the Jewish homeland is the second important factor. The idea for a Jewish state dates back to the Zionist movement begun in Basle in 1897 by Theodore Herz (1860–1904). The dream was not to be fulfilled easily, but early in the twentieth century Tel Aviv began as the first entirely Jewish city. In 1917 the British foreign secretary, Balfour, issued a Declaration saying that Britain supported the idea. Palestine came under British control after World War I. Then the Jews began to move in more and more. As a result of a United Nations decision in 1948 they took over the government of Israel, and Orthodox Jewish standards (kosher food in the army, no public transport on the Sabbath, etc.) were maintained. The Jewish State was born.

There are three main Jewish groups in Britain today: Orthodox, Liberal and Reformed.

Orthodox Jews are those who believe that God revealed to His Chosen People all they needed to know in the Torah (the Jews' holy book) once and for all. Its 613 instructions (mitzuots) must be interpreted and obeyed. The best known interpretation is the Talmud (see p. 57). These cover behaviour and diet as we shall see. They believe God is all-powerful and all-knowing. A few of them believe the Jews should have waited for the Messiah to come to start the

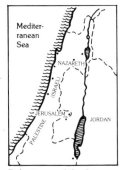

Palestine and Jordan in 1948

State of Israel. The majority of English Jews are Orthodox ones, under the leadership of the Chief Rabbi of the United Congregation of the Commonwealth.

Liberal Jews (called Reform Jews in the USA) originated in Germany under David Friedlander (1756–1834) in the nineteenth century as a group which felt that the Torah contained God's 'teaching' rather than His 'law'. They argued that although its rules on good behaviour must be obeyed, its rules on rituals, such as Sabbath observance, were not divine. They should be altered as times changed. For them the Torah is a collection of people's thoughts about God and how He should be served. They point out it contains some primitive ideas and errors which need updating; as God used men to tell others, the messages could get distorted in the telling. So their synagogues and services differ from the Orthodox ones and they are less strict and precise. They feel Jews must keep up to date and change with the times, whereas Orthodox Jews argue that as God's rules are eternal, they must be obeyed in the form in which they were given. They claim God does not interfere with the laws of nature, and play down the role of miracles. For them the parting of the Red Sea is a legend.

Reform Jews (called Conservative Jews in the USA) also originated in Germany, under Zachariah Frankel (1801–1875) when it was felt the Liberal Jews had gone too far in their free ways. The sect caught on in the USA where it now has 1½ million followers. They disagree as to whether the Torah is the only revelation of God to Man, and they do not believe it is all God's work and so divine. They think God may want all the ritual rules kept and so try to apply them in modern ways as we shall see. Many of them support Zionism, but think emigrating (alijah) to Israel is not essential, only desirable. They do not look for a Messiah coming to start his Kingdom in Jerusalem.

There are some 12 million Jews today, of whom 410 000 live in Britain. Jews believe all religions have their routes to God and that Judaism is a good route for themselves. There are Jews of all races and nationalities.

12. *Compare Buddha's teaching on suffering with the beliefs of the Jews. Take care to show the different stages in thought which the Jews had on the subject. Look ahead to Buddha's Four Noble Truths (pp. 85–7) before answering.*

13. *State briefly why the Jews believe they are a people selected by God for particular care in return for their religious duties to Him. Does their history justify their claim?*

14. *List all the points made describing God and His ways, attitudes, etc., and say which prophets made which points. What points do you consider the most important and why?*

15. *(a) Does God intervene in history or has He no control over what men do or what natural events and disasters occur?*
    (b) Give examples, ancient and modern, great or small, to support your opinion.

16. *When the Jews suffered, their leaders said it was God's judgement on them and so it was their fault for not keeping to the contract or covenant with Him. Why do you think the leaders said this rather than saying it was God's fault and He had let them down?*

17. *(a) Why did God need prophets to explain what He and His methods were like?*
    (b) What might have happened to Judaism if there had been no prophets to give God's attitude to matters when problems arose?

18. *(a) Summarize the main differences so far mentioned between Orthodox, Reform and Liberal Jews.*
    (b) Why do Orthodox Jews insist the Torah's rules must all be kept while other Jews say they can be changed?

CHRISTIANITY

Jews, Christians and Muslims have a common belief in there being one God. They agree with the Westminster Confession of 1648 which says:

> *There is but one only living and true God, who is infinite in being and perfection . . . invisible, without body, parts or passions, immutable . . . eternal, incomprehensible, almighty . . . working all things . . . most loving, gracious, merciful, long suffering, abundant in goodness and truth, forgiving . . . sin; the rewarder of them that diligently seek Him; . . . most just and terrible in His judgements, hating all sin, and who will by no means clear the guilty.*

Jesus. But what makes Christians distinctive from what Jews and Muslims believe is their acceptance of Jesus as the Son of God, and not just as another prophet (John 14:9; 20:28; Mark 1:10−11). Jesus is unique in being both God and Man. Christians argue that the Jewish prophets had merely paved the way for the coming of God's Son to make the truth clear and provide a way of salvation for mankind. Jesus' perfect example showed people what God wanted them to be like (Mark 1:14−15).

Jesus was born in Bethlehem, probably sometime between 2 and 6 BC (our 'AD' calendar is not completely accurate). According to the stories of his birth he had a human mother, Mary, but no human father. So it is claimed he was both God and Man when he was on earth. Mary was told that God's Holy Spirit would overshadow her and she would conceive a son. Some Christians argue that Jesus had to be conceived without a human father because he was uniquely the Son of God.

19. *Interview the innkeeper about the events connected with the couple who arrived seeking shelter and whom he put in the stable (Luke 2:1−20; Matt. 2).*

Jesus seems to have lived a quiet life as a carpenter until he was about 30 years old. Then he led his missionary life for some three years until the closing events of his earthly life. His mission began when he was baptized by John the Baptist and received God's Spirit (Mark 1:1−11). He was immediately put to the test by the devil Satan before starting his teaching career (Matt. 4:1−11).

Moving among the social drop-outs, Jesus concentrated his teaching on the rapidly approaching coming of the longed-for reign of God on earth, the Kingdom of God. He told special stories (parables) which stressed that the 'zero hour' was near and people must make a decision to trust God completely. Coming into Galilee he said 'The time is fulfilled; and the Kingdom of God is at hand; repent and believe in the gospel (good news)' (Mark 1:14−15). Jesus cured the lame and the blind miraculously, as signs that the age of salvation was dawning (Matt. 8:1−14; 9:1−8, 18−31). His exorcisms (expelling of evil spirits from people) marked the opening assault on the forces of evil (Matt. 8:16, 28−34; 9:32−34).

Who is baptizing whom?

20. *Give brief summaries of (a) cures, (b) exorcisms done by Jesus. Comment on what interests or surprises you about them.*

21. *Jesus compared the Kingdom of God to a number of things including a mustard seed, treasure and a fishing net*

(Matt. 13:31–49). Explain the Kingdom in terms of (a) a mustard seed; (b) a fishing net.

Jesus urged Jews to respond to the coming of God in the person of himself (Matt. 10:37–42; 11:28–30), stressing the matter was urgent. This led him to press everyone who believed him to adjust their behaviour quickly (Mark 1:14–15). His followers should love others without exception he argued. Their relations with each other must match God's with them (Luke 6:32–36; Matt. 5:43–48). The more they loved the bad characters of this world, the more they would appreciate God's love for all people (Matt. 25:24–46; Luke 10:29–37). He stressed that a person's attitudes and motives counted most of all (Matt. 15:11–20; Mark 7:1–23) and he set high standards for his followers to copy (Matt. 5:5–9, 21–24, 27–32, 38–48; 6:1–4, 24–33; Luke 18:9–14). But he offered salvation as the prize (Matt. 7:21; 18:1–5; John 5:21–24; 6:48–51, 54; 11:25–26; 14:6).

22. *(a) Look up the Bible references given above and summarize Jesus' teaching on (i) good behaviour; (ii) salvation.*
(b) How can a Christian obtain salvation?

Like some other Jews, Jesus simplified the Jewish Law by reducing it to two commands, 'Love God and love others as much as yourself' (Mark 12:28–31; Luke 6:27–28). He taught his disciples (followers) that they were God's sons rather than His slaves. They could approach God in an intimate, personal way as Father (Matt. 6:7–18; Luke 10:21; 23:34, 46; John 14; Rom. 1:7). He gave them the Lord's Prayer, which begins with the common Jewish formula, 'Our Father in heaven'. One modern version of the Bible gives the Lord's Prayer as follows:

Our Father in heaven, we honour your holy name. We ask that your kingdom will come now. May your will be done here on earth, just as it is in heaven. Give us our food again today, as usual, and forgive us our sins, just as we have forgiven those who have sinned against us. Don't bring us into temptation, but deliver us from evil. Amen (Matt. 6:9–13)

(Amen is a common ending to prayers which means 'so let it be'.)

When he appointed twelve disciples as followers and aides it seemed to some a sign that he was about to start a Messianic community (God-like community run by a Saviour) to replace the Twelve Tribes of Israel (Matt. 4:18–22; 10:1–42; Mark 1:16–20; 3:14–19). Under these circumstances it was not surprising that his controversial views and huge outdoor meetings attracted the attention of powerful Jewish religious leaders. They feared their people might be misled with false hopes. The political situation did not help as the Romans were occupying the land and Jesus' efforts might be seen as aimed at starting a popular nationalist uprising. The result was that the Jewish leaders pressed the Roman governor, Pilate, to find him guilty of pretending to be the expected Messiah (political and religious king) when he entered Jerusalem in triumph (Mark 15:2, 9, 26). Anticipating arrest, he had invented a unique commemorative-style meal for his followers when he broke bread and blessed it and wine at the Last Supper (Mark 14:22–25; see also Exod. 24; Isa. 42:6). However, his view of the Messiah differed from that of the Jews (see pp. 99–100) for he saw his role in terms of the Suffering Servant of Isaiah (Isa. 42:1–2; 49:1–6; 50:5–9; 52:13–53:12): 'He was despised and rejected of men . . .'. Jesus saw his mission as one which involved suffering and death for the sake of others. He came 'to minister, and to give his life as a ransom for many' (Mark 10:45) and so re-establish the good relations between God and people which had been broken by sin.

The Last Supper.

The difficulties of securing a conviction and sentence at his political trial can be seen from all the problems which arose from the time of his arrest onwards (Matt. 26:45–27:27; Mark 14:41–15:15; Luke 22:47–23:25; John 18:1–19:16).

23. *Summarize the trial sequence, from the time of Jesus' arrest until Pilate's condemning him to death, using any two of the Gospel accounts. What differences can you find in the two accounts you have selected?*

Jesus was flogged before being made to carry the beam of the cross from which he was to be crucified. Thus he paid the supreme sacrifice of surrendering his life for others. His disciples put his body in a tomb (Matt. 27:26–61; Mark 15:15–47; Luke 23:25–56; John 19:16–42). These events are commemorated by Good Friday.

24. *Summarize the story of Christ's last hours, from when Pilate handed him over to the troops to his burial, using any two of the Gospel accounts.*

Two days after Good Friday Jesus' body had disappeared, the stone in front of the tomb having been rolled away. All that remained inside were the bandages that the body had been wrapped in. The disciples were in some confusion, the more so when Jesus appeared to them alive again. He was not a ghost as the wounds he had

Jesus on the cross
as depicted in a
modern film.

suffered were there to touch. Christians believe that he ascended bodily into heaven for as the unique Son of God he could not end his life like others (Matt. 28; Mark 16; Luke 24; John 20–21). His rising is commemorated by Easter Sunday and his ascension on Ascension Day.

25. *Give brief descriptions of all his appearances after he rose again. Comment on what interests or surprises you.*

The Trinity. Before he left his disciples Jesus gave them instructions to carry on his mission. He promised to send them God's Holy Spirit to aid them, and this promise was fulfilled (Luke 24:49; John 20:21–22; Acts 2:1–33, 38). This led to the teaching that God is Three-in-One (Tri-unity, Trinity): God the Father, God the Son and God the Holy Spirit (2 Cor. 13:14). The Godhead can appear to us in three forms just as water can be ice, liquid or steam, namely God *over us* (the Father), God *with us* (the Son, Christ), and God *in us* (Holy Spirit or Ghost). The first viewpoint stresses God's immeasurable greatness before which all should bow humbly. The second shows His love for mankind in sending His Son. The third provides His followers with comfort and guidance. God is one being or 'substance' but can be 'seen' as three 'persons' or 'channels of communication'. Some Christians tend to emphasize one viewpoint more than others, so they disagree in some ways about how God should be approached and what the Christian life should be.

26. *The Jews claim that God controls history and they are His Chosen People, while Christians claim that God entered history personally in the form of Christ. What is the difference between these views and the effect they have?*

27. *Jesus was a poor man who travelled only some 90 miles (145 km) from his birthplace, wrote no great books, lived and worked with the poor and outcasts, and died a criminal's death; yet he altered the course of history as the founder of Christianity. Why? How?*

28. *It is claimed that Jesus freed people from three intolerable burdens: (a) fear, even of death; (b) guilt over sin; (c) selfishness, and that he gave them a new birth into life. See 1 Pet. 1:2–25; Rom. 3:9–31; 5:3–6:11; Gal. 5:19–24. How could this be so?*

St Paul. It was an intelligent Jew called Saul, who had been persecuting the Christians before he was converted and changed his name to Paul, who was to open up the new faith for all people and not just Jews (Acts 9:1–22). This split the movement for a while. It was Paul who stressed that Jesus should be called the Christ (Greek for 'Anointed One'). He argued that people were affected by original sin which had become inborn in them (Rom. 5:12–21). To overcome this you must believe Jesus is the Christ and be baptized as his self-sacrifice on the Cross atoned for (pardoned) this sinfulness (Rom. 6:3–11). The resurrection was his triumph over sin in the world (Rom. 5:18–19). Paul's letters in the New Testament helped Christians to understand a lot more about their new faith.

Catholic and Orthodox Churches. There are 983 million Christians today. Over the centuries they have become split into many different denominations and sects—some major, some minor. The first split resulted from the Roman Empire breaking up into eastern and western parts. The Christians of the Eastern or Byzantine Empire looked to Constantinople as the centre of what became known as the Orthodox Church. This church became divided into fourteen self-governing churches under Patriarchs (senior bishops), for example those of Constantinople, Jerusalem, Russia and Greece. They allow their parish priests to marry but not their bishops. There are now 100 000 Orthodox Christians in Britain.

The Western European Christians came to see Rome as their centre, and today the Roman Catholic Church has 615 million members, of whom 6 million live in Britain. Their head is the Pope. He is supported by a college of cardinals (senior bishops) from all over the world. When a Pope dies the cardinals are locked up in the Vatican (pope's palace) until they have elected a new one. No Roman Catholic clergy are allowed to marry.

Protestant churches. In the sixteenth century some Christians broke away from the Roman Catholic Church. These groups are called Protestants because they protested for one reason or another against the Pope's power and his Church's teachings. Protestant churches also allow their clergy to marry. A German called Martin Luther was one of the first to challenge the Roman Catholic Church in a period known as the Reformation. His actions in 1517 led to the foundation of the Lutheran Church, and John Calvin's actions in Switzerland in 1536 led to the start of the Calvinist Church. In 1534, in the reign of Henry VIII, the Church of England broke away from Rome to become England's national or 'established' church, with the sovereign at its head. Twenty-six of its leading bishops now sit in the

House of Lords. In Scotland, Ireland and Wales the protestant episcopal church is no longer 'established', being free of parliamentary control.

The Church of England is divided into dioceses (large geographical units) presided over by bishops, who are based at cathedrals. There are some 18 000 smaller units called parishes which are under the control of parish priests (rectors or vicars). Deans are in charge of cathedrals and are aided by priests called canons; archdeacons supervise the clergy and church property over set areas; deacons are trainee priests; curates assist parish priests. The governing body of the church consists of bishops, clergy and laity (ordinary members). It is called the General Synod.

There are a number of 'noncomformist' denominations which have broken away from the Church of England.

The Baptists (founded in England in 1612) insist on adult believers' baptism (see pp. 191–3). They are supervised by the Baptists Union which is subdivided into provinces under general superintendents. Their chapels are run by ministers (clergy) and their congregations.

The United Reformed Church was formed in 1972 with the coming together of the Congregational and Presbyterian churches, some 2000 churches in all. It is run by a General Assembly, 12 synods and numerous district councils.

The Society of Friends (Quakers) was founded by George Fox in the 1660s. There are about 20 000 Friends in Britain, worshipping in 400 meeting houses. They have no clergy, but elect members to be elders and overseers to take charge of meetings. They have local, district and national meetings. They have no set form of service, no sacraments and no creed, but trust in God's Spirit to guide them.

The Methodists were founded by John and Charles Wesley, and the Methodist Church broke with the Church of England in 1784. There are some 40 million Methodists in the world, of whom 730 000 are in Britain. The Methodist Conference is divided into 34 districts and then into 900 circuits under superintendent ministers. Some 20 000 lay preachers assist the ministers, who can only stay in one posting for five years. Women have been allowed to become ministers since 1974. Each congregation is divided into classes of 10–12 members whose commitment is checked annually.

John Wesley.

... on an international scale The Salvation Army provides **352** children's homes and nurseries, **481** hostels for the homeless and transient, **117** homes and centres for the treatment of alcoholics, **130** hospitals, clinics and dispensaries, **36** maternity homes, **10** institutes and centres for the blind, **10** leagues for the deaf and dumb, **21** homes and institutes for the handicapped, **110** remand, probation and approved homes, also schools, **874** primary, secondary and vocational training schools, **150** industrial homes and workshops, **3** leprosaria, **150** holiday homes and summer camps, **18** convalescent homes, **10,000** missing persons traced and found each year, **96** community centres, **15,175** evangelistic centres.

The cost is enormous. In order to help others

THE
SALVATION
ARMY

continues to need your help.

Salvation Army fund-raising poster. To what extent do the details given show that a 'military' style campaign is needed?

The Salvation Army was founded by William Booth in 1865, and it now has 3 million members using 111 languages in 83 countries. Its leaders hold 'military' style ranks with a general in overall command. Lieutenants, captains, majors, etc. are its ministers. They are posted every 3–4 years from one citadel ('fort' or base) to another. There are 1250 citadels in Britain. Men and women can become officers, but officers must marry officers if they wish to marry. They specialize in the care of the rejects and failures of society, and march into battle with their bands against evils such as drink, drugs and poverty. Their Missing Persons Bureau traces some 10 000 missing people a year. They accommodate 200 000 homeless each night and provide 2000 million meals a year in Britain.

The Pentecostal Churches consist of the Elim Church, founded in 1915 with 2500 in 310 congregations, the Assemblies of God in 1924 with 60 000 in 541 congregations, and the West Indian New Testament Church of God with 20 000 in 74 congregations. They concentrate on the gift of the Holy Spirit at Pentecost (Acts 2:1–4). In addition to adult baptism they expect members to be baptized by the Spirit, and speaking 'in tongues' occurs at their services (see p. 193). This emphasis on 'Baptism in the Holy Spirit' has spread to other churches in what is known as the Charismatic Movement. Pentecostalists also believe that people can be 'devil-possessed'. This means that they are controlled by the devil or evil spirits, causing sins such as drunkenness and violence, or severe illness. Some people can remove demons and this is called exorcism.

Christianity began as a missionary religion to proclaim the 'good news' and has swept across the world over the centuries. It has numerous missionary societies today attached to its different churches. The Church Missionary Society of the Church of England is one example. It has hundreds of workers preaching, educating and healing in different parts of the world. The existence of the World Council of Churches shows the breadth of Christian witness.

29. *Make a table of the different Christian churches and denominations under the headings: (a) name; (b) when started; (c) main features.*

ISLAM

Muhammad and Allah. 'Islam' means 'submission to God'. God is called Allah (Allah; Al = the; lah = God), and submission to Him will bring peace. The prophet Muhammad ('highly praised') was born

*MEN, GODS
AND HISTORY*

The main areas of
Islam today.
Muslims face
towards Mecca
when praying (see
p. 113). Which
compass direction
do they face from
(a) London,
(b) Rabat,
(c) Tehran and
(d) Dacca?

in the trading centre of Mecca on Monday 20 August AD 570. His
father had just died and his mother died when he was six. As an
orphan he was sensitive to human sufferings. He started work as a
shepherd boy for his uncle, Abu Talib. In AD 594 he worked for a
merchant and the next year he married his widowed employer,
Khadija. He was 25 and she was 40. They had a number of children
all but one of whom died young. But it was a happy marriage.

Muhammad was a gentle, sensitive and helpful man who traded
honestly. He was known as the 'upright, trustworthy one'. He was
disturbed by the lawlessness and immoral behaviour of those around
him and by their futile idol worship. Possibly he heard of the Jewish
and Christian beliefs in one God and the importance these two
religions attached to their holy books. Certainly he must have turned
over in his mind the problems of his countrymen. Then in AD 610,

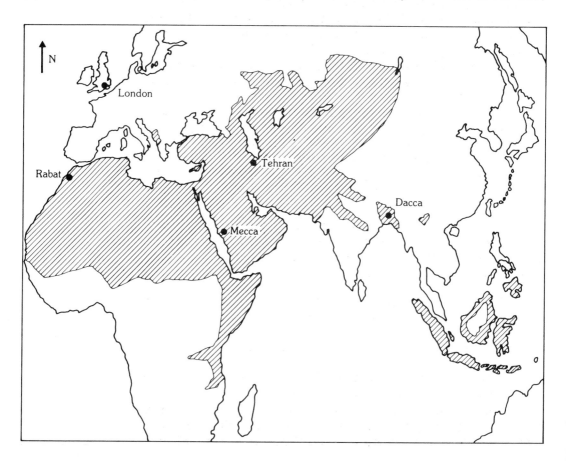

during one of the all-night vigils he used to keep in caves or the wilderness, he had a revelation from the angel Gabriel:

> He came to me while I was asleep, with a piece of brocade whereupon was writing, and said, 'Recite!' [The word here is 'iqra' which means 'recite after me'; Muhammad himself could not read or write.] I said, 'What shall I recite?' . . . 'Recite, in the name of thy Lord who created man from clots of blood. Recite! Thy Lord is wondrous kind, who by the pen has taught mankind things they knew not'. So I recited it, and he departed from me. And I awoke from my sleep, and it was as though these words were written on my heart . . . When I was midway on the mountain, I heard a voice from heaven, saying, 'O Muhammad . . .' I raised my head . . . to see, and lo, Gabriel in the form of a man, with feet astride the horizon, saying, 'Muhammad! Thou art the Apostle of God and I am Gabriel'.

Terrified, Muhammad ran home. His wife said he must be either a prophet or mad, and she thought he was a prophet. His first revelation was on Lailat-al-Qudr, the Night of Power, and it is commemorated during Ramadan (see p. 117).

In a number of revelations Muhammad received the Koran from Gabriel. 'We have made this Koran easy for you in your own tongue' (Koran, Surah 44:58) so 'that you may understand' (Koran, Surah 43:3). So for the next ten years Muhammad preached about Allah, the One and Only God, the Compassionate and Merciful, to the tribesmen who came to Mecca on business or as pilgrims to the Ka'ba (see pp. 118–20). The Meccans worshipped natural objects made of stones and wood. He warned them that this was idol worship and they would suffer on the Day of Judgement (see p. 226). His views were a threat to the trade centred on the idol worship there. Also he called for higher moral standards, which was unpopular. His claim that all were equal in Allah's eyes was dynamite to the class-ridden Meccan people. So opposition to him built up and he and his few followers were pelted and stoned.

30. *What evidence is there that Muhammad received the Koran from Allah rather than writing it himself?*

31. *Why were Muhammad's views rejected at Mecca?*

By AD 619, 200 had accepted Muhammad's message. They were mainly slaves or poor workers. In 622 a group from Yathrib (later called Medinat-al-nabi, City of the Prophet) asked him to help the faithful there. His journey to Medina is called the Hijrah or Hegira ('breaking with old ties'; 'migration') and Muslims date their calendar from this turning point in their history. AH 1 means Anno Hegira 1. En route there Muhammad and a friend hid in a crevice as Meccans tried to find them. His frightened friend said, 'We are but two'. 'No', said Muhammad, 'We are three for Allah is with us'. After three days in hiding they escaped.

At Medina Muhammad preached about Allah in opposition to the idol worship. He ceased to be a despised preacher and became in turn a statesman, judge, general and teacher. He was both a religious and a political leader which meant that his judgements were seen as Allah's commands pronounced by His prophet. He called for an end to idol worship, immorality and alcoholism. He developed Medina as a rival trade centre to Mecca. In addition, he hoped that Jews there would accept the message and see him as the Messiah as he too preached about one God. But they rejected him and said no Arab could be the Messiah. At Medina he issued the first charter of freedom of conscience in human history when he said that Jews (and Christians) 'shall . . . practise their religion as freely as the Muslims'.

Muhammad's wife died in AD 619 and the custom of the land led him to accept that he could have several wives. Nine or 14 have been mentioned, but he was never married to more than four at one time. When he married Zainab, who was divorced from his close friend Zaid, he removed the idea that divorce degraded a woman. He married other women when he was between 55 and 60 years old, sometimes to cement relations with various tribes and sometimes to shelter widows during periods of war. He raised the status of women and insisted that sex should only take place within marriage (see p. 199). Muhammad was a man of burning sincerity and magnetic personality.

If he was to establish Allah's rule on earth Muhammad believed he would have to set up an independent state based on Allah's laws. This meant fighting for Medina's independence from Mecca. Thus until his death in 632 war was almost continuous. The fighting he regarded as jihad (holy war) for the faith, which would lead to life in Paradise for those who fought in it. In 624 at the battle of Badr his 300 defeated the Meccans' 900 (Surah 8:11–12, 42–44), but they suffered at Uhud in 625 (Surah 3:120–126, 143–154) when 9000 attacked their 700. Muhammad was wounded. But in 630 his 10 000 captured Mecca easily. He destroyed all 360 idols and then circled the Ka'ba there before rededicating it to Allah.

32. *Jihads are of two kinds. The Greater Jihad is the struggle to purify oneself. The Lesser Jihad is a war fought in the last resort*

Arabia

● MEDINA
● MECCA

Arabian Sea

What happened at Medina and Mecca?

after all peaceful attempts have failed. It is not an aggressive war.

(a) What wars have been fought by people in the name of their religion?

(b) Do you think they were justified today?

(c) Do people who fight in holy wars usually win?

Muhammad died in 632. Whereas Jesus had emphasized that God is a Father of His people, Muhammad stressed His compassion as the majestic powerful God who shows mercy. Muslims' prayer is an act of submission to Allah. Islam means 'submission' and Muslim 'a surrendered man' (active participle of 'Islam'). Muslims claim that Allah only reveals what He wants, not what His nature is really like. They think Christians go too far in thinking they know His nature when they call Him Father. They deny Jesus is God's Son as that would reduce God to human level, they claim. They deny that the Holy Spirit is part of the Godhead, saying spirit is part of God's creation.

The Muslim equivalent of the Lord's Prayer is:

In the name of Allah, the Merciful, the Compassionate.
Praise be to Allah, the Lord of the worlds,
The Merciful One, the Compassionate,
Master of the day of doom.
Thee alone we serve, to Thee alone we cry for help!
Guide us in the straight path,
The path of them that Thou hast blessed,
Not of those with whom Thou are angry,
Nor of those who go astray.

(Surah 1)

33. *Compare this prayer with the Christian Lord's Prayer on p. 28.*
    (a) Have they any points in common?
    (b) What different pictures of God do they conjure up in your mind?

The Koran describes Allah with 99 'Beautiful Names' and Muslims have 99 beads on their rosaries (subha) to help them remember them. The key names are Compassionate, Merciful, First and Last, Almighty, Creator, Giver of Life, Provider, Guider, Forgiver and Judge. 'Father' is not one of the 99.

Spread of Islam. Unlike many religions, Islam spread like a hurricane, so that between AD 635 and 651 Egypt, Palestine, Syria, Iraq and the Persian Empire were overrun.

Inevitably Islam became divided into sects, largely for political reasons. When Muhammad died, his friend Abu Bakr was elected his successor (or kalif) instead of his cousin Ali. Ali became the fourth kalif but was later assassinated. Ali's supporters (the Shi'a or Shi'ites) refused to accept the later kalifs and would only support Ali's relatives. The opponents of the Shi'ites became known as the Sunni. Today the Sunni make up about 80 per cent of the Muslim world; the Shi'ites live mainly in Iraq, Iran, Lebanon and India.

The division between Shi'ites and Sunni is also expressed in differences over beliefs and practices. Both consider the Koran infallible (i.e. it cannot be faulted), but the Shi'ites also believe in the infallibility of the imāms or kalifs, successors to Muhammad in their interpretation of the Koran, claiming that they were as sinless as him. They say there were 12 Imāms. The last, Madhi, vanished in AD 880, and it is believed he will return again. This reminds one of the Christian expectation of Christ's return.

Sufis (literally 'wearers of undyed wool', hence austere people) belong to the mystical sect of Islam. Their burning love for Allah draws them closer to Him through the use of self-control and denial of worldly pleasures. They concentrate on prayer and spiritual exercises such as dances which involve whirling round and round ('whirling dervishes'). They began in the seventh century AD among the Sunni and there are numerous different groups now, including some in Britain.

Recent history. Islam, once the fastest-spreading religion in history, is now trying to grow again. Modern states such as Pakistan, and Iran (under Ayatollah Khomeini), attempt to enforce the law of Allah. In the Middle East, Arabs have realized the power of oil and use this to gain influence in non-Muslim countries, regardless of colour or race. This is the modern form of jihad or missionary work, by which Muslims hope to extend their faith throughout the world.

In the unorthodox Black Muslim movement in the USA, Islam attracts many who feel downtrodden. Mosques are now being built in Britain where 1 million of the world's 850 million Muslims live (35 000 Muslims live in Birmingham alone). The largest single Islamic country is Indonesia with 100 million.

34. *Compare the lives of Muhammad and Jesus.*
    (a) What is particularly different about what they did?
    (b) What is strikingly similar?

35. *Compare the Christian and Muslim views of God.*

36. *Why did Muhammad reject the idea of Jesus being God's Son and accept him only as a prophet?*

SIKHISM

Guru Nanak (AD 1469–1538), the founder of Sikhism, was born in Talwandi village, now called Nanakana, in Pakistan. His father, Kalu, was a well-known officer and a Hindu. At Nanak's birth the midwife saw a dazzling line round the baby's head, and this led a local brahmin (Hindu priest) to say that Nanak would be a great man, a king or a guru (wise teacher). His father took him away from school early on when he spent too much time thinking about God and not doing his work. He was given a brahmin tutor instead. Nanak asked him, 'Can you tell me, sir, why should I be a Hindu at all? Is it not good to be just a man?' Kalu and the priest were very annoyed at this and Nanak was packed off to be a cowherd.

One day he fell asleep under a tree and the cattle got into a cornfield and ate the crop. The angry farmer took the cattle away and told the police chief who in turn set off with Kalu to find Nanak. When they got to the field they found the corn was as good as ever! It seemed like magic and Nanak came to be accepted by many as 'a man of God'. When he was a teenager he had Muslim as well as Hindu friends. When Kalu told him off for having Muslim friends, he replied, 'There's no Hindu or Muslim. We are all brothers'. Kalu was angry because Nanak kept giving away his clothes, books, food and money to poor boys, and so he decided he must put his son to the test. He gave him 20 rupees to go to a city and set himself up as a merchant. But Nanak used the opportunity to preach his friendship-faith as he went through the villages, and when he got to the jungle he used the money to buy food for 20 hermits who lived there praying to God. Returning home empty-handed he was slapped by Kalu.

At 18 Nanak got married and became a storekeeper. One day he went to the river to bathe and did not return. Three days later he was found at prayer. He said God wanted him to work for Him. He was asked if he meant for the Hindus or the Muslims, and he replied neither as they were brothers in God's eyes. He then began a 30-year missionary journey in which he covered thousands of miles on foot. In one village he stayed with a carpenter, Lalo, and shared his simple food. A rich man, Malik, invited him to a feast and he went reluctantly, taking some of Lalo's simple food with him. When everyone had gathered, Nanak stood up with Lalo's food in one hand and Malik's in the other. He squeezed the two handfuls, and from Lalo's came drops of milk and from Malik's, blood. He denied that this was magic and said it was the truth for a poor man's food was clean as it was worked for, whereas a rich man's was not as it was not obtained by honest work, but by making others work until they dropped. Malik quietly bowed low before Nanak and promised to treat his workers better in future.

When he went to the Muslim holy city of Mecca, Nanak lay down to rest in such a way that his feet pointed towards the Ka'ba. This made the priest Rukandin furious as Nanak's position insulted Allah. Nanak apologized and asked, 'Could you turn my legs to the side in which there is no God?' But each time Rukandin moved him round and looked up he found the Ka'ba was still in front of Nanak's legs. Rukandin was dumbstruck. Nanak told him, 'God does not live in one place. He lives everywhere'.

Nanak eventually reached Hardwar on the R. Ganges. A crowd was splashing water in the direction of the sun where they believed their ancestors now lived. Nanak started splashing water in the opposite direction and got told off for being so stupid. He replied that his farm 300 miles (483 km) away had not had any rain for a year and he was sending it water. They asked him how could the water possibly reach his farm and he pointed out that theirs had a much longer way to go to reach the sun! So the people stopped and listened to him and he told them to serve the living and not the dead.

On one occasion Nanak was travelling through Bengal, and one village refused him and his companion the food they had begged for, whereupon he said, 'May these people stay in this village for ever'. At the next village the two were given food and he prayed, 'May the people of this village scatter'. His companion was puzzled and asked him why he blessed the bad and cursed the good. Nanak pointed out that he wanted the example of the good villagers to be spread around, while the bad ones should be confined where they were so that they did not spread their bad customs.

When he was 70, Nanak gave up his journeyings and started a farming commune. He knew he had to choose a successor and after a hard day's work he thought of a test which would help him choose wisely. A heap of wet, muddy grass was lying in the fields and he asked his two sons to carry it home. 'What for? We don't need it at home', said the elder. 'It is wet and muddy and will spoil our clothes', said the younger, and added, 'Ask one of your Sikhs'. Nanak replied that his sons should work as hard as his Sikhs. Immediately a Sikh,

Guru Nanak

Lehna, ran forward and picked it up. Nanak was now convinced his sons were too proud and lazy to become his successors, but he decided on a further test. Another day he dropped a rupee into a deep pool of cold, dirty water. No one, including his sons, wanted to get wet to recover it. But Lehna jumped in and got it without complaining. After a while Nanak asked him if he felt cold and Lehna replied, 'No, I don't, my Lord. I enjoy working for you. It keeps me warm'. That evening Nanak appointed him his successor, naming him Angad (literally 'my limb', myself). During the night Nanak died.

37. *What are the main events in Nanak's life which particularly interest you? Why?*

38. *Compare the ways in which Jesus and Nanak preached or demonstrated their beliefs.*

Gobind Singh. Sikhs believe their gurus (wise leaders) are men who have achieved moksha (spiritual liberation, freedom from rebirth). They are perfect men who have been sent to earth once more to preach God's message. The Sikhs had ten gurus from Nanak to Gobind Singh (1666–1708). Gobind was guru at one of the many times when the Sikhs were persecuted by the Muslim Mogul Emperor of India. He realized that a strong organization was essential if Sikhism were to survive. The emperor had executed the previous guru, and had one boiled to death and another sawn in half while alive. So in 1699 Gobind called the Sikhs together at Anandpur. He stood in military uniform with drawn sword in front of a tent, and cried three times, 'Is there anyone of you who will give his head to prove his faith in me? I want a head!' One Sikh got up and said, 'Lord, you can have my humble head. There can be no greater gain than to die under your sword'. Gobind took him into the tent; a thud was heard and blood flowed out. Gobind emerged with dripping sword and cried, 'Is there any other true Sikh who will offer his head?' Twice more he called and another came forward. Five times in all this frightening ritual was enacted before he and the five emerged from the tent. They were all dressed in saffron uniforms and carried swords. To an astonished audience he announced that the five were now his brothers in the cause as they had passed the toughest test. He declared his intention to start the Khalsa ('pure ones') army of soldier-saints, a brotherhood in which all were equal. They took the surname Singh ('lion') and demonstrated their equality and unity by consuming amrit (sugar and water mixture) and received the five K's in a ceremony (see pp. 199–202). Twenty thousand Sikhs were then

Guru Gobind Singh

Two Sikh gurus. Describe Guru Nanak to someone who has not seen this picture. What differences are there between him and Guru Gobind Singh? (Look at the clothes and facial expressions.)

43

'baptized' into the Khalsa that day. Gobind told them they must never shrink from the enemy but help the poor and protect the weak. They must not smoke or use drugs and should not cut their hair.

39. *Write a one-act play on Gobind's founding of the Khalsa. Read about the five K's on p. 201 before doing so.*

The fighting continued and Gobind's four sons sacrificed themselves for the cause. The two youngest, aged 9 and 7, were bricked up alive in a wall in 1704. Gobind died in 1708 as a result of being stabbed by a Muslim retainer. He was known to his followers by numerous names, some of which have been translated as follows:

> *Pious, Profound, Perfect and Princely Prophet,*
> *Painstaking, Prominent, Powerful and Pitiful Patriot,*
> *Platonic, Practical, Prudent and Pacific Philosopher,*
> *Progressive, Popular, Proficient and Prolific Poet,*
> *Promising, Predominant, Patient and Potent Politician,*
> *Paternal, Polite, Pleasant and Peaceful Personage.*

> *Subtle, Serious, Sober and Stately Seer,*
> *Sympathetic, Strong, Soothing and Successful Saviour,*
> *Sweet, Supreme, Sacred and Simple Saint,*
> *Scientific, Sound, Shining and Significant Scholar,*
> *Skilful, Sensible, Sagacious and Sane Statesman,*
> *Selfless, Stout, Splendid and Steady Soldier,*
> *Sincere, Silent, Superfine and Social Sage,*
> *Smiling, Shielding, Striking and Spiritual Sovereign.*

40. *Take two or three other letters of the alphabet and see how many words you can write down which could be applied to Gobind Singh.*

41. *What happened when an Islamic jihad and a Sikh Khalsa met in India? See if you can find out both for Gobind's period and the late 1940s.*

Nam. Sikhs believe in one God whom they call Nam ('Name'). Nanak wrote, 'There is one God . . . the All-pervading Creator, without fear, without hatred, immortal, unborn, self-existent! God sustains all and is a personal God who is close to men's hearts. He controls history.' Nanak wrote:

> *By His writ some have pleasure, others pain,*
> *By His grace some are saved,*
> *Others doomed to die, relive and die again.*

Gobind made his view of Nam clear when he wrote, 'God has no marks, no colour, no caste and no ancestors, no form, no complexion, no outline, no costume and so He is indescribable. He is fearless, luminous and measureless in might'. Of Man's relations with God, he wrote:

> *As sparks flying out of a flame*
> *Fall back on the fire from which they rise,*
> *As dust rising from the earth*
> *Falls back upon the same earth;*
> *As waves beating upon the shingle*
> *Recede and in the ocean mingle*
> *So from God come all things under the sun*
> *And to God return when their race is run.*

Notice that Nam does not become incarnate, that is He does not come to earth in any human form, but He is called Father. Guru Arjan (1563–1606) said, 'He dwells in everything; He dwells in every heart'. Sikhs treat the Guru Granth Sahib (Sikh holy book, see pp. 64–5) with devotion like the Christians treat their Bible and the Muslims their Koran.

42. *Compare the Muslim idea of God with that of the Sikhs. Is the Sikh idea nearer that of the Muslims or the Christians?*

Recent history. Sikhism began as an attempt to combine Hinduism and Islam and suffered a lot of persecution from both as a result. There have been many divisions among the Sikhs in their 400-year history. They suffered in great massacres, nearly half a million dying in 1947 when the Punjab was divided between Pakistan and India through their territory. The survivors were driven out of Pakistan and some went to E. Africa or Britain. Others continue to live in India. There are now about 15 million, of whom half a million live in Britain.

43. *Make a table listing the words or phrases used to describe (a) Brahman; (b) the Jewish God; (c) the Christian God; (d) Allah; (e) Nam. Then add a further column (f) with words or phrases which appear in all the other columns. Finally add a column (g) containing words or phrases you would use to describe God.*

44. *Draw a world map and mark in the areas of the different religions. Mark in the total membership figures for each religion as part of the key.*

3.
BOOKS TO READ

All the main religions of today possess holy books of some kind, often dating back a very long way. Holy books are usually ones which contain teaching revealed by God or gods and so they are of very special value to their religions. Their contents may have been built up over a thousand years, as with the Jewish holy books, or quite a short time, as with Islam's Koran which was finished within 40 years.

We shall see that some religions revere their holy books as so much the very word of God that they will not allow them to be criticized in any way. Such books are regarded as infallible; that is, they tell the truth and cannot be faulted. People who believe in the literal truth of such books are often called fundamentalists.

Holy books are usually given a place of honour in the worship building and may be ceremoniously carried in during services. Readings from them are considered most important and a sermon (instructive talk) may be based on some passage from them. This liturgical (service) use of holy books will be dealt with more in Chapter 5. Most Hindus, Orthodox Jews, Muslims and Sikhs insist that when their scriptures are used in services they are read in their original languages as God revealed them in those languages.

The contents of holy books are varied. They are likely to contain some historical facts as well as biographies of leading characters, rules to be followed, songs or poems to be recited, and myths. Myths are stories of God or gods, people and events. They are designed to explain matters which would otherwise not be easy to put into words. For example, the story of Adam and Eve explains the need for people to find God, ask His forgiveness and obey Him in future.

HINDUISM

Hindu sacred writings are of two types:

(1) Sruti, or Shruti ('hearings') which the rishis (holy men) heard

from the gods. Thus they are eternal and were in existence when the rishis discovered them. They include the Vedas and the Upanishads.

(2) Smriti, or Smrti ('memory') which were remembered from generation to generation then written down by wise men. This means that they are considered as lower than the Sruti. If there is anything in Smriti which conflicts with Sruti, the Sruti point is taken as correct. They include the Mahabharata, Ramayana and the Laws of Manu.

Sruti. The Vedas ('Knowledge of God') are four books recorded in Sanskrit between 1500 and 800 BC. The first books are the Karma Kanda ('work portion') while the Upanishads or Vedanta are the Jnana Kanda ('knowledge portion'). The first section of the Vedas is the Samhitas ('collection') of chants. The second is the Brahmanas ('belonging to brahmins'), the prayer book section with rules for sacrifices and rituals. Sacrifices serve three purposes:

(1) Gifts to persuade gods to give people long life, health and wealth.

(2) Sin offerings to remove guilt.

(3) Communal meals with the gods so that those who join in acquire the gods' virtues.

One of the four Vedas is the Rig-Veda (Veda of Praise), which consists of ten volumes (mandalas) containing 1017 hymns to nature gods, each made up of a number of verses (mantras). These hymns reflect the nomadic life of people who cry out to their favourite gods as they charge into battle, rejoice in the sun's rising or feel lonely on a silent evening.

The 108 Upanishads (meaning 'sit down near your teacher') were recorded between 800 and 300 BC. They are also known as the Vedanta ('end of the Vedas') as they used to be the third section of the Vedas. Set in quiet forest glades, they consist of discussions and teachings that gurus (teachers) had with their disciples about Brahman, atman, karma and transmigration. They answer the question 'Who are you?' by saying that you are not the clothes you wear, nor the things you eat, nor the face you have; your real self is your atman (soul), which you will find when you join Brahman. They stress that the millions of gods of the Vedas are really one, Brahman, which is the energy source behind them all. Life is a quest to over-come problems. They offer the yogas (ways) to salvation to enable

you to find your atman and so cease to return continually to earth.
For example:

From the unreal lead me to the real!
From darkness lead me to light!
From death lead me to immortality!
He who inhabits water . . . fire . . . the sky . . . heaven . . . the sun
. . . the moon and stars . . . darkness . . . light . . . He is your Self
[atman], the Inner Controller, the Immortal.

Smriti. Mahabharata (Story of the War of the Bharatas) and
Ramayana (Adventures of Rama) are long collections of stories
(epics). They attempt to get to grips with the mysteries of chaos and
misery in human life and show how order and purpose in life would
eventually prevail. They claim that history goes in cycles. The world
starts in good order or righteousness (dharma) and then goes
through four ages (yugas) in which goodness weakens until it is
necessary for the gods to destroy the world and start again.

The Ramayana is set at the end of the second yuga, when
goodness is still basically intact but under serious threat. The
adventures were put together in Sanskrit by Valmiki, a wise man, in
about 300 BC. Prince Rama, heir to the kingdom of Ayodhya, is
exiled when his step-mother tries to get her son made heir. Rama, his
wife Sita, and his brother are sent to the forest home of the demons.
The demon king, Rvana, abducts Sita and takes her to his island
kingdom, Sri Lanka. Eventually monkeys, led by the monkey-god
Hanuman, link tails to provide a bridge for Rama to rescue Sita.
Rama (an avatar of Vishnu, see p. 10) is the ideal good ruler whose
faith withstands the demons' wiles. Sita proves her loyalty, when
Rama doubts it, by walking through fire. So good conquers evil by a
display of manly courage, and a woman's virtue is maintained.

The Mahabharata is the world's longest poem, consisting of
three million words and it is set at the end of the third yuga. It tells of a
tragic war between two sets of cousins, the Pandavas and the Kurus,
or Kauravas, of the Bharata royal family, which ushers in the Kali
yuga, the final age of disorder and wickedness in which we now live
today. It was compiled perhaps about 200 BC by a vyasa (editor)
who was told by Brahma to get Ganesha, the elephant god, to take it
down at his dictation.

The Pandavas and Kurus both wanted control of Elephant City,
a kingdom whose ruins are near Delhi. The Kurus became jealous of
the heroism and goodness of the five Pandava brothers, and tried to
burn them in their palace. The Pandavas, however, secretly hid in
the forest disguised as brahmins. The story centres on how the five

face the crisis. The eldest hates war and wants to turn from the world like a Buddhist monk. The second thinks only of fighting on, while the fourth and fifth are too young to help. The third, Arjuna, dislikes war but is nevertheless a great warrior. Eventually he emerges from the forest to win an archery contest and hence a princess in marriage. He alone was strong enough to draw the bow and hit the eye of a revolving target five times. So the Kurus had to recognize the five were still alive and share the kingdom with them. But they succeeded in tricking them by a game of dice and after some years the war was renewed.

The climax is a section of the Mahabharata called the Bhagavad Gita (Song of the Lord) consisting of 700 verses written between 400 BC and AD 100. In it Arjuna hesitates before the final battle at Kurukshetra as he is shocked at fighting his relatives. He orders his chariot driver to withdraw, but the man argues with him. Gradually Arjuna realizes the man is in fact Krishna, the god, who has appeared to teach him the truth. Krishna argues that because the world is threatened with chaos it is Arjuna's duty to restore order and not simply fight for his own gain. He must face up to life and serve God as revealed in Krishna. What Krishna asks for is love, 'Just fix your mind

Krishna as charioteer to Arjuna.

upon Me, the Supreme Personality of the Godhead, and engage all your intelligence in Me. Thus you will live in Me always'.

Krishna assures Arjuna that those who die in battle live eternally, for none really die. So Arjuna, aided by Krishna, fights and wins over the Kurus with all their material forces. In a sense Arjuna represents Man's soul and the chariot his body while the chariot's motion is time and the battlefield the world.

The poem commands personal devotion to a personal God and this form of life and worship is called Bhakti Yoga (see p. 71). In overcrowded, poverty-ridden India it is the most popular Hindu scripture today.

The Yoga Sutras (Yoga Exercises) were written in AD 100–200 (see pp. 72–3). The Puranas ('old writings') were written about 1000 years ago to popularize the religion of the Vedas. They were written in the language of the time for ordinary people to read. They illustrate the main religious points by means of stories about the world's creation, destruction and re-creation and the lives of the rishis, kings and gods.

The Laws of Manu ('man', a kind of Adam) has 12 books with 2685 verses, and was written in 200–100 BC. They give detailed instructions on what men may or may not do, marriage laws, diet rules, daily rites and laws, and so on:

> Coveting the property of others, thinking in one's heart of what is undesirable and adherence to false doctrines are three kinds of sinful mental action. Abusing others, speaking untruth, detracting from the merits of all men, and talking idly shall be four kinds of evil verbal action.

The Tantra ('Rule System') are magical and religious books made up of talk between Shiva and Shakti about creation, destruction, worship, etc., in which the power of the female is dominant.

1. List the titles, dates and main subjects of these Hindu books.

2. Draw a picture or series of pictures from some of the stories in these books.

SHINTOISM

Although the word 'Shinten' means 'a collection of sacred books', Shintoism has no holy book comparable to those of other religions, but it has got the Kojiki (Records of Ancient Matters) which was finished in AD 712 and covers events to AD 628. It contains myths and historical stories about creation, gods, men, the nation, customs and ceremonies. The story of Izanagi and Izanami is in it (see pp. 12–13).

The Nihongi or Nihon Shoki (Chronicles of Japan) gives different versions of the same creation myths and legendary figures as the Kojiki, and covers to AD 700; it was compiled in AD 720. For example:

> *Of old, Heaven and Earth were not yet separated . . . They formed a chaotic mass like an egg which was of obscurely defined limits and contained germs . . . Heaven was therefore formed first, and Earth was established subsequently. Thereafter Divine Beings were produced between them.*

The purpose of these books is to make clear the origin of the Imperial Throne with its clan lineage.

3. *What does a religion lack if it has not got a 'bible'? Why cannot the two Shinto books be considered as 'bibles'?*

4. *Are books of myths and legends any real religious help today?*

TAOISM

There are two main books from about 300 BC and a collection of books compiled in the fifteenth century AD:

Tao Te Ching (pronounced 'Dow Deh Jing'), means The Way and its Power, or, The Book of the Right Way. It is the basic guidebook said to be written by Lao-Tse. It is like a popular bedside book today. If it was written by him, it would date from the sixth century BC, but it was more likely written by an unnamed person between 350 and 300 BC. It has 81 short chapters and teaches that there is a way (Tao) which if taken will show how a perfect balance in one's life can be reached. But it is a cryptic book, which has been understood in different ways. Man can possess three great treasures, it claims:

> *I have Three Treasures. Guard them and keep them safe.*
> *The First is Love.*
> *The Second is Moderation.*
> *The Third is Never be first in the world.*
> *With love, one will have courage.*
> *With moderation, one will have power to spare.*
> *Through not trying to be first in the world, one can develop talent and let it grow.*

Men should live according to nature and so it is opposed to too much government activity and too many laws. It is against war too.

He who by Tao proposes to help a ruler of men will oppose all conquest by force of arms; For such things are wont to rebound. Where armies are, thorns and brambles grow, . . . And what is against Tao will soon perish.

Book of Chuang Tzu. It is thought that Chuang Tzu (369–286 BC) actually wrote little of it. Its 33 chapters are made up of essays and stories, and it is important as it explains the Yin–Yang idea that nature is controlled by continuous transformations as the two forces rock to and fro.

Tao Tsang is a collection of books compiled in AD 1436. It consists of 1120 volumes which contain material from much earlier centuries. It is divided into the San Tung (Three Vaults) and the Ssu Fu (Four Supplements). The first two San Tung contain texts for meditation and rituals, while the third has the 24 registers of the names and functions of the spirits discovered by Chang Tao Ling, the first Heavenly Master and founder of Tao Chiao, Religious Taoism. The Ssu Fu contains the Tao Te Ching and an alchemy section. The volumes have spiritual charts, illustrations, magical rites, charms, cures, blessings and hymns.

BUDDHISM

Tripitaka (Three Baskets) are the scriptures of the Theravāda or Southern Buddhists, written in Pali. The original texts have long since been lost and the earliest surviving fragments date from 250 BC. The title refers to the way baskets of earth are passed from hand to hand in building, implying that baskets of wisdom or traditions are passed from person to person.

The Vinaya Pitaka (Discipline Basket) is the first basket. It gives rules for monks and nuns.

The Sutta Pitaka (Teaching Basket) contains the teachings of Buddha and his followers. These are debates with Hindu priests who challenge them. It contains stories of Buddha, a description of the 32 superman marks which he had on his body, and an account of his descent to the world to give us his teachings. There are 547 Birth Stories about Buddha's previous lives as a bird, stag, hare and man.

As a stag he sacrificed himself to save the herd; as a hare he hurled himself into a fire to feed a starving brahmin. Finally, it contains the Dhammapada, the Way of Virtue, or Path of Teaching, which in 26 chapters gives the Four Noble Truths and the Eightfold Path (see pp. 85–90). Its 423 verses are often learnt by heart.

Do not speak harshly to anybody; those who are spoken to will answer thee in the same way. Angry speech breeds trouble, you will receive blows . . . To wait on mother and father, to cherish child and wife and follow a quiet calling, this is true blessedness . . . To give alms, to live religiously, to protect relatives, to perform blameless deeds, this is true blessedness. . . . To cease from sin, to refrain from intoxicating drinks, to persevere in right conduct, this is true blessedness . . . Patience and pleasant speech, contact with holy men, religious conversation in due seasons, this is true blessedness. Penance and chastity, discernment of the noble truths and the realization of Peace, this is true blessedness.

5. *Compare these statements with the Beatitudes (Blessednesses) given by Jesus in Matt. 5:1–12.*

The *Abhidhamma Pitaka* (Higher Teaching Basket) has long explanations and comments on Buddha's teachings. *Milinda-Panha* (Questions to King Milinda) was written in the first century AD and deals with the questions this Greek king put to the monk Nagasena about Buddhism:

The King asked, 'Is it true that nothing transmigrates, and yet there is rebirth?'
'Yes, your majesty'.
'How can this be? Give me an illustration'.
'Suppose, your majesty, a man lights one lamp from another—does the one lamp transmigrate to the other?'
'No, your reverence'.
'So there is rebirth without anything transmigrating'.
'Does the Buddha still exist?'
'Yes, your Majesty, he does'.
'Then is it possible to point out the Buddha as being here or there?'
'The Lord has passed completely away in nirvana, so that nothing is left which could lead to the formation of another being. And so he cannot be pointed out as being here or there'.
'Give me an illustration'.
'What would your Majesty say if a great fire were blazing, would it be possible to point to a flame which had gone out and say that it was here or there?'

'No, your reverence'.

'In just the same way . . . the Lord has passed away in nirvana
. . . He can only be pointed out in the body of his doctrine, for it was
he who taught it'.

Other Buddhist Books. The Mahāyāna, or Northern Buddhists,
accept the Tripitaka but have other books as well. They are the Sutras
('threads'), a collection of rules or sayings. There are so many of
them that no man has read them all. The Diamond Sutra or Scripture
compiled in the fourth century AD, deals with Buddha's knowledge
and teaching. It says a Bodhisattva's (saviour's) job is to save all
beings.

The Lotus Sutra or Lotus of the Wonderful Law was written in
the second century AD. It has been called the 'Gospel of half Asia'. It
pictures the Buddha sitting on a Himalayan peak, announcing to
thousands a new way for all to be saved. He points out that a
Theravāda monk's life is too narrow as it results in only a few being
saved. From now on a large raft (mahāyāna) will enable all to cross
the sea of life to be saved.

6. *List the names and summarize the contents of (a) Southern
    Buddhist and (b) Northern Buddhist books.*

The Diamond
Sutra.

JUDAISM

The Tenakh (or Jewish Hebrew Bible) is the Old Testament of the Christian Bible but in a different book order. The Greek translation is called the Septuagint (meaning '70') as it was translated by 70 people in 270 BC. It consists of 24 books divided into three sections: (1) the Torah (Law); (2) the Prophets (Nevi'im); and (3) the Writings (Ketubim).

(1) The Torah, meaning 'guidance' or 'teaching', is made up of five books: Genesis, Exodus, Leviticus, Numbers and Deuteronomy. Genesis deals with the beginning of the universe and early life on earth. Exodus describes how the Israelites escaped from slavery in Egypt. Leviticus lays down rules on the jobs of priests and (among other things) how to deal with sacrifices and leprosy. Numbers deals with Jewish history from the time the Jews left Mount Sinai until they approached Canaan, the promised land, and shows how their leader Moses built them up into a nation. Numbers refers to the census taken at the time. Deuteronomy (the 'second book of the Law') reviews the events of the earlier books and concludes with some strong statements by Moses on how the Jews are to live. It includes the Ten Commandments (Deut. 5:1–22).

7.   Read Gen. 1–2 and summarize these chapters.

8.   Read Lev. 5 and name the different types of sacrifice mentioned. Describe one of the types in detail.

9.   Read Lev. 13–14 and state the main rules for leprosy cases.

(2) The Prophets are books dealing with Jewish history from the time of Joshua. Holy people called prophets disclosed various aspects of God to the Jews and guided them in their understanding and worship (see pp. 22–3). The books include Joshua, Samuel, Amos, Isaiah, Jeremiah and Ezekiel. Jews regard the Torah books as more important than the Prophets, whereas Christians do the reverse.

(3) The Writings deal with human problems, such as family relations, social and business matters, manners and moral behaviour. Among the numerous books that make up this section is the Psalms, which deals with the whole range of human life at its best and worst. The book Ecclesiastes argues that everything in this world is impermanent and worthless. Pleasure is short-lived and wisdom gives a wise man no advantage over a fool when they both die

(Eccles. 2:13–16). Wealth has nothing to do with merit or ability but just chance; moreover it cannot be taken with one at death (Eccles. 9:11). Good and bad people are treated alike so good behaviour seems pointless (Eccles. 9:2). Although earthly life is transitory, and fleeting, it is not pointless; it is a riddle which we do not yet know the answer to.

10. *Produce some evidence for and against Ecclesiastes' arguments about life.*

The Book of Job is the story of a good man who suffers horribly, so raising the question of why do people suffer. It stresses that suffering is not the result of one's sins as the sinful prosper and the good suffer. It concludes that suffering is a mystery.

11. *Read (a) Pss. 5 and 12 and (b) Prov. 23:29–35 (on alcoholism). Summarize what they say in modern English.*

The Torah can also refer to the Prophets and Writings when it is used in the synagogue (see pp. 136–7). It is highly honoured by Jews as they regard it as a sacred object in their ritual. It sums up the learning, wisdom and love of God which is involved in their faith. The Torah scrolls used in the synagogues are handwritten on parchment.

Studying the
Torah.

Talmud. Second in importance to the Tenakh is the Talmud (meaning 'teachings', 'tradition'). This is a huge collection of traditions to explain the Torah, as well as the oral law handed down by word of mouth from previous generations. It was completed in the fifth century AD. It is the main Jewish textbook for social and religious laws as it was compiled from the writings of over 1000 contributors. Its 63 sections contain legal rulings, stories, history, discussions between scholars, thousands of parables, biographies and humorous anecdotes in 6000 pages and 3 million words. The legal rulings are called Mishnah and deal with the laws on agriculture, the Temple and sacrifices, cleanliness and impurity rules. The Gemara are the rabbis' explanations of the Mishnah, printed below each Mishnah. Here are some examples from the Talmud:

- *Give every man the benefit of the doubt.*
- *One good deed invariably leads to another; an evil deed always brings another in its wake.*
- *Do not threaten a child; either punish him or forgive him.*
- *A classroom should never have more than 25 pupils.*
- *When you encounter a child whose head is as solid as iron, you may be sure that his teacher did not have a pleasant way of explaining things.*
- *Always begin the lesson with a humorous illustration.*
- *There are four categories of pupil: the sponge — he absorbs and retains everything; the funnel — everything that goes in comes out; the sifter — he remembers the trivial and forgets the significant; the sieve — he retains the important and sifts out the incidental.*
- *Judge a man not according to the words of his mother, but according to the comments of his neighbours.*

12.   *Give your opinion on what the Talmud says about schools and schoolchildren.*

The Midrash (meaning 'to search out, expound') deals with legal, moral and devotional teachings, and includes the well-known saying, 'All is well that ends well'. It includes the oldest legends and fables of the Jews.

For Orthodox Jews the Torah and its interpretation, the Talmud, are the Word of God and must be kept as divine. Reform Jews do not believe that God actually delivered the whole Torah and argue that human errors have crept in. They believe God is definitely concerned about its good behaviour rules, and maybe its ritual ones too. The Liberal Jews see the Torah as 'teaching' rather than 'law' and so argue that it can be changed. This means rituals are not divinely binding.

The Holy Bible (Greek 'biblia' means 'books') consists of the Jewish Old Testament (Old Covenant) in Hebrew and the New Testament (New Covenant) in Greek. The latter's contents were not finally decided until AD 367. Although it was clear that certain books should be included there were a number on the borderline. Even today the Roman Catholic Bible contains a section of Jewish writings called the Apocrypha which are not accepted by Protestants. The New Testament consists of 27 books including: (1) the four Gospels ('good news') named after early Christians Matthew, Mark, Luke and John, which recount Jesus' life on earth; (2) Acts of the Apostles by Luke; (3) 21 Epistles ('letters') mainly by Paul; (4) the Book of Revelation. The Gospels and Acts were all probably written at different times between about AD 60 and 100. The Epistles' dates vary from about AD 48 to about AD 140, and Revelations was written in about AD 90. By including the Old Testament in the Bible, Christianity is the only religion to include all the scriptures of another religion with its own.

The Gospels came to be written down for several reasons. The original eye-witnesses of Christ's earthly life were dying out, while the spread of Christianity made it impossible to keep in personal contact with all members and the persecution of Christians ordered by Emperor Nero in AD 64 gave a feeling of urgency to the matter. Errors would creep in if there was no book to lay down the truth. The gap between the Old Testament and the Epistles needed filling with the story of Christ's earthly life and the early life of the Church.

The four Gospels record Jesus' life and teaching. Matthew's, Mark's and Luke's are similar because Mark's Gospel was probably used as a basis for the other two. Hence they are called the Synoptic Gospels. Presumably each author wanted to give to the story the emphasis which he thought would suit his particular readers. The result is that the Gospels are not straightforward biographies but books designed to proclaim Jesus as the expected Messiah, the Saviour whom God sent to mankind. We have already studied their content in Chapter 2 (pp. 27–31). They contain numerous parables (stories with a meaning), healing stories and comments by Jesus. John's Gospel begins each chapter with a story about Jesus and then goes on to comment on it afterwards.

13. *Look in the Gospels for the birth stories of Jesus. Summarize them, pointing out how they differ.*

14. Read Matt. 20:1−16 and then rewrite it in a modern setting in England.

The 'Good News' was that the reign of God was near. All should repent of their sins, and Jesus had explained what was involved in starting a new life. Some may have thought he was about to start a national uprising against the Romans and the Gospels record the desperate attempts made to have him found guilty and condemned to crucifixion (death on a cross). They describe the event and then the astonishment of the disciples (Jesus' followers) when they find he has vanished from the tomb. Eye-witness accounts of the risen Christ are given.

Acts starts with Peter and his companions preaching the new faith and how a persecutor of theirs, Saul of Tarsus, becomes converted and is renamed Paul. Paul then goes on to bring the gospel to Gentiles (non-Jews) when he sees it has world-wide implications and is not a religion solely for the Jews.

15. Read Acts 2:44−47. How did the early Christians live?

16. Read Acts 5:7−7:3; 7:51−60. Describe how the first Christian to die for his faith was handled by the authorities and what he said at his trial.

17. Read Acts 9:1−30. Put in your own words what happened to Paul. What explanations can you give of these events?

The Epistles (epistolē is Greek for 'letter') are letters by Paul and others to groups of Christians they have started at Rome, Corinth, etc., and to friends such as Timothy and Philemon. They explain Christian beliefs, and argue that Jesus is the Messiah whom the Jews expected. They claim he is God's Anointed One, the Son of God in fact. They present a new way of thinking about God, stressing that He is Love.

18. Read 1 Cor. 7:26−40. What does this indicate about what early Christians thought was about to happen?

19. Read Eph. 3:1−11. State in your own words what Paul's message is. Why might it disturb the Jews?

The Book of Revelation was written to encourage Christians who were facing persecution by Nero and other Roman emperors. Its strange visions of heaven and warfare cannot be taken literally.

Most Christians are prepared to analyse and criticize the Bible in an effort to find the truth from the fiction about their faith, although they hold it in respect and use it regularly in services. Sermons often explain its meaning. Jesus is regarded as more important than the Bible in contrast to the Sikhs, for example, who respect their holy book more than their founder.

ISLAM

The Koran or Qur'an (meaning 'recitation') is the sacred book which Muhammad received as revelations from Allah via the angel Gabriel over a period of 20 years beginning in AD 610. An official version was compiled in about AD 650. It is different from the other books we are considering because it is the only one collected by one person. It is a little shorter than the New Testament and contains 114 surahs (chapters), which, except for the first surah, are arranged in order of decreasing length from Surah 2's 286 verses (ayats) to Surah 114's six verses. Events are described in reverse order, the shorter chapters dealing with earlier events and the longer ones later matters. Because of this some translations reverse the order of surahs.

It is claimed that the original Koran is on a tablet beside Allah's throne in heaven and that every word is Allah's: 'There is no doubt in this book'; ' "I have perfected revelation for mankind", said Allah'. The Koran is to Muslims what Christ is to the Christians, the Word of God, but in the form of a book instead of a man.

Muhammad could not read or write and so he could not have written the Koran himself, argue the Muslims. He memorized it and

(a) Extract from a sixth-century bible discovered in England in 1982. The extract is from Ecclesiasticus and the language is Latin.
(b) Extract from the Koran. What is the language?

(a)

(b)

60

dictated it to scribes. It is said that after Muhammad's death, Abu Bakr ordered Zaid to write it down and he did 'from pieces of paper, stones, palm leaves, shoulder-blades, ribs, bits of leather and from the hearts of men'. In Arabic it is in rhyming prose and Arabic copies are used in mosques although translations are used in private. Because it is Allah's word no criticism of the text is allowed.

Every chapter except one begins, 'In the name of God, the Compassionate, the Merciful'. Chapters headed Mecca and Medina show where they were revealed, while others are after such names as Abraham, Joseph and Mary, or after animals, such as the Cow, the Ant and the Bee.

20. (a) *Summarize how the Koran came to be written and explain the layout of the book.*
     (b) *What is the proof of its divine origin?*

Adam, Abraham, Joseph, David, Solomon and Jesus are referred to as prophets and honoured as true messengers of God. Abraham revealed there was only one God; Moses gave the Ten Commandments; and Jesus ('Isa') gave the Golden Rule of 'Love your neighbours as yourself'. Thus Islam follows on from Judaism and Christianity, paying respect to those religions, but also claiming that until Muhammad received the Koran the revelation of God was not complete. Muslims claim that Judaism and Christianity are superseded by Islam:

> He has revealed to you [Muhammad] the Book with the truth, confirming the scriptures which preceded it; for He has already revealed the Torah and the Gospel for the guidance of men, and the distinction between right and wrong. Those that deny Allah's revelations shall be sternly punished; Allah is mighty and capable of revenge. Nothing on earth or in heaven is hidden from Him . . . It is He who has revealed to you the Koran. Some of its verses are precise in meaning — they are the foundation of the Book — and others are ambiguous (or allegorical). Those whose hearts are infected with disbelief follow the ambiguous part, so as to create dissension by seeking to explain it. But no one knows its meaning except Allah. (Surah 3:3–7)

21. *How does the Koran get around the fact that some of its verses are difficult to understand?*

> This Koran could not have been composed by any but Allah . . . It is beyond doubt from the Lord of Creation. If they say: 'It is your own invention', say: 'Compose one chapter like it. Call on your false gods to help you, if what you say be true!' (Surah 10:37–40)

22. Why will Muslims not criticize the Koran?

So far as Christianity is concerned, the chief point is that Islam denies that Jesus was uniquely the Son of God. He is seen simply as a great prophet:

Speak nothing but truth about Allah. The Messiah, Jesus, son of Mary, was no more than Allah's apostle . . . So believe in Allah and His apostles and do not say, 'Three' (i.e. Trinity) . . . Allah is but one God. Allah forbid that He should have a son. (Surah 4:171)

Jesus' birth is mentioned twice in the Koran:

When the angel said: 'Mary! God has chosen thee and purified thee and chosen thee above the women of the world . . . be obedient to thy Lord and humble thyself . . . God gives thee good news with a word from Himself whose name is the Messiah, Jesus, son of Mary, worthy of regard in this world and the hereafter, and one of those who are near to God . . .' she said, 'My Lord, how shall there be a son born to me as no man has touched me and I am not unchaste?' He said, 'So shall it be, God creates what He pleases; when He has decreed a matter, He only says to it, "Be", and it is'. (Surah 3:40–46)

And she conceived him and then withdrew herself with him to a remote place. And the throes of childbirth compelled her to betake herself to the trunk of a palm tree. She said: 'Oh, would that I have died before this' . . . Then a voice called out to her . . . 'Grieve not'. (Surah 19:22–24)

It goes on to say that Jesus will heal the blind and lepers and bring life to the dead (Surah 3:18). But his crucifixion is denied.

And [the Jews] saying; 'We have killed the Messiah, Jesus, son of Mary, the apostle of God'; and they did not kill him nor did they crucify him, but he was made to resemble [one crucified] . . . and they killed him not for sure'. (Surah 4:157)

In fact, Muslims find it hard to accept that a prophet as great as Jesus could have suffered such a humiliating death. Because of this, some Muslims argue that someone who died on a cross was mistaken for Jesus. Others say he was put on the cross but revived when placed in the tomb. Nothing on the resurrection or ascension into heaven is mentioned.

23. Compare the Koran's references to Jesus' birth with those of Luke 1:26–55; 2:1–20.
(a) How does the Koran suggest the birth was quite unique?
(b) Why are these two versions of Jesus' birth so vital to the two religions concerned?

24. How does Islam link up with Judaism and Christianity?

25. (a) Why would the references to Jesus as the Messiah upset the Jews?
    (b) Is the meaning of Messiah different for these three religions?

26. Why must the Koran deny the crucifixion and the resurrection of Jesus if it is to be taken as God's Word?

The Koran's main message is that Allah is immaterial, invisible, almighty, the creator, the merciful, the judge, the kindly one, the wise, the life giver, the avenger, the forgiver. In all, 99 Beautiful Names are ascribed to Him. Man is Allah's supreme creation for the great, good world He created. Man's soul lives for ever. There will be a Day of Judgement, which will be considered in Chapter 8 (see p. 226). Clear directions are given on worship, marriage, divorce, women's position, fasting, almsgiving, pilgrimage and many other matters. Although the Koran may not be on display in a mosque, passages are used in prayer. Friday sermons are based on it. Before reading the Koran a Muslim will always wash carefully. Many learn it by heart and are awarded the title of Hafiz.

Hadith. Besides the Koran there is the Hadith ('saying'), the traditional sayings of Muhammad which record the Sunna, the rules of life. There are three kinds:

(1) A saying of Muhammad.

(2) An action or practice of his.

(3) His silent approval of someone else's action.

They can also be classified as Sahih (sound), Hasan (good) and Da'if (weak) or Saqim (infirm) according to how genuine they seem to be after extensive checking by thousands of scholars. In the Sunna the details of when to pray and give alms are spelt out as the Koran says little beyond 'pray and give alms' (see pp. 116–17). Several Hadith collections have been made and Bukhari's (AD 810–870) fills 97 books. He writes:

> Abdallah reported that 'Al-Fadl told us: "Isma'il told us on the authority of Yaha that he heard Abu say, 'I heard Ibn Abbas say, "When the Prophet . . . sent Mu'adh to the Yemen, he [Muhammad] said to him, 'You will come upon some of the People of the Book [Jews, Christians], so the first thing you will call on them to do is to profess the Oneness of God . . . When they have learned that, inform them God has prescribed . . . five ritual prayers a day . . . inform them that God has imposed zakat [see p. 116] on their possessions.'

27. (a) How many people passed along orally Muhammad's
    words before they were written down by Bukhari in the extract?
    (b) Why do you think some Muslims criticize the Hadith?
    (c) How are Muslims to treat Jews and Christians?

Sunni Muslims accept six collections of the Hadith while Shi'a
Muslims accept their own five collections. The Hadith is open to
criticism by Muslims.

SIKHISM

The Adi Granth ('original' or 'first' book) was compiled in AD 1604
by Guru Arjan. It is regarded with great respect (see pp. 150–2).
Arjan collected the preachings of six gurus and 12 non-Sikhs
together and wrote them down in Punjabi, the language of north-
west India. The teachings include 5894 hymns by Sikhs, Hindus and
Muslims in the 1430 pages. Nanak had written over 900 hymns and
Arjan included 2216 verses of his own. There are 31 tunes (ragas) for
these hymns. Guru Gobind Singh completed the book by adding
works by his father, Guru Tegh Bahadur. He declared that the
Granth would be his successor as Guru of the Sikhs. It was then
called Guru Granth Sahib (meaning 'Teacher Book, Sir'). Thus after
ten gurus there were to be no more gurus but the Granth would be
their living voice to men. It is treated with great reverence and its
pages are not touched by unwashed hands. When it is carried into a
room, everyone stands and bows towards it. In its presence Sikhs are
named, baptized and married.

At the beginning is the Mool Mantra (sacred chant stating Sikh
beliefs):

> There is one God
> Eternal Truth is His name:
> The Creator, devoid of fear and hatred
> Immortal, unborn, self-existent,
> Great and bountiful . . .

On the beginning of things, the Granth proclaims:

> In the beginning there was darkness; there was no earth or heaven,
> naught but God's unequalled being. There was no day or night or
> moon or sun, no life, no voices, no wind, no water . . . no continent,
> no hills, no seas, no rivers . . . nor the Hell nor Heaven of the
> Hindus, nor birth, nor death, nor did anyone feel pain or pleasure.
> There was no Brahma, no Vishnu, nor Shiva of the Hindus. There
> existed but the one God.

It offers the following advice:

Let compassion be thy mosque, let faith be thy prayer-mat, let honest living be thy Koran, let modesty be the rules of observance, let piety be the fasts thou keepest . . . The foolish who drink wine are the maddest of all. The true drunkards are those imbued with the name of God . . . Human birth is a rare fortune; it does not take place again and again . . . Pilgrimage, austerity, mercy, almsgiving and charity bring merit, be it as little as the mustard seed . . . Live amid the hurly-burly of life, but remain alert. Do not covet your neighbour's possessions. Without being devoted to God's name we cannot attain inner peace or still our inner hunger.

There are no story sections in the Granth. Few Sikhs own personal copies as this would involve setting aside a room in their home as a gurdwara (temple) to house it as they honour it so highly. It would also involve the owner in the daily task of having a pre-dawn bath before he read it and then in the evening a further reading followed by meditation.

The Dasam Granth is another collection of poems by the tenth guru ('das' means ten) Guru Gobind Singh. He wrote enough to fill 1428 pages. The collection making up the Dasam Granth was compiled in 1734 after his death. It is not held in such honour as the Guru Granth Sahib.

28. *What criticism of Islam does the Granth make and what would Muslims think of these criticisms?*

29. *What Hindu beliefs are rejected in the Granth? What would Hindus think of these rejections?*

30. *Make a table with columns headed: (a) religion; (b) holy book; (c) date of writing; (d) author, if known.*

31. *(a) Which religions take their basic book to be so holy as to be above criticism?*
    (b) Why do they do this?
    (c) What effect might such a view have on their religion?

32. *Describe the use made of their holy books by: (a) Christians; (b) Sikhs, during their services. (See pp. 141–2, 150–2 for further information.)*

33. *The scriptures of the world's religions are made up of very different types of literature. Illustrate this point by reference to the scriptures of two religions.*

4.
ON THE ROAD

Once you have become a member of a group or organization you are expected to obey the rules. If you do not do so, you will not get the full advantages of membership. Comparing the rules of one school with those of another can be an intriguing task as the differences may tell you a lot about the two schools, although by and large you will find the rules are similar. As you read this chapter compare each religion's rules. Ask yourself: what are these rules for? Are they designed to make you worship God properly or to ensure you live peacefully with your neighbour? The latter rules may be similar to those any country has to prevent crime. Do the rules suggest that good behaviour—a moral life—is an essential part of a life acceptable to God? Whereas a government makes laws on murder and adultery for the peace of the community, a religion may also do so because it claims God expects good behaviour.

But joining an organization has a purpose beyond that of obeying rules. A religious group is there to help and guide its members to find God or the truth about life here and hereafter. Each religion explains how to set off on life's journey. There is a right road to follow, they claim. If you step out along it you will 'get there in the end'. Not surprisingly, many religions means many roads are pointed out. But they may run parallel to each other. As the Vedanta Hindus say, 'God has made different religions to suit different aspirants, times and countries . . . One can ascend to the top of the house by means of a ladder or a bamboo or a staircase or a rope, so diverse are the ways and means to approach God, and every religion . . . shows one of these ways . . . The devotee who has seen God in one aspect only, knows Him in that aspect alone'. So let us examine the recommended routes and see what they have in common and what alternatives they offer.

HINDUISM

Rules. The Hindus have a set of clear-cut rules divided into two parts. The first part, Yama (abstentions, things not to be done) are:

(1) Do not destroy or injure anything.

(2) Do not lie.

(3) Do not steal.

(4) Do not be envious.

(5) Do not overeat or overdrink or over-indulge in sex.

The second part, Niyama (observances, things to be done) are:

(6) Keep yourself clean inside and out.

(7) Be contented.

(8) Practise self-discipline, tolerance, patience and mental calmness.

(9) Educate yourself.

(10) Try to surrender your mind to the Higher Power.

1. *Only Rule 10 refers to God; all the others refer to human weaknesses and characteristics. Only Rule 10 says 'Try': the rest are orders.*
   (a) Why do you think this is so?
   (b) Should a set of commands include more about our relationship with God?

Class and caste. It is claimed that Brahman assigned separate duties and jobs to those who sprang from his mouth, arms, thighs and feet. This means that every Hindu is born into a jati (birth caste group) and a varna (occupational class) and must follow the dharma (duty) of that position. The four varna classes are:

(1) Brahmins, priestly class, with varna colour of white.

(2) Kshatriyas, warrior and ruler class, with varna colour of red.

(3) Vaisyas, farmer, merchant and minor official class, with varna colour of yellow.

(4) Sudras, unskilled workers, with varna colour of black.

Besides them there are the pariahs, the 'outcasts' or 'untouchables', who do menial work.

A jati consists of about 1000 families with similar occupations, customs and marriage arrangements. Each village may have many jatis, one for each job; the landowner's jati being the superior one.

Three thousand jatis exist to cover all the occupational groups in India, and they are particularly important among the lower classes. Some jatis are regarded as 'impure' and thus 'untouchable', such as leather-workers, liquor distillers and butchers. Other trades are considered better, such as that of a tailor. The great holy leader Gandhi (1869–1948) did much to undermine this caste system by encouraging his followers to clean toilets, a job normally reserved for outcasts.

Hindu rules make various requirements depending on one's class. Brahmins can only eat rice cooked by brahmins, but vegetables cooked by anyone. Only brahmins can repeat the Vedas (see p. 47) while low-class Hindus must not do so. The lower classes may drink liquor but brahmins may never do so. It is a brahmin's 'dharma' (rule of life, duty) to study, while a kshatriyas should fight or rule, and so on.

2. Design posters to explain (a) the varna class system, (b) jati caste system.

3. Why do you think leather-workers, liquor distillers and butchers are in the untouchable jatis?

4. (a) Make a list of jobs done by Englishmen today, together with rules that these jobs impose on them.
    (b) How does your list compare with that which would affect Hindus under their system?

5. Comment on these Hindu sayings:
    (a) He who is calumnious (given to slander) has the character of a cat.
    (b) A sacrifice is obliterated by a lie and the merit of alms by an act of fraud.
    (c) Never do to others what would pain yourself.
    (d) Children should be considered lords of the atmosphere.
    (e) Love is all important, and is its own reward.

The Hindu paths. Hindus do not think about sinfulness as Jews and Christians do. Their gods and goddesses got married, had children, quarrelled, made friends, and so on. They were not concerned about sin in the way God is for the Christian. So the Hindu does not see the need to start on the road of life feeling himself to be a sinner. Instead, he knows that he has a dharma to perform. If he does his dharma, he will be able to cope with the dukkha (painfulness of life). The law of karma (you get what you deserve) is ever in his mind.

The problem a Hindu faces is maya, which is the name for all visible things which we mistakenly assume to be 'real'. We think things are real when they are not. They are really all illusions as they will all pass away one day. Chairs, houses, people, animals and so on are just illusions as they will not exist for ever. The word 'real' means something that will last for ever. Only Brahman is real. So the Hindu needs to follow the road to help him solve the confusion in his mind as he keeps thinking that things around him are real whereas they are only maya.

He claims there are four paths (yogas) which you can follow to obtain moksha (release from the worldly life; salvation). Different paths for different kinds of people. 'Yoga' also means 'yoke', and, as a yoke disciplines and unites two animals for ploughing, so yoga disciplines a person and brings him into unity with Brahman.

Jnana Veda Yoga (Path of Knowledge or Realizing) is the shortest, steepest, hardest path up the hill of life. It involves stopping caring about things and people. It means using all the powers of your brain to distinguish what is really yourself inside you from what you appear to be. If you try really hard you will find your true self, your real self, called your 'atman'.

He is myself within the heart, smaller than a grain of rice, smaller than a mustard seed; He is myself within the heart, greater than the earth, greater than the heaven; He is myself within the heart, He is that Brahmin . . . He who inhabits the nose — the organ of speech — the eye — the ear — the mind — the skin — He is your self, the Inner Controller, the Immortal. (Upanishad)

To follow this path you must divide your life into four sections. In practice few reach the last stage, however.

Stage One, the brahmacharin (student or immature stage), is for 8–20-year-olds, for study and character building. You must learn the rules of personal purification which involves bathing twice a day, good conduct, and so on.

Let him not injure others in thought or deed; let him not utter speeches which make others afraid of him, since that will prevent him from gaining heaven . . . Let him abstain from honey, meat, perfumes . . . substances flavouring food, women . . . and from doing injury to living creatures . . . from the use of shoes and an umbrella, from desire, anger, covetousness, dancing, singing . . . from grumbling, idle disputes . . . and lying, from looking at or touching women. (Laws of Manu, 200 BC)

6. *What kind of person will you become if you follow these rules?*

7. List (a) the rules you agree with, (b) the ones you do not agree with.

Stage Two. Grihastha (householder stage), for 20–50-year-olds, is when you earn your living, marry and have a family. You should choose a job suitable to your class, and speak, eat and dress in a way befitting your calling.

Stage Three. Vana Prastha literally means 'retirement as a hermit to search for the truth'. It begins with the birth of your first grandchild.

> *When a householder sees his skin wrinkled and his hair white . . .*
> *then he may resort to the forest . . . Abandoning all food raised by*
> *cultivation, and all his belongings, he may depart into the forest,*
> *either committing his wife to his sons, or accompanied by her . . . Let*
> *him wear a skin or tattered garment; let him bathe in the evening and*
> *in the morning, and let him always wear his hair in braids; the hair of*
> *his body, his beard, and his nails being unclipped . . . and give alms*
> *(or water, roots, fruit) according to his ability . . . Let him live without*
> *a fire, without a house, wholly silent, subsisting on roots and fruits.*
> (Laws of Manu)

8. List what a hermit gives up.

9. Do Hindu children care for their hermit parents or not? If not, what would the hermit parents miss which elderly parents in the West expect from their children?

Stage Four. Sadhus, or samnyasins, are holy men. Reaching this stage involves becoming a wanderer possessing only a loin cloth, food bowl and water pot, but freed of worries and duties. Only a very few women become sadhus.

A sadhu.

> *Take no thought of the future, and look with indifference upon the*
> *present. Departing from his house fully provided with the means of*
> *purification let him wander about absolutely silent and caring nothing*
> *for enjoyments that may be offered to him. Let him always wander*
> *alone, without any companion, in order to attain final freedom . . .*
> *He shall neither possess a fire, nor a dwelling, he may go to a village*
> *for his food, but be indifferent to everything . . . concentrating his*
> *mind on Brahman. A potsherd in place of an alms bowl . . . coarse*
> *worn-out garments, life in solitude and indifference towards*
> *everything, are the marks of one who has attained liberation . . . Let*
> *him bless when he is cursed . . . sitting (i.e. in yoga position) . . .*
> *entirely abstaining from enjoyment.* (Laws of Manu)

10. List the changes between the Third and Fourth Stages.

11. What attitude to worldly things is a holy man required to have and why?

Bhakti Yoga (Path of Love and Devotion) is the second path, and it is the most popular of the four. Instead of using your brain to search for the truth, you use your emotions, your feelings. Parents should love their children, children their parents, and so on. God loves you, so you should love Him.

> *All that you do, all that you eat, all that you offer and give away . . . should be done as an offering to Me. Thus you will be freed of all reactions to good and evil deeds; and by this principle of renunciation you will be liberated, and come to Me . . . Whoever renders service unto Me in devotion is a friend; and I am a Friend to him . . . Engage your mind always in thinking of Me, engage your body in My service; and surrender unto Me . . . Completely absorbed in Me, surely you will come to Me. (For anyone devoting himself to Me) I am the swift Deliverer from the ocean of birth and death . . . Just fix your mind upon Me, the Supreme Personality of Godhead . . . thus you will live in me always.* (Bhagavad Gita)

12. *Could a Christian follow this path to his God? Give your reasons for or against.*

13. *Would this path appeal to you or not? Why?*

14. *In what ways is this path easier to follow than Jnana Veda Yoga?*

Karma Yoga (Path of Works) is the third path. The more you do things without thought of gain for yourself, the less self-centred you will become. 'One to me is loss or gain, one to me is fame or shame, one to me is pleasure, pain'. What makes you work is your devotion to God, not your desire for more money or power. If you yourself do not count, you are freed from yourself. Work must be done as a sacrifice to the gods; otherwise it is selfish. Regular worship is essential. You must build up merit. The Laws of Manu lay down diets, home and public rituals and duties for each class, including those for birth, marriage, and so on.

Each home has a Pūjā, a shrine room or at least a god-shelf with a picture or statue of a god. Before dawn the Hindu utters the sacred sound OM or AUM which symbolizes the whole world, past, present and future. It is the mystical word for the Triad (threesome) of Vishnu, Shiva and Brahma. It is pronounced AA-OO-M; AA is the deepest note, produced in the chest; OO takes the vibration through the open mouth; M is pronounced softly with the lips together. If it is intoned properly he can feel his inner self withdrawn from his body. He also utters the name of his god and ties a coif of hair and marks his

71

forehead with ash or paste. Then he sits bare-chested and bare-foot, facing east. He meditates, and touches his body at six points to express the presence of God in his physical being. He bathes and at midday meditates again, offering flowers, food and light to God. His final worship is in the evening. Each day he must honour his parents and ancestors, and give shelter to guests or alms to the poor as well as feeding animals, especially cows. Even a starving family will divide its food into three portions: for guests, animals and themselves. In fact a Hindu's whole life is an act of religion as he makes a ritual of the simplest acts of washing, working and praying. Temple worship (pujas) is described on pp. 126–7.

15.   *Why does a Hindu do good works?*

16.   *How important do you think routine is to the followers of Karma Yoga?*

17.   *Explain the meaning of OM for a Hindu.*

Raja Yoga (the 'kingly' Path of Psychological Exercises) is the fourth path. In life you get so swamped with things to do and problems on your mind that you cannot see where you are going or what you are like, so this path is the one designed to clear your head and calm your thoughts. There are eight steps to follow.

Step One. Yama (self-control) is 'abstaining from harming others, from falsehood, from theft . . .'.

Step Two. Niyamas (observances, see p. 67) involve making your relations with others pure and devoted to God so that you gain supreme happiness.

Step Three. Asanas consist of 86 body positions for meditation. The Lotus position involves keeping your eyes half-open and focused on your nose or stomach. If you close your eyes you will daydream; if you keep looking around your mind will wander. Cross your legs to numb their nerve ends and start to control your breathing for Step Four.

Step Four. Pranayama is controlled breathing, in which you aim to breathe in slowly (count 16 slowly), hold your breath (count 64) and then slowly let your breath out (count 32). Try this out for yourself by starting with numbers such as 6, 24 and 12 as you will find it very hard to do. When you get into the daily rhythm of quietly doing this you will be able to release your mind and think of nothing, no earthly thing, as the remaining steps show.

A yoga position. What indicates his state of mind?

Step Five. Pratyahara is 'being alone', withdrawing your mind from things around you so that you have complete mastery over all your senses of smell, touch and hearing.

Step Six. Dharana is 'concentration', fixing the mind on some divine thing.

Step Seven. Dhyana is 'meditation', allowing your mind 'an unbroken flow of thought toward the object of your concentration', losing all sense of time and space.

Step Eight. Samādhi is 'becoming absorbed into atman', perceiving 'the true nature of the object shining forth, not distorted by the mind of the perceiver' (Yoga Sutras). Then you will find your real self, your atman, for you will have completely forgotten all your worries and hopes. You will have become detached from everything around you. You will have overcome the aches and pains of your body, the itches and fidgeting. Time stops, eternity is with you, as you hold your breath and almost stop living.

18. *Hindus keep their eyes half open when meditating; Christians close theirs when praying. What are the merits and weaknesses of these two methods?*

19. *Raja Yoga is designed to help you find reality, so how does it also help to make you cope with life more easily? What do local advertisements for yoga classes claim for those taking a course?*

20. *Why will this method involve years of practice to really achieve success?*

21. *Which of the four yogas would you prefer to try and why? Put them in your order of preference and say what you would find particularly difficult when trying each.*

22. *St Paul talked of Christ living in him and the Holy Spirit working in him; a Hindu talks of God being in himself. What conclusions can you draw from these viewpoints?*

Pilgrimages. Possibilities are almost limitless as rivers, mountains, coasts and their meeting places are considered holy. Benares is the most famous as it is situated on the holy R. Ganges where it is joined by the R. Varuna. As Shiva is said to have once lived there it is that god's special centre. Rama is also worshipped there and the annual Dussehra festival re-enacts the Ramayana story (see p. 48). To die in Benares and have one's ashes cast into the Ganges is the desire of all Hindus. Pilgrims take bottles of Ganges water home with them. At

Hardwar, at the head of the Ganges, ashes are also committed to the river as the name means 'The Lord's Gate'. Both cities are visited by pilgrims to perform ceremonies on behalf of their relatives and record events in their own lives. Vrindaban on the R. Jumna is visited as the birthplace of Krishna and the pilgrims follow a route recalling events

Benares on the River Ganges. Priests sit under the shades to teach. A temple's sikhara (see p. 126) is on the left. People stand in the water to pray and immerse themselves completely. Notice the sacred thread worn by those on the right (see pp. 178–80).

of his youth. Pilgrims pay priests to guide them through the complicated rituals which often involve the payment of money at various stages. Some crawl round the sacred place and this act of circling is called 'pradakshina'. Hindus are convinced their pilgrimages will be of lasting value in this life and the next.

23. *What reasons would a Hindu give for making a pilgrimage? How could he become a victim of commercialization?*

SHINTOISM

Standards of behaviour. Shintoists believe that people are born innocent of evil and so are essentially good. So too is the world as it is the kami-controlled world. Since the Shintoist does not have to root out inherited evil, he does not think a set of behaviour rules necessary. He argues that as he was born with the kami spirit in him he will know right from wrong in his heart. All he has to do is to follow his conscience. To have a set of behaviour rules would make him inferior to animals as they know what to do instinctively.

24. *Why are parents and teachers likely to disagree with the idea that following your conscience is sufficient? Can you run (a) a school, (b) a religion, (c) a country, on the assumption that conscience is sufficient?*

A Shintoist's religion does not set out to tell him whether his conduct is good or bad; instead it seeks to free him from his worries. He will not think of his attitudes or actions as sinful so much as shameful to his honour.

25. *What is the difference between 'sinful' and 'shameful'?*

To maintain his honour a Shintoist will observe high standards of behaviour. The way (michi) of the kami is vitally important to him. Michi is the essence of human life as it links him to the will of the kami and is the natural way to live. If he is to live an honourable life he must be sincere, honest, tolerant and generous. There are no real objections to drinking or indulging in sex. People's values are constantly changing, say Shintoists, and what may be the 'done thing' in one place or circumstance may not be elsewhere in different circumstances.

Some Shintoists, called Tenri-kyo, believe there are Eight Dusts which fall on the mirror of one's soul so that the mirror no longer reflects a true picture. The Dusts are covetousness, meanness, undisciplined love, hatred, revenge, anger, pride and selfishness. They are all to do with human relationships and they show that a Shintoist may find it difficult to live up to his conscience. But he will not blame himself so much as the magatsuhi (evil spirits) as they are the cause of evil (maga). His soul is good, but his flesh and senses can fall victim to the magatsuhi. To solve the problem he has to wipe the Dusts off and the mirror will be pure again.

26. *(a) Are there any other 'dusts' you could add to the Tenri list?*
(b) Are the eight all essential?
(c) Compare the basic Shinto belief about being born with the knowledge of right and wrong with the Tenri belief about Man's nature. Which is more likely to be right in your opinion, and why?

Purification. You can purify yourself by means of two ceremonies. These will cleanse you so that you do not have to feel personally sorry for your weaknesses, make a personal confession or ask for forgiveness. Notice the contrast here with the Christian who feels guilty if he has sinned in some way. Here are the two ceremonies:

Misogi (or Kessai). You must eat simple food in small quantities, avoiding meat, tea, coffee and alcohol, and take a cold bath or shower after a hot bath. For the best effect you should take your cold dip in a river, the sea or under a pounding waterfall, preferably naked or in a thin white robe. If no water is available, then you sit on a mountain top in a biting snowstorm. You should spend an hour each morning and evening in meditation, sitting in an awkward position, with little or no clothing, even if your skin turns blue. Notice the sharp contrast to the Hindu's comfortable meditation position.

Harai (or Oharai). This involves a white-robed priest 'paying' offerings on your behalf while waving a purifying wand (nusa, or haraigushi) made of long paper streamers and a few flax ones. He will wave it over his shoulders, left, right and left again. He may carry out the purification rite for your new car or house to make them safer.
    Both rites end with the same prayer:

Awe-inspiring, august Izanagi, when thou performed misogi-harai, facing the sun, in the plain covered with green trees at the mouth of a river, the great Kami of Purification, Haraedo-no-Kami, appeared. Give us purification for every kind of sin, blameable action or

Harai Purification. The priest is using his haraigushi wand to purify the car.

Misogi Purification. What are the main differences between Hindu meditation and Shinto purification?

pollution. *Cause the Heavenly Kami, the Earthly Kami and the august 80 myriads of Kami, all together, to give us purification. Please listen to me and augustly speak.*

27.   *With Misogi, what connection do Shintoists assume between bodily punishment and purification?*

28.   *With Harai, what must be the source of the priest's power to purify?*

Daily worship. Every Shintoist has his local guardian kami, and every house, workshop or office has its kamidana (god-shelf), with three boxes, containing shintai (god emblems), such as a hair, paper or a stone, to the 'Kami of the World', the local kami and ancestors. Each day you must purify yourself the Temizu ('hand water') way which means rinsing your mouth and pouring water over your finger tips. Then you offer rice and tea before saying your prayers of thanks. You can hang up ema (small wooden prayer tablets) on which you write your prayers—for example, 'I would like to find a nice girl to marry. I am fond of children so I think I can be a good father. Please help me'. There are four reasons for such daily actions:

(1) You must tell the kami what you have been doing—school-children will report their marks, even before telling their parents what they were.

Kamidana. How does the kamidana bring worship alive in a Shinto household?

77

(2) You must say your thanks for blessings received.

(3) You must offer praise to the kami.

(4) You must pray for the community and perhaps for yourself.

29. How does having a kamidana (a) at home, (b) in the office, help to bring Shintoism into daily life?

Pilgrimages are very popular and there are pilgrim associations to help you to visit as many as possible. It is almost a tourist industry. At the shrine you will throw a pebble to the komainu (dog statues) or torii (arch) (see pp. 127–9). Pilgrims like to collect the shrines' rubber-stamp seals in their 'stamp-books'. The seals state the temple's name and its kami's characteristics and the type of worship offered to him. The most famous shrine, at Isé, is described on p. 129. Every Shintoist is expected to make a pilgrimage there once in his life.

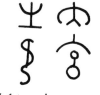

Isé temple stamp.

One hundred thousand visit Mount Fuji each year doing the eight-hour climb in straw sandals (waraji). There are six routes, each with ten resting huts.

TAOISM

Yin and Yang. Taoists believe self-discipline is better than discipline imposed by a set of rules. Consequently there is no list to be kept.

The Way (Tao) the universe works is governed by the twin forces of Yin and Yang. Watching nature at work the Chinese concluded that all nature is busy—things happen as the seasons come and go. There is a rhythm behind it all. Nature is full of energy. The active energy the Book of Chuang Tzu (see p. 52) called Yang and the quiet energy Yin (literally the 'sunny side' and the 'dark side' of a hill). Yang is sometimes symbolized as a dragon, while Yin is a tiger, but the usual pattern (Tai Chi) resembles two tadpoles. Yang is shown in red or white and Yin in blue or black. They are the balancing powers in life. Yang can be seen as summer, Yin as winter; or Yang as masculine and Yin as feminine; and so on. They overlap each other as the diagram shows. Each invades the other's hemisphere and establishes itself (the 'eye' dots) in the very centre of its opposite's territory. The message is that life is not clear-cut, a case of good or evil, right or wrong. Life is a mixture, a balance of good and evil. Yang is the power in life which produces all firm, solid warm things; Yin, the power that gives soft, moist changeable things. In life

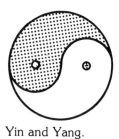

Yin and Yang.

the two powers are balanced, and life, like a wheel, rolls forwards and backwards. So sometimes nature and your life are governed by Yang and all is well, while sometimes Yin is in control and things go badly. When one or the other energy gets out of control they get 'out of balance'.

This leads Taoists to argue that they cannot state what is fixedly good or evil as some religions bluntly do. Good and evil are relative to each other. A farmer's neighbour said he was sorry to hear the man's horse had run away. 'Who knows what is good or bad?', replied the farmer. Next day the horse returned bringing a drove of wild horses it had found. The neighbour congratulated the farmer on his luck. 'Who knows what is good or bad?', he replied. The next day the farmer's son broke his leg trying to ride one of the wild horses. The neighbour said he was sorry. 'Who knows what is good or bad?', the farmer replied. Then soldiers came to force all healthy young men into the army, but the son was not drafted because of his leg. Thus Yang and Yin alternate in life. 'The Way to do is to be'.

30. *Write a story, fictional or true, in which good and bad, happiness and misery keep alternating. At the end of each event put 'yang' or 'yin' in brackets to indicate which is in control at the time. Make sure one event follows on from the previous one as in the story above.*

31. *Some religions say man is born good but sinks into evil due to his own weaknesses and the corruptions surrounding him. Other religions hint that man is even born in sin, perhaps inheriting it.*
    (a) Are Taoists more honest and truthful in their assessment of a person's nature?
    (b) Is it better to say someone is born positively good or bad, or, that he is born with a mixture of good and bad in him?

How can we cope with the Yin–Yang to-and-fro movement in life? Taoism split into two broad sects in its efforts to answer this problem. The Tao Chia or Philosophical Taoism (wise thinkers' way) says that we should harness ourselves to the movement of the Way (Tao) the universe moves. The Tao Chiao or Religious Taoist sect says you should call on priests to control the gods with their rituals.

The Tao Chia method. Nature's energy is effortless; it flows rather than struggles. If we can use our energy as effortlessly as nature does, we will live naturally—as we are designed to do. So quieten yourself, your senses and your appetites and you will gain an inner vision of the Tao (the Way) which you are to follow.

I have Three Treasures. Guard them and keep them safe.
The First is Love.
The Second is Moderation.
The Third is Never to be first in the world.
With love, one will have courage.
With moderation, one will have power to spare.
Through not trying to be first in the world, one can develop talent.
(Tao Te Ching; The Way and Its Power)

32.   *Are these three treasures sufficient to guide one through life?*
      Why has Lao-Tse put them in this order?

Just as Shintoists respect and hold nature in awe, so Taoists claim the Way is that of nature, or natural forces. If you want to become perfect you must not obstruct the ways of nature, but serve them. The way of life is called Wu-wei, meaning 'non-effort', being receptive to life and what it brings and not resisting it. Life is a mystery but it has a rhythm to it. Your aim must be to be active as well as relaxed and free from tension.

According to the Tao Chia method: 'One may move so well that a footprint never shows; speak so well that the tongue never slips, reckon so well that no counter is needed'. How can you be superactive and relaxed simultaneously? Taoists say water is the best example of Tao as it supports objects and carries them effortlessly. Its pattern is humility. Water behaves naturally. The Chinese for a swimmer is 'one who knows the nature of water'. A swimming instructor tells his pupils not to fight the water but to float on it. So one who knows the nature of the basic life force knows it will sustain him if he stops thrashing about and trusts it to buoy him up and carry him along:

Those who flow as life flows know
They need no other force;
They feel no wear, they feel no tear
They need no mending, no repair.

Water goes round obstacles, adapts itself to its surroundings and seeks the lowest levels; it is infinitely supple and yet incomparably strong:

Man at his best, like water
Serves as he goes along;
Like water he seeks his own level,
The common level of life.

'Muddy water let stand will clear'. So you should take life as it comes, be humble, oppose aggression. Do not over-assert yourself or be over-ambitious:

> *Standing on tiptoe a man loses balance,*
> *Admiring himself he does so alone . . .*
> *At no time in the world will a man who is sane*
> *Over-reach himself,*
> *Over-spend himself,*
> *Over-rate himself.*

While Westerners talk of 'conquering' nature, by climbing Everest or damming rivers, Taoists talk of 'befriending' it. Some religious people claim they are nearer God on mountain tops, but Taoists seek ravines which receive all things in them. They build their temples to blend with nature, not to stand out provocatively. Some religions expect you to strive beyond your limits, but Taoism does not expect you to do so.

33. *Taoists see the wheel of life as one which rolls backwards and forwards rather than one which is propelled along to the end of the journey of life.*
    (a) Do you think this means one can take life easily and not set out to achieve a definite goal?
    (b) Should one take life as it comes or make something positive of it?

The Tao Chiao method. The aim of this Power (Te) is to achieve immortality and control the forces of Yang and Yin to one's advantage. It is claimed this can be done by alchemy in one of two ways. Wai Tan (External Elixir) involves the use of chemicals, drugs and metals. Nei Tan (Inner Elixir) works by priests controlling the spirit world so as to draw on the strength of the spirits. Alchemists claimed that special gold could be made, which, if eaten, would give you immortality. Long-life pills were another speciality. But the Nei Tan method of the Taoist Master priest lives on today. Training in spirit control is a very long and complicated one. The priest must summon spirits out of his body (Fa-lu rites meaning literally 'lighting the incense burner'). He can then unite himself with the Tao (Way) by his k'o-i, meditation rituals, and use this power (Te) over spirits of heaven, earth and the underworld, before returning them to his body. His rank is decided by his knowledge when he qualifies. The pass grade he gets will decide how many spirits he can control on his Lu (list). Grades 6 and 7 entitle the holder to a Lu of 10−14 spirits; grades 4 and 5 have a Lu of 24; grades 2 and 3 require a knowledge

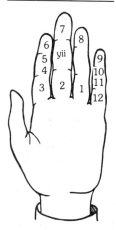

Symbols of the spirits. If the master touches (a) 2, (b) 3, which spirits will he summon?

of thunder magic against black magic, while grade 1 needs knowledge of the Yellow Court Canon. Both men and women can qualify. In addition to knowing many secret words and movements, he has to learn which joints of the left hand to touch with his left thumb.

The 12 months of the year are represented by the 12 organs of the body from whence the spirits emerge to bless men. The 12 are symbolized by the left hand's joints. The positions (shown in the illustration) represent: (1) gall; (2) liver; (3) lungs; (4) big intestine; (5) stomach; (6) spleen; (7) heart; (8) small intestine; (9) bladder; (10) kidney; (11) shoulders; (12) belly tubes. For example, the god of the east, who controls spring and rain, dwells in the liver; the god of the west, who controls autumn and harvest, and leads men in war, dwells in the lungs; the god of the centre, who holds the power which overcomes the winter's damp and cold and is the source from which wood grows and in which metal hides, dwells in the spleen (press yii for him).

Masters who specialize in the exorcism of evil spirits are not popular figures as their visits are always to do with sickness and death. Their training involves running and jumping with weights on their shoulders so as to be able to jump great heights without them during the rituals. They strengthen their wrists by hitting hard things as exorcism involves somersaults in mid-air and fighting demons with swords. A Master will have a large team to aid him so that if he is famous the cost of his services will be high.

The Master's closest secret is his list of the spirits' names, faces, clothes and weapons, without which his ritual would be useless. Among the six Chia demon spirits is Chia-tzu, who is 12 feet tall, rat-faced, yellow-haired and bearded, and armed with a bow, sword and shield. He can move mountains, plug up the sea, and shrink or stretch the earth with his 100 000 spirit troops. Another demon spirit is the violent, merciless Chia-hsu, who is nine feet tall, with a man's face, snake's body, golden crown and yellow robe. He is armed with a spear made of eight snakes, stones and arrows; he commands 100 000 troops. If Chia-hsu draws a line on the ground a river appears; he can make cliffs, drill wells, invade cities, and so on. Offerings of wine, dried fruit and meat are made to all six demons in sacred areas. The Master draws the shapes of the spirits in the air, recites and makes sword strokes. The six are summoned 12 times in 60 days before he can control them and their armies. Once in control he can get them to defeat enemies in battle, cure illness and exorcize spirits. He needs to be a strong-minded Master to cope with these demons and he expects to die young from the exhaustion of these rituals. To end with he cuts a white cock's comb and lets out some of its blood which he and the spirits will drink.

Thunder magic is a highly prized art and requires a high-ranking Master. It is a purification rite to deal with black magic. On the first day after the New Year when thunder occurs, he faces the thunder and breathes in the electrified atmosphere which circulates through him until it reaches his gall bladder where it will be stored for later use. To use it, he breathes through his nose and the vapours will mix with saliva which is swallowed and sent to the furnace of the belly. He repeats this until he stops breathing altogether in meditation. Thunderblocks (vajra) of carved datewood are used in the elaborate rituals for summoning the thunder power from the gall bladder. He uses the thunder power to cure illness and expel evil, as well as to control the sun's rays for exorcisms.

34. *Draw a picture of what you would imagine a Chia demon to look like.*

All traditional Chinese homes will have a god-shelf facing the front door. On it is a picture of Tzau Wang, the kitchen god, his wife, horse, dog and chicken, with ancestral plaques and photographs on either side. Two candles, three wine cups, a basket of flowers, fruit and a small urn for joss sticks are on the shelf too. The New Year Festival connected with Tzau Wang is described on pp. 162–3.

Followers of Tao Chia argue that Lao-Tse would not have accepted the Tao Chiao way of priestly magic.

Tzau Wang, the kitchen god.

BUDDHISM

The Five Precepts. Buddhists try to practise five basic guidelines known as the Five Precepts (Pancha-shila, or, Pans'il):

(1) Do not kill, humans or animals.

(2) Do not steal.

(3) Do not be unchaste.

(4) Do not lie.

(5) Do not drink intoxicants.

   Monks have an additional five:

(6) Eat moderately and before noon.

(7) Do not look at dancing, singing or drama.

(8) Do not use perfumes or ornaments.

(9) Do not use comfortable beds.

(10) Do not accept gifts of gold or silver.

Sometimes five others are observed:

(11) Do not gossip.

(12) Do not be envious.

(13) Do not be malicious.

(14) Do not swear.

(15) Try to learn the truth.

35. (a) Is it true to say that the Five Precepts deal with human weaknesses whereas the monks' precepts deal with luxuries?
(b) Why do you think monks must obey additional precepts?
(c) Should people who set out to be religiously special have to obey such extra rules as part of their calling?
(d) What is the aim behind such rules and are they helpful?

36. Buddha argued that first we act, then we put into words what we have done and finally we think about the matter; in the West we say that we think of something, put it into words and finally act on it. For example, Buddha would say, 'Root out killing and you will end hatred', while a Westerner, influenced by Christianity, would say, 'Root out hatred and you will end killing'.
(a) Which is more likely to be true in practice?
(b) Give other examples aimed at good behaviour and present them in a
    (i) Buddhist way, (ii) Western way.

It is important to realize that the Buddhist road does not lead to a Being in the sense of a creator God which other religions believe in. For them life is not a preparation for eternity, but a way of living out your present life until you reach the highest good. Buddha's teaching (dharma) works because it offers a solution to this life's problems and not because it taps supernatural resources to aid you. Freedom is your quest. Your aim is to develop yourself from an ordinary person into an extraordinary or enlightened person—the superior species.

Buddha argued that you had to know where you were going to start from before you could set off on life's road. He saw a person's chief problems as ones of suffering and self-deception, and so he listed Four Noble Truths or sensible ideas, in the same way that Indians then diagnosed illnesses.

First Noble Truth, Dukkha. Dukkha means 'suffering'; something which is not perfect or permanent, hence 'imperfection', 'impermanence'; 'ill-fare' as opposed to 'welfare'. Buddha meant that we are all suffering from a kind of illness. For us all life is made up of unsatisfactoriness or suffering. He was not trying to frighten us, simply to alert us to the position we are in. There is no need for us to panic or get depressed, since Buddha has a ready cure.

There are three kinds of Dukkha:

(1) Suffering—headaches, bereavements, etc. A mother giving birth suffers pain; being born is painful; a baby might be deformed; growing old is painful.

(2) Unsatisfactoriness is part of pleasure as pleasures do not last, so in the end they are unsatisfactory.

(3) Ordinary life is unsatisfactory until one becomes enlightened.

Dukkha is the symptom of life's disease. Just to exist seems Dukkha, so do not get angry about it; instead hunt for its cause and cure. Like a doctor treating his patient, Buddha went on to diagnose the disease.

37. List examples of Dukkha under headings (1) and (2) above.

Second Noble Truth, Samudaya. Buddha saw the origin (Samudaya) of life being full of Dukkha as being caused by our craving (tanhā) for things—our passionate greed for pleasures, power, wealth and our own opinions. These are the sorts of things which give rise to quarrels. They even cause countries to fight because of their greed for economic wealth, political power and social wellbeing.

Buddha claimed that we cannot blame a god for all this Dukkha. The immediate problem is to cope with Dukkha, and any attempt to define God can be left aside for the time being. He argued that people have made up two false ideas in their minds. To give them a feeling of safety they have conjured up the concept of a god, some great Being who protects people. Then to satisfy their worry that they will become totally extinct when they die, people have invented the idea of everyone having an immortal soul. These two false ideas simply console people in their fears and desires and show how ignorant they are.

If Dukkha is not caused by some Being, then where does it come from? It must have a human cause. Eat too many cream buns and you will see. Admittedly you could suffer due to someone else's selfish action (e.g. a motorcyclist breaking the speed limit injures you) but mainly you are to blame due to your selfishness. Worldly life is wanting pleasure and prosperity and these things will not satisfy you in the end. To desire such things is not 'sinning' in the Christian sense of disobedience to God. It is just that you are ignorant about how you cause Dukkha for yourself.

Our selfish craving even leads to us wanting to be reborn again and again so that we can continue to gratify our desires (see p. 219). Buddha used the word 'karma' in a different way to the Hindus. For him it did not mean that at rebirth a person was up- or down-graded according to how he had behaved for there is no divine judgement to face. Instead he meant that karma is a theory of cause and effect. Our cravings cause the effect of our being reborn. So how can one stop this cycle? How can one cure this 'disease'?

38. Briefly say why Buddha decided humans cause their own Dukkha.

Third Noble Truth, Nirodha. The doctor's prognosis—the cure —is the Third Noble Truth. It involves overcoming selfishness and releasing yourself from your cravings. Dukkha disappears when you cease (Nirodha) wanting things. If you continue to live on a worldly plane or level you will be dogged by the Five Mental Hindrances, which Buddha likened to impure water:

(1) Greed, for food, sex, etc.—like water discoloured by bright colours.

(2) Hatred—like boiling water.

(3) Sloth, torpor, keeping your cravings for sensuous desires —like water choked with weeds.

(4) Restlessness and worry—being unable to settle down to anything—like water whipped up into storm waves.

(5) Doubt, indecision, a lack of faith or trust—like water full of mud.

Fourth Noble Truth, Magga. This is the Middle Way (Magga) of the Eightfold Path—a kind of moral and mental development scheme designed to raise you from the worldly to the spiritual plane of life. It is a Middle Way as you do not have to follow the extremes of being a hermit or living an extravagant life. Instead of allowing your life to go on like a vicious circle (sleep—wake—sleep; love—hate—love) you can improve yourself and climb the spiral (the creative spiral) of life, going up and up as you go along. Buddha stressed that everyone can do this, and so one should be optimistic, not pessimistic, in the face of Dukkha. It is like a mental disease which can

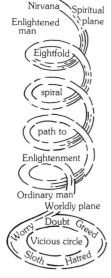

The Eightfold Path to Enlightenment.

be cured when the cause or secret of the illness is discovered and understood by the patient.

The Dharma-chakra, the wheel of the law, has eight spokes for the eight steps involved in the course of treatment prescribed. No pill-taking is involved; you go into rigorous habit-forming training, but of a different kind to that which your games coach instils into you. The goal is enlightenment, rather than winning a race, but the specialist training to climb the spiral is just as essential.

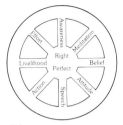

Dharma-chakra, the wheel of the law.

39. (a) Do you think Buddha is right in seeing suffering as the starting point of the journey? What alternatives are there?
(b) What do you think of his diagnosis and prescription? Give your reasons.
(c) Give examples of how you have suffered
(i) due to the actions of others,
(ii) due to your own actions.

Eightfold Path. Although the steps are numbered you do not necessarily have to climb them in that order as they are all linked together and so you can tackle them together. The object is to enable you to break away from the worldly plane of unwholesome thinking (akusala) and set off for the spiritual plane of wholesome thinking (kusala). Then you will be able to stop your cravings and so stop being reborn. With your cravings gone you will be enlightened, free from the karma force which has kept you going round and round. You will find nirvana when you will be free from all worries, obsessions, complexes, etc. Your 'mental health' will then be perfect. You do not have to wait until you are dead to 'attain' the bliss of nirvana as you can find it in this life. Notice this contrast with other religions which say you cannot reach heaven until you have died. As we shall see, nirvana and heaven are rather different.

As you follow the steps you will find they cover three essential things:
(i) Good behaviour (Sīla) — steps 3, 4 and 5.
(ii) Mind control (Samādhi) — steps 6, 7 and 8.
(iii) Wisdom (Pannā) — steps 1 and 2.

Notice as you go through them that they do not include prayer, worship or ceremony, which religions normally include. This is because Buddhists do not believe in God. With no God, you can have no outside help along the path — it is all up to you.

Step 1: Right/perfect viewpoint. Be wise and start by believing the training scheme is the right one to cure you. In other words, accept the Four Noble Truths; accept that life is painful and unsatisfactory, and that something better is possible. You need a vision of what you might become. Then you will see things as they really are, and have a penetrating understanding of life.

Step 2: Right/perfect attitude or purpose. Be wise by being determined to succeed; having your heart in the task; setting out unselfishly. True wisdom requires some noble qualities in you.

Step 3: Right/perfect speech. The language you use matters. Unwholesome words are harsh and false ones; wholesome words are true and helpful.

Step 4: Right/perfect behaviour or action. Obey the Buddhist directives—the Five Precepts. Live an unselfish, charitable life; keep regular hours; help the sick; and so on.

Step 5: Right/perfect livelihood. Choose your job carefully for the more it helps others the more it will raise you to the spiritual plane. Butchers are frowned on because they destroy life. Change your environment for this will change your level of consciousness. For example, a mountain holiday will enlarge your vision of the greatness of creation.

Thus Steps 3, 4 and 5 are aimed at making you a better person for you will not be able to climb higher unless you behave well. Next come the mental, mind-training steps.

Step 6: Right/perfect effort. Use your willpower to stick to your moral standards and make a right use of your energies to produce good and not evil. This involves mind training which is called meditation (bhāvanā). It means cleansing your mind of all unwholesome thoughts, worries, lusts, etc., and cultivating wholesome thoughts, joy, peace of mind, etc.

At this step you should try a meditation called Samatha or Samādhi. It existed before Buddha's time but is one which he used and Buddhists still use. It is simply designed to help you to concentrate your mind, not an easy thing as you must have discovered when your teacher has told you off for inattention. It takes about 20 minutes and involves sitting comfortably on cushions. It calms your restless mind by fixing it on an object (kasina)—for example, your breathing. The aim is to pull yourself together. Each of us is made up of a number of part-selves—the dutiful self (we do our work), the disobedient self (we are lazy), and so on. We hardly know which of these selves we really are. In fact, we have got to bring our real self into being by mind control. You divide the time between these four stages:

   (i) concentrate on your breath as it moves through your nose;
  (ii) relax, breathe quietly; count 1–10, 1–10, etc., after each breath;
 (iii) count 1–10, 1–10 before each breath;
 (iv) cease counting and concentrate on the rhythm of your breathing.

     Another meditation is Metta Bhāvāna ('Bringing love into being'):

   (i) Think about yourself—remember happy times; wish yourself well.
  (ii) Think of a good friend of the same sex and age—wish him/her well.
 (iii) Think of a neutral person—the postman, ticket-collector—wish him/her well.
 (iv) Concentrate on an enemy or someone you do not get on with well—wish him/her well.
  (v) Concentrate on all four—then all in the room—the town—the country—overseas. . . .

     So you will expand and radiate the warmth of your love. Besides Metta Bhāvāna there are three other meditations which collectively are known as Brahma Vihāra (Four Sublime States). The others are:

   (i) Karuna (having compassion), understanding the suffering of others and making plans to help.
  (ii) Muditā (having sympathetic joy), feeling happy about the joys of others.
 (iii) Upekkhā (being well balanced), having a balanced, steady mind without tempers or depressions or over-excitement.

     But these meditations will only help you live happily in this world. They will not give you complete freedom or insight into the truth. So you must take another step.

Step 7: Right/perfect awareness or mindfulness. Now you will use Buddha's Vipaassana, 'insight' meditation, to get insight into four main objects—things; yourself; other people; reality of truth. This is the crucial step which prepares your mind for the final step. It requires you to have a flow of wholesome, good thoughts uninterrupted by any unwholesome bad ones of the Five Mental Hindrances kind. It is not a question of trying to judge whether things, yourself or other people are good or bad, right or wrong. It is simply an investigation carried out by your mind to observe and examine things, emotions, people, etc., in a calm, detached way. Suppose you want to meditate on why you are very angry and filled with hatred. You must not keep thinking of 'my angry mind', but imagine you are outside yourself looking at 'an angry mind' in action. Have you noticed that someone who is angry is not mindful of his anger until the moment he becomes aware he is angry—then his anger subsides as he has grasped what is happening to him and can master it. Once you can stand outside yourself and see yourself as you really are you can get control of yourself. Then you will improve yourself; you will cope with all your cravings. The aim of this step is to improve yourself by working directly on controlling your mind.

Step 8: Right/perfect absorption, enjoyment or meditation. Now meditation reaches its peak and you will become 'absorbed'—just as soap powder is absorbed in water, said Buddha. You will find bliss and ecstasy. You will discard all desires, worries, thoughts, etc., and find nirvana. You will see everything in its true place and realize that all earthly things are unsatisfactory and impermanent. Nirvana will give you release from all the limitations of your human self. Nirvana means literally the 'going out' or 'cooling off' of a flame. Thus your earthly self is 'extinguished' as you reach the 'incomprehensible, indescribable, inconceivable, unutterable' state of nirvana:

> If you ask, 'How is nirvana to be known?', it is by freedom from distress and danger, by confidence, by peace, by calm, by bliss, by happiness, by delicacy, by purity, by freshness. (Milinda Panha)

You can reach this state in this life and continue in it when your human self dies (see also pp. 219–20). A person who has reached nirvana is called an arhat, or arahat.

40. *Is mind training really the way or should one try and find the truth elsewhere and by other means?*

41. *What problems would you face trying to follow the Eightfold Path? Give examples.*

The two types of raft. All Buddhists talk of crossing the sea of life—the great sea of self-desire—on rafts (yāna). They leave the shore of death and reincarnation, fear and peril for the land of nirvana. The Southern Buddhists are sometimes known by the word Hīnayāna, meaning small raft, as they see the craft as one designed to get an individual to nirvana by his own efforts in contrast to the Northern Buddhists' Mahāyāna, big raft, which carries many at one time. The difference between the two ways is illustrated in the story of four men, who, crossing a desert, came upon a high-walled compound. One, determined to find out what was inside, scaled the wall, shouted for joy and jumped over. The second and the third did likewise, but when the fourth got to the top and saw the garden with sparkling streams and delicious fruit, he resisted the temptation to jump down, remembering the other wayfarers in the desert. He climbed back down and devoted his life to directing others to the oasis. The first three were Southern Buddhists and the fourth a Northern one.

Hīnayāna monks. The aim of the Southern Buddhist is to become an arhat, to attain nirvana, by meditation and wisdom while caring little about helping others to find nirvana. The wisdom route is almost exclusively for monks. He must do six things:

(1) Feel joy for the Buddha because he is following his teaching.

(2) Live a moral life by walking the Eightfold Path.

(3) Practise patience.

(4) Do good works.

(5) Meditate.

(6) Turn towards Buddha.

In Thailand Buddhist boys spend one to four months in a monastery at teenage. First they are dressed in rich clothes (as Buddha was once a prince), then in rags with their heads shaved (as Buddha gave up riches to become a holy man), and finally in the saffron robes of a monk. Men can become monks temporarily or permanently. You can gain merit by becoming a monk for a week or several years if you wish. Monks say masses for the dead to help them build up merit for the next life. They rise before sunrise at the sound of a drum. After prayers, they wash, sweep their cells and filter their drinking water to ensure no insects are killed accidentally. Then they set off in a line to collect food from housewives. The donors thank the monks for accepting their food offerings. If the monks thanked the donors they would rob them of their due merit. It is better to give than to receive. The monks eat twice a day, both meals being before midday because after that they may only drink. They study and pray, receive friends, and give advice to any who ask for it. Their brotherhood of monks is called the Sangha. There are Sanghas for nuns too. In Thailand there are 150 000 bhikkhus (fully fledged monks), 90 000 samaneras (novices) and 2000 chees (white-robed nuns),

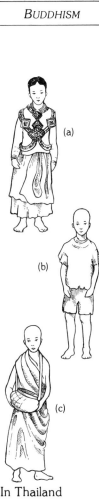

In Thailand Buddhist boys go through changes of clothes to make them realize Buddha was once a prince (a), gave up all to become a holy man (b), and favoured the middle way of a monk (c).

Burmese Buddhist monks with their begging bowls. Why do the donors thank the monks and not the monks the donors?

who tend to be aged and homeless women. There are 120 000 dekwats (temple boys), who live in monasteries and perform serving duties. Monks wear yellow in Burma, red in Tibet and grey in Korea.

42. (a) What benefits do you think you would get from being a temporary Buddhist monk (i) at teenage, (ii) later in life?
(b) Do you think all people would benefit from some kind of monastic life for short periods in their lives? If so, why?

Northern Bodhisattvas. Mahāyāna Buddhism began just before Christianity was founded. It stressed love of others and putting oneself last. Anyone can become a buddha as Buddha is the mind which is enlightened. A Northern Buddhist seeking to guide others to nirvana is called a Bodhisattva (one who has the essence, sattva, of enlightenment, bodhi), a saint who gives up his own hope of reaching nirvana for the sake of others. Anyone can become a Bodhisattva. To do so you must do ten things, the same six as the Southern Buddhists and also:

(7) Tell others what you have seen.

(8) Remain quiet and serene in spite of your exciting news.

(9) Proclaim the faith.

(10) Using all the powers and characteristics of a buddha, show sympathetic love for others.

The Northern way is designed for the layman rather than the monk. 'I surrender my all to promote the welfare of others,' said Santiders, a seventh-century poet. You can pray to a Bodhisattva for help to find the way to nirvana.

43. *Which is better, to be an arhat content with having found nirvana for oneself, or a Bodhisattva showing others the way? Give reasons for your answer.*

Zen. One branch of Mahāyāna Buddhism is called Zen (Ch'an in Chinese). 'Zen' is a Japanese word which today implies a belief in the suddenness and directness of enlightenment—it comes in a flash after long study and meditation. To become a Zen master (Roshis) you have to go into training in a monastery to undergo Zazen, Koan and Sanzen. Zazen is seated meditation which takes place in the monastery's semmon dojo (meditation hall), a long narrow building where the monks sit to meditate. The abbot lights an incense stick to mark the time, then two monks rise, bow before the shrine to Buddha and collect a keisaka (piece of wood) and proceed to walk up and down the lines whacking anyone who falls asleep. When the incense stick has burnt to the end the abbot sounds a bell to mark the beginning of an exercise period. This involves a quick march round the hall until another stick is burnt out. Then back to meditation, and so on for three hours.

Twice a day the monks have a 'sanzen' (interview) in which they are asked how they are getting on with solving their 'koans' (problems, riddles or crazy puzzles). The monk bows before his master as bells are rung and then the question-and-answer session begins. Here are some examples:

(1) When a man comes to you with nothing, what would you advise?
Answer: Throw it away.

(2) What did your face look like before your parents begot you?

(3) A fable says, 'A cow passes by a window. Its head, horns and four legs all pass by. Why did not the tail pass by?'

(4) We all know what two hands clapping sound like. What is the sound of one hand clapping?

(5) A long time ago a man kept a goose in a bottle. It grew larger and larger until it could not get out any more. He did not want to break

the bottle, nor did he wish to hurt the goose; how would you get it out? 'There, it's out', was the reply. In this story the goose represents the man and the bottle the circumstances in which he lives. Either he must abandon the world or be crushed by it—a suicidal dilemma. But the moment he finds a way through he has a flash of satori (instinctive experience of enlightenment) and the goose is out of the unbroken bottle. He has escaped from his imaginary prison which consisted of the rigid way of life he had created for himself over the years.

The object of setting these topsy-turvy problems is to show you that your intellect, your brain power, is insufficient. The problems lead you into a cul-de-sac for the ordinary thinking mind can find no way out. The problems destroy your usual thinking process in order to make you see beyond what the mind can think of. To see beyond, you must first exhaust your thinking process and then break out of the cul-de-sac. You abandon your thinking for intuition—a flash of sudden insight—which enables you to bridge the gap. The mind is then freed; you have had a mystical experience, a heightened sense of reality, so that you now view things from an entirely different angle.

44.   What is meant when one says, 'She grasped the point intuitively (instinctively) without pausing to think?' Is this an example of solving a koan?

45.   Try to solve a koan set for you by someone else.
(a) Why is it difficult to solve?
(b) If you spent two hours a day for a month trying to solve it, what effect might it have on you?
(c) What do all koans have in common?

46.   How might a satori experience alter a person's life? Can a satori be taught or only experienced?

47.   Is there knowledge to be discovered in ways which are beyond man's thinking mind to find?

Pure Land Buddhism. Other Northern Buddhist sects are the Jodo-shu and Shin ones, called Pure Land sects. They claim all you have to do is to trust Amida, Lord of the Western Paradise or Pure Land, and you will reach there because of his merit, not your own. Salvation is by faith in him alone and this will enable you to bypass karma's effect of rebirth (see p. 219).

The Ten Commandments. When Moses was having a difficult time leading the Jews away from slavery to a new freedom, he needed a basic set of minimum rules to control them. These Ten Statements or Commandments he secured from God as a result of consulting Him on Mount Sinai (Exod. 19–20; Deut. 5:6–21):

(1) I am the Lord your God.

(2) You may worship no other god but me. You shall not make yourselves any idols; any images resembling animals, birds or fish. You must never bow to any image or worship it in any way; for I, the Lord your God, am very possessive; I will not share your affection with any other god.

(3) You shall not take the name of God irreverently, nor use it to swear to a falsehood.

(4) Remember to observe the Sabbath as a holy day. Six days a week are for your daily duties and your regular work, but the seventh day is a day of rest and on that day you shall do no work . . . for in six days the Lord made heaven, earth and sea and everything in them and rested on the seventh day.

(5) Honour your father and mother.

(6) Do not murder.

(7) Do not commit adultery.

(8) Do not steal.

(9) Do not lie.

(10) Do not be envious of other people's property or circumstances.

48. (a) *How does this set of rules show how important God is in the Jewish life?*
   (b) *What picture of God do they conjure up in your mind?*

49. *Some argue these rules were designed to cope with a crisis period in Jewish history. Do they show this or are they suited to any conditions?*

50. *The Ten Commandments have been used as the basis of many of the world's sets of moral and legal rules. Find out what part of the clothing of judges, barristers and clergymen in England show this and explain how.*

These Ten Commandments are just a few of the 613 in, for example, Exod. 21–23, 34; Lev. 1–27 and Deut. 5–31. These chapters give precise directions on how Jews were to behave. The Jews' delight in keeping their rules comes from a sense of obeying God's will if they do so.

51. *Examine the examples of Exod. 21:16, 18–19, 22–24, 33. Summarize them briefly and give your opinion on them.*

52. *Leviticus deals with sacrifices to God as well as health hazards such as leprosy.*
    (a) Read chapters 1–3. Why are the rituals so clearly stated?
    (b) Read chapters 13–14 on leprosy. List (i) the priest's duties, (ii) what the leper is to do when he gets leprosy and when he is cured, (iii) what is to be done with affected clothing?

53. *Lev. 11:2–23 and Deut. 14:3–21 give details of what you may or may not eat. Make a list of (a) permitted, (b) forbidden beasts. Dietary rules are part of Jewish worship (see p. 99).*

54. *(a) Read Deut. 22:22–27. Is this a fair law for women in the two cases?*
    (b) Read Deut. 24:5. How long is the honeymoon period granted?
    (c) Does Deuteronomy combine gentleness with being severe?

The Hindus believe the world we live in is an illusion (maya) and that we have to escape from it to find real life in eternity. But for the Jews there is no such illusion in life; life here is *real* life, leading to another real life after death. The Jews see God controlling history, ensuring His Chosen People win their battles when they deserve to and lose them when they need punishing for their poor behaviour. For the Jews, God is righteous and just. He is not unfair or un-reasonable. He also shows loving-kindness, so He treats people like His children, praising or telling them off as necessary.

The Sabbath. If Jews are to secure God's favour they must keep His commandments and observe the Jewish way of life as He chose them to do just that. Strict or Orthodox Jews will observe the Sabbath (Friday evening to Saturday evening) by not doing any work (see the Fourth Commandment). They will not travel, use electricity or write on the Sabbath and may even go to the extent of not putting up an umbrella as that is like putting up a tent. Some Jews will use inter-leaved toilet paper so as not to work by tearing off a sheet. Jews feel that each age reveals a new significance and value in Sabbath-keeping. For example, not using the telephone on the Sabbath is a joy for an office-bound Jew. The pressures of the twentieth century

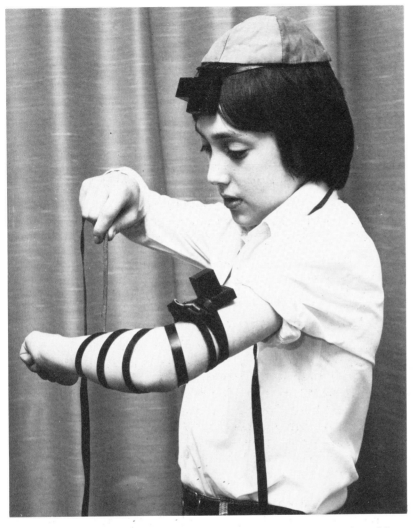

Boy putting on a tefillin. What two things has he got on his head? What effect is the lengthy task of putting on the tefellin likely to have on him?

are kept at bay for better things such as family life and worship. Many Reform Jews will allow the use of transport to the synagogue but no-where else on the Sabbath, while Orthodox Jews insist on walking there. In an emergency one can break the Sabbath so long as murder, idolatry and adultery are not committed. Thus, when Israel was attacked on the 'Sabbath of Sabbaths' (Yom Kippur) in 1973, she mobilized her forces against Egypt and Syria.

Daily prayers are said at home as much as at the synagogue and especially on the Sabbath. An Orthodox or Reform Jew puts on a cappel or yarmulke (small round cap) and straps on tefillin or phylacteries, one to his forehead to remind his brain to think of his faith and another to his left arm (left-handers put it on their right arm) to encourage him to take action about his beliefs as it is near his heart. Tefillin are small black leather cubes (with each side 25–50 mm) containing four little parchment squares called the Shema (the Belief), stating what Jews believe about God and His care for them (see Exod. 13:1–10, 11–16; Deut. 6:4–9; 11:13–21). When praying, Jews wear a tallith, silk or wool prayer shawl round their shoulders (Deut. 22:12; Num. 15:38–40). In 1982 a tefillin cost £42 and a tallith £20.

Jews regard the day as starting at dusk so the Sabbath begins on Friday evening when the mother lights the Sabbath candles, saying, 'You are our Light, O Lord, and our Salvation. In your name we kindle these Sabbath lights. May they bring into our household the beauty of truth and the radiance of love's understanding'. A clean cloth is put on the table. The father sits at the head of the table with two loaves representing the double portion of manna (possibly plant

Sabbath meal.

lice or gum resin), which the Israelites were allowed to gather on their desert journey 3000 years ago (see Exod. 16; Num. 11:4–35). He takes a cup of wine and recites the Kiddush (blessing) and the Genesis verses on the creation and the need to rest on the Sabbath. All drink from the cup, hands are washed, and the bread is broken. The bread has been freshly baked and is called challah.

55. *Why do you think the mother and not the father initiates the Sabbath ceremonies?*

56. *(a) What is your opinion of the Sabbath ceremonies beginning in the home rather than in the synagogue?*
(b) Would all religions benefit by having a regular weekly cere-monial meal at home?

The main service for Liberal Jews is on Friday evening but for others it is on the Saturday (see p. 137).

The Jewish kitchen plays a vital part in religious life at home, as several Torah laws refer to diet. Many suggest that the strict hygiene rules became religious ones, so that an observer of these rules cannot serve pork, or meat from the hindquarters of any animal. A full list of permitted (kosher) and forbidden (treyfah) foods is given in Leviticus, chapter 11. Meat must have blood drained from it so it is bought from a kosher butcher who slaughters animals according to the slaughter laws. Meat is soaked in cold water for half an hour, rinsed and sprinkled with salt to extract the remaining blood. An hour later it is washed before being cooked. In fact it will not taste different from normally prepared meat. Meat and milk may not be cooked or eaten together so rice pudding cannot follow a meat course, nor can you have butter on a chicken sandwich. White coffee after chicken and chips is also banned. A long gap after meat eating must occur before any milk can be consumed. Housewives have to have two sets of saucepans, cutlery, cloths and two wash basins to keep these foods separate.

The Messiah. From what has been said we can see that Jews consider duty and tradition to be extremely important. In the synagogue one prayer always said is the Alenu, beginning 'It is our duty to praise the Lord of all things, to ascribe greatness to Him who formed the world'. The ritual of the kitchen and the meal table and numerous annual festivals (see pp. 165–71) commemorating historic events in Jewish history, are the aids which keep them on the road. Notice that they do not usually do anything similar to eastern meditation as training the mind is not so important to them as doing their duty. Strict Jews look to the future when a 'Messiah' will come to set up God's Kingdom on earth. This Messiah is seen as a human being who is specially gifted with leadership and wisdom. Other Jews have reinterpreted the Messiah belief into meaning that society, not a single person, will eventually usher in the Kingdom by its goodness. Bible references to this are: Isa. 2:4; 11:1–10; Zech. 14:9.

57. *The Hindus argue that you must escape from the life of illusion here to the real world of eternity; the Jews see God's control of this life and the final coming of the Messiah as showing that life now is real. Compare the two opinions and say why you prefer one of them to the other.*

58. *Can God show His care and love, or His justice and judgement, unless He intervenes in the events of history?*

59. *Do you think doing things in a traditional ritual way helps you to worship and understand God better?*

60. *Why do you think some Jews are so very strict about the Fourth Commandment? Try to defend them in your answer.*

Pilgrimages. Jews have not been expected to go on any pilgrimages since the destruction of the temple in AD 70. The Wailing or Western Wall of this temple is a pilgrims' place of prayer, however. It is all that remains of the temple built by Herod the Great and others on the site of Solomon's temple. Some kiss the stones as they pray and many weep openly. Some push papers with prayers on into the cracks.

In recent years Jews have taken to visiting Yad Vashem in Jerusalem where there is a memorial to six million Jews who died in the Holocaust of Hitler's extermination campaign. Yad Vashem means 'A Place and a Name' (quoted from Isa. 56:5). The place is a bare room lit by a candle with the names of the concentration camps inscribed on the floor. The Holocaust Museum is nearby.

CHRISTIANITY

The commands of Jesus. Christians accept not only the Jewish Ten Commandments but also Christ's summary of them:

Love the Lord your God with all your heart, soul and mind. This is the first and greatest commandment. The second most important is similar, Love your neighbour as much as you love yourself. All the other commandments, and all the demands of the prophets stem from these two laws and are fulfilled if you obey them. Keep only these and you will find that you are obeying all the others. (Matt. 22:37–40)

61. (a) Is Jesus right in saying if you keep his two commandments the others will all be obeyed?
(b) Is it better to have just two all-embracing directions than a lengthy set of detailed rules?
(c) Would this work if applied to your school?

62. Notice how Jesus takes it for granted that people's thoughts and attitudes lead them to do things. Which religion held the opposite view? We looked at it earlier in this chapter.

In fact, Jesus did explain and elaborate on his basic rules. For example, he said:

> You have heard it was said, 'Do not commit adultery'. But now I tell you; anyone who looks at a woman and wants to possess her is guilty of adultery with her in his heart. (Matt. 5:27–28)

> You have heard that it was said, 'An eye for an eye, and a tooth for a tooth'. But now I tell you: do not take revenge on someone who does you wrong. If anyone slaps you on the right cheek, let him slap your left cheek too . . . When someone asks you for something, give it to him. (Matt. 5:38–42)

> You have heard that it was said, 'Love your friends and hate your enemies'. But now I tell you; Love your enemies and pray for those who mistreat you. (Matt. 5:43–44)

There are other points in Matt. 5:5–7, 9, 21–24; 6:1–4; 18:1–5.

63. (a) Think about all these teachings of Jesus and then say why Christianity is a very tough religion to follow.
(b) Is Jesus really demanding too much of his followers?
(c) What effect would living by his standards have on your character?

Modern ideas. Over the centuries the churches have brought out more detailed sets of rules for themselves. The Society of Friends (Quakers) will not fight under any circumstances. Their Peace Testimony proclaims:

> We utterly deny all outward wars and strife, and fightings with outward weapons, for any end, or under any pretence whatever; this our testimony to the whole world . . . we certainly know . . . that the Spirit of Christ . . . will never move us to fight and war against any man with outward weapons. (*Declaration from the Harmless and Innocent People of God,* presented to Charles II, 1660)

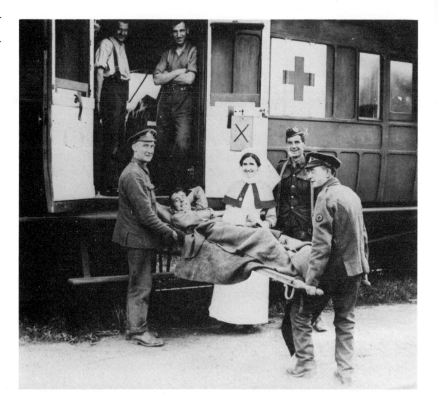

Quakers in action during the First World War.

64. (a) *Should all Christians never fight under any circumstances?*
    (b) *Under what circumstances do you think they could fight?*
    (c) *How would you explain to a non-Christian that Christians have often fought Christians in the last 2000 years?*

65. *Quakers also refuse to take oaths as that involves taking the name of God 'in vain'. What do they do when required to tell the truth in court today?*

The Salvation Army are firmly against drinking alcohol as they daily come up against the effects of over-drinking in the people they seek to save. In 1980 they were running 52 homes and centres for the treatment of alcoholics.

66. *The Salvation Army believes that you must practise what you preach. Should other Christian churches stop members drinking?*

Salvation. Christianity is based on the belief that Jesus is part of the Godhead, not just a great human being. Other religions see their founders as outstanding humans. Christians argue that God appeared on earth in the form of a human being to demonstrate His love by sacrificing Himself for the failings of people, so following the Christian road involves believing at the outset in who Jesus is and what he did on earth.

The Christian has to find his way to salvation although it is equally true to say God may seek to find him. He wants to be saved from his sins, his weaknesses and from himself. He hopes he will then be received into heaven when he dies. He does not believe in re-incarnation so that there is a sense of urgency about being 'saved' as he does not know when he will die. Jesus had a number of things to say about salvation:

Not every person who calls me 'Lord, Lord', will enter the Kingdom of Heaven, but only those who do what my Father in heaven wants them to do. (Matt. 7:21)

The training of church leaders in Africa.

Remember this, unless you change and become like children you will never enter the Kingdom of Heaven. The greatest in the Kingdom . . . is the one who humbles himself and becomes like this child. (Matt. 18:1–5)

I am the resurrection and the life. Whoever believes in me will live, even though he dies. (John 11:25–26)

I am the way, the truth and the life; no one goes to the Father except by me. (John 14:6)

67. *Summarize Jesus' teaching on salvation and how a person can achieve it. See Matt. 7:21; 18:1–5; John 5:21–24; 6:48–51; 11:25–26; 14:6. Which Hindu yoga is the closest to the Christian road to salvation?*

68. *Jesus told his followers how they should behave. See Matt. 5:5–9, 38–47; 6:24–33; 7:1–5, 12.*
    (a) Which points do you think you could succeed in following and which do you feel are beyond you? Give your reasons.
    (b) If a community followed these directions would it live in peace and happiness?
    (c) Do you think people could follow such directions without being religiously minded?

69. *Why does the Christian have to consider his life and beliefs with some urgency compared to the Hindu?*

The Christian argues that by praising God, loving Jesus and allowing yourself to be guided by the Holy Spirit in you, you will be freed from fear, even fear of death, and released from any sense of guilt or sin. You will be free to serve others in love. You will be 'born again' when you accept what Christ did for you and turn to follow him. For example, John Wesley, the eighteenth-century founder of Methodism, called on people to accept Christ as their Saviour. William Clowes wrote what it was like to be converted:

The power of Heaven came down upon me and I cried for help to Him who is mighty to save . . . I felt my head splitting and when the change was taking place, I thought within myself, What is this? This, I said, is what the Methodists mean by being converted. Yes, God is converting my soul. In an agony of prayer I believed He would save me. Then I believed He was saving me. Then I believed He had saved me. And it was so.

Some Christians will tell you that that they were brought to this point by Jesus seeking them rather than they turning to him.

The 'evangelical' or 'low church' branch of Christianity emphasizes that Christ died for your sins, and if you really believe this you will have a place in heaven because of his merciful sacrifice, and not because of your own efforts to be good. You are 'saved' when you accept Christ as your Saviour, and it is then your duty to show this by living a Christian life. The 'catholic' or 'high church' branch argues that you must humbly live out the good Christian life in the hope that his death together with your own efforts will ensure a place for you in heaven.

Contact between God and a Christian can occur in various ways. Some people use their reason to try to work out whether Christianity is true. Others see glimpses of God through beauty and love of others. Sometimes, though, people experience the Christian faith through suffering or feelings of their own inadequacy as these hymn verses show:

Abide with me; fast falls the eventide
The darkness deepens; Lord with me abide!
When other helpers fail and comforts flee,
Help of the helpless, O abide with me.
(H F Lyte, 1793–1847)

Just as I am, though tossed about
With many a conflict, many a doubt,
Fightings within, and fears without,
O Lamb of God, I come.

Just as I am, thou wilt receive,
Wilt welcome, pardon, cleanse, relieve;
Because thy promise I believe,
O Lamb of God, I come.
(Charlotte Elliot, 1789–1871)

The Lamb of God is Jesus and many Christians have found strength through meditating on His cross:

When I survey the wondrous Cross,
On which the Prince of glory died,
My richest gain I count but loss,
And pour contempt on all my pride.

See from his head, his hands, his feet,
Sorrow and love flow mingled down;
Did e'er such love and sorrow meet,
Or thorns compose so rich a crown?

Were the whole realm of nature mine,
That were a present far too small;
Love so amazing, so divine,
Demands my soul, my life, my all.
(I Watts, 1674–1748)

Christians also see God as their Father too:

> No earthly father loves like thee,
> No mother, e'er so mild,
> Bears and forbears as thou hast done
> With me thy sinful child.
>
> Father of Jesus, love's reward,
> What rapture will it be
> Prostrate before thy throne to lie,
> And gaze and gaze on thee.
>
> (F W Faber, 1814–1863)

70. The idea of Jesus being a slaughtered 'lamb' on a 'Cross' seems very gory. Why should it appeal to Christians?

71. What does the writer F W Faber long for and why?

Fellowship with other Christians is very important too. Jesus said that if two or three were gathered together in His name He would be there with them (Matt. 18:19–20). Together they can create an atmosphere which helps them to find God.

Hands in prayer.

Prayer is essential for the Christian although no set times or positions are laid down. Reading the Bible can take up part of his devotional time. Prayer can take many forms and may be spoken out loud or silent:

Praise—telling God that you appreciate His greatness.

Thanksgiving—for all the good things of life, for God, for Jesus, and so on.

Penitence—saying sorry to God for wrong doing.

Intercession—prayer for other people, especially those in need or who are sick, or for ourselves.

Prayer is not only about talking, though, but about listening to God. Silent contemplation has always been regarded as important: 'Be still and know that I am God' (Ps. 46:10).

Contemplation includes meditation. The Christian quietens his brain and imagination to find an inner peace. He may find it helpful to repeat a phrase such as 'Lord Jesus Christ, Son of the Living God, have mercy upon me, a sinner', or 'My God I want thee; help me to want thee more'.

72. What other religion(s) involve the repeating of a 'mantra' (phrase)?

73. Look up Ps. 46:10. How does this express contemplation?

Some Christian saints have become so engrossed in contemplation that they have seemed to enter a 'void' when God is absent. St John of the Cross called this the Dark Night of the Soul.

74. *Does the experience of a 'void' in prayer remind you of another religion?*

Beyond this painful experience, some saints have felt a release into love and ecstasy, a feeling of God Himself.

Variety in Christianity. For the Roman Catholic, God's presence today is brought out by the splendour of candles, incense and processions, while the Quakers believe that worship should concentrate on the Holy Spirit, which, they claim, can best be found in a plain room in the midst of a quietly praying congregation. Between these two extremes the various churches offer a variety of ways.

The Virgin and Child—a sculpture which many Roman Catholics would find helpful.

The Roman Catholic Church also requires you to make regular confessions of your failings to a priest, whereas such confessions in the Church of England are voluntary and rare. The priest and penitent (sorry person) usually sit in two halves of a 'confessional'. This is a cubicle divided by a wall in which there is a screened grille through which they talk. The priest must never tell anyone what he hears in confession and he will tell the penitent what penances he should do. Penances might involve saying certain prayers or putting a wrong right. Rosaries are used to count the prayers. A full rosary has 15 sets of ten beads, with single larger beads between sets, and a crucifix (a cross with Jesus on it); a lesser rosary has five sets. The Creed (statement of beliefs) is on the crucifix: 'Our Father' (Lord's Prayer: Matt. 6:9–13) on the larger beads; 'Hail Mary full of grace' (to Jesus' mother) on each of the small beads; and the Gloria ('Glory be to the Father . . .') on the chain.

Some Christians recall Jesus' sacrifice by making the sign of the Cross on their chests as they enter a church or when praying. An Orthodox Christian puts his thumb and two fingers together for the three Persons in one Godhead, and bends the others into his palm (Christ with God and Man). Then he touches his forehead, chest and right and left shoulders with the three fingers as the head is the centre of his mind and the chest, his feelings and inner self and the shoulders, his physical strength.

The Salvation Army sees the Christian's duty as a 'military' operation in which 'soldiers' march behind the flag to take

Christianity on to the streets and particularly to deprived areas. Their vocabulary is military: 'knee drill' for a prayer meeting, 'cartridge' for a donation. Its full-time leaders have officers' ranks and they and all its members buy uniforms to wear. Officers only stay at a citadel (i.e. a 'fort') for three to four years before being posted elsewhere so as to keep them fresh on the job. Members are expected to devote most of their free time to 'fighting the battle' for Christ. Care of tramps, drunks and drug addicts, unmarried mothers, runaways and so on is uppermost in their efforts. If someone comes forward to the penitent's form or mercy seat (bench in front of the congregation) during a service in the citadel, the whole congregation will stay there for however long it takes for that person in need to find help in Christ. That person's soul is considered so precious that the pattern of the service must be changed to one of care and help.

75. *The Salvation Army is against alcohol and the Quakers are flatly against fighting.*
   (a) Why do they think it vital to be so rigid on these points?
   (b) Should Christian groups all take firm stands on such matters? If not, why not?

Wesley's 'method' involved doing three things each day: prayer, Bible study and a charitable deed. He saw the need for Christians to be methodical in their lives. Bible study is a basic part of the Christian's life as is daily private prayer. There are no rules on washing or praying in a precise position or at a definite time. Praying morning and evening is simply suggested. Some churches have 'house groups', small groups meeting in private houses for Bible study, discussion and prayer.

76. *Does the Methodists' 'methodical' approach offer an aid to keeping up one's faith?*

Christians may serve others through their church, at work or at home, as well as through welfare organizations. They may see evil in the world but often want to transform the world with God's help. As God loves them and forgives them, so they can love and forgive others.

77. *In what ways could a Christian serve God and other people (a) at home, (b) at work?*

78. *Name any Christian organizations that help the needy.*

Some Christians find it helpful to go on a retreat—that is, a quiet weekend or longer at a centre where they can receive instruction and fellowship with others of like mind. Usually quiet is observed for much of the day to allow for personal reflection and prayer. Christians find the experience very refreshing.

Some Christians concentrate on worship in a particularly solemn and humble way, while others stress the joy of their faith. So worship ranges from that provided by the cathedral choirs to pop groups with guitars. You can express your worship by reciting set prayers and attending elaborate services or you can make up your own prayers with others or alone.

Pilgrimages are not essential although 'high-church' followers like to go on them. Ancient holy wells have become 'christianized' in some cases, but most sites are those where some historic event occurred. Canterbury Cathedral attracted pilgrims to the scene of Archbishop Thomas à Becket's killing, for example. More recently pilgrimages have centred on places where visions of the Virgin Mary have been seen and miracles recorded. Knock, a village in County Mayo, Ireland, was the place where two women saw her in 1879. Since then cures have occurred there. Lourdes in France has been the centre for cures since Bernadette Soubrious saw Mary in 1858 on 18 occasions. Her visions were very vivid ones. She was made a saint by the Pope in 1933. About a million people go there each year and most are seriously ill or handicapped. For most of the year two 'jumbulances' carrying 24 pilgrims, including a doctor and nurses, regularly leave Britain for Lourdes.

79. *Some Christians put a lot of trust in repeating set prayers, possibly using a rosary, while others prefer to make up their own prayers spontaneously. Give reasons for and against each way and then say which you would prefer.*

80. *Is the main purpose of prayer to praise God or to petition Him?*

81. *Does the strength and weakness of Christianity lie in the wide range of approaches it offers to its followers? List points which provide (a) strength, (b) weakness.*

82. *(a) What makes a place into a centre of Christian pilgrimage? Give examples.*
   (b) Have pilgrimages a value today?

Obedience to Allah. Islam agrees with Judaism and Christianity in seeing God's role as one of ruling while Man's is one of obeying. God has given Man command over nature, but expects to be served in return. This does not make Man a slave of God, but gives him the dignity of being the most superior creature on earth. In all three religions Man is God's tenant controller of the world on God's behalf. Like a tenant farmer he can farm the land provided he pays his due to his overlord. So Man must act in a responsible way and must ask himself if he should 'misuse' nature by making nuclear bombs or allowing abortion. The Koran (Surah 2) points out that the angels thought God was taking a big gamble in setting Man over the world. They thought they ought to rule it. However, God got all of them to change their minds except Satan. Man's task is to prove God was sensible in giving them power. Satan spends his time trying to prove he is right by making people not act responsibly. It follows that for Muslims it is essential that they keep Allah's laws if they are to live up to God's requirements for human beings.

Muslims and Christians disagree on one important point. While Christians argue that all people have sinned and need to be 'saved' by God's grace, Muslims say that people have not 'fallen' and so do not need a 'saviour' to 'save' them.

A Muslim will point out that you are born innocent—free from sin—and you are just as inclined by your human nature to do good or evil. This is because you are free to obey God or not as you like. You are not compelled like a puppet to do either good or evil. You are capable of doing *both*. You have the chance to prove yourself by worship and good deeds. You are entitled to take pride in doing so. But if you deliberately reject Allah's call, you do evil and so deserve punishment.

Rather than upset you by saying you are born with inescapable sin, Islam reassures you. You are born with eyes and ears, an active mind and a heart—all of which will aid you to learn of Allah and serve Him. It is stressed that good can be achieved in this world and, as a Muslim, it is your duty to see to this. The 'other world' after death will be one of reward or punishment depending on what you have done in this life. If you serve Allah you will have happiness here and hereafter. You must remember that you are God's tenant controller or manager (khalifah) on earth and have a responsibility towards Him. The rules of Islam must be understood in this context.

Coming after Judaism and Christianity, Islam could draw on

their commandments. Among the 6239 verses of the Koran can be found Nos. 1 and 5–10 of the Ten Commandments, with different wordings. For example:

> Thy Lord has commanded that you shall not serve any but Him and that you do goodness to your parents . . . Do not kill your children for fear of poverty [NB This rules out birth control and abortion today]. And go not nigh to fornication, for it is an indecency . . . And do not kill anyone whom God has forbidden except for a just cause . . . Do not say, if people do good to us, we will do good to them, and if people oppress us, we will oppress them, but resolve that if people do good to you, you will do good to them, and if they oppress you, do not oppress them in return . . . Repel evil with that which is better.

The Shar'ia (The Clear Path, Islamic law) tells Muslims how to lead their lives. It lays down how to apply the points made in the Koran and the Sunnah (Muhammad's practices and thus recommendations) of the Hadith in daily life (see pp. 63–4). There are five grades of Fard (obligations) to be followed, namely: (i) binding; (ii) recommended; (iii) indifferent; (iv) disapproved of; (v) forbidden. The first four are called Halal (permitted) while the fifth is Haram (forbidden). Among the Fard are the Five Pillars (see p. 112) as well as ones on trade and political matters, even one on how to cut your nails. A recent leaflet on the Shar'ia's rules on dress says, 'Do not ape the trends set by money-making non-believers in Paris and London', arguing that it is wrong to 'mould one's social life according to that of non-believers', and calling on Muslim parents to 'stop this total imitation of Western attire and vulgarity'. Eating is governed by such laws as: eat with the right hand, using the thumb, index and middle fingers, the fourth finger being used if the food is very soft. One may not blow on hot food, or express one's dislike of any food. In other words, have good table manners.

Harsh punishments are set down to deter people. This was felt better than imprisoning people as that would deprive them of their God-given freedom. 'The man who steals and the woman who steals, cut off their hands as a punishment' (Surah 5:38). But the verse goes on to suggest that it is only habitual thieves who are to lose a hand; the first offender who is repentant is forgiven. If one steals for the sake of one's starving family one would not be punished. The point is that if there is a social security scheme for all there is no excuse for theft. Where there is no scheme, there may be an excuse. Another harsh punishment, recommended in the Koran (Surah 24:1), is this: 'The adulteress and the adulterer, flog each of them a hundred stripes'. This is not necessarily put into practice.

Muhammad believed that Christians were wrong to think Jesus was the Son of God. He saw Jesus as just a prophet. He stressed that Allah (God) was almighty ('Allahu Akbar') and that people were His slaves. 'Muslim' means a 'surrendered person', just as 'Islam' means 'submission' to God. God is set apart from people, and not to be seen in quite such a personal way as Christians see God. So you should humbly plead for mercy, forgiveness and guidance. Allah will be merciful to those who humble themselves before Him.

> O my Lord! If I worship thee from fear of hell, burn me in hell; and if I worship thee from hope of paradise, exclude me thence; but if I worship thee for thine own sake, then withhold not from me thine eternal beauty. (Rabi'a, female poet and mystic)

The Five Pillars. Islam lays down a clear, straightforward road for its followers, namely, do your duty. There are five requirements called the Five Pillars of Islam. In diagram form the four minarets (towers) and the dome of the mosque (place of worship) emphasize this.

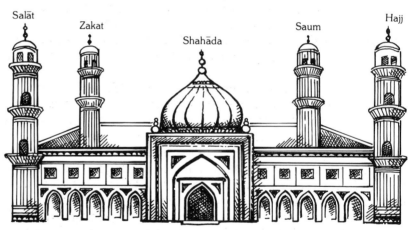

The Five Pillars of Islam in diagram form. List the meanings of the Five Pillars in English.

The First Pillar: Shahāda or Kalimah (declaration of truth). You must accept that 'There is no god but Allah, and Muhammad is His Prophet'. This will make you aware of what the universe stands for and how you fit into it as Allah's servant.

The Second Pillar: Salāt (regular worship). This consists of rakats (prayer sequences) five times a day, as follows:
    At daybreak (fajr): two rakats
    At midday (zuhr): four rakats
    In the afternoon ('asr): four rakats

In the evening (maghrib): three rakats
At night ('isha): four rakats.

The aim of this regular prayer is to strengthen the Muslim's ties to Allah and develop his love for Allah so as to appreciate His Mercy, Power and Glory.

The muezzin (caller) calls the faithful to prayer (azzan, 'call to prayer') from the top of the minaret by shouting, 'God is the greatest. I bear witness that there is no God but Allah. I bear witness that Muhammad is the messenger of Allah. Come to prayer. Come to security. God is the greatest'. Each time, a Muslim must carry out different acts of devotion, each with a set prayer and position to take up. The illustrations (pp. 114–15) make these clear. If you are a Muslim, this is what you do.

Before you can begin, you must make yourself thoroughly clean. This procedure (wudu) removes dirt and also purifies you from any defilements as well as helping you to concentrate on Allah. First, you wash your hands, then your mouth and nose, before the whole of your face. After that, you wash the right hand and forearm, then the left, before wiping your head with your hand; finally, your ears and feet. Parts are repeated three times. 'Believers, when you rise to pray, wash your faces and your hands as far as the elbows, and wipe your heads and your feet to the ankle', says the Koran (Surah 5:6).

Next you face Mecca, the direction of which can be found by looking for the mihrab (niche) on the qibla (direction) wall of the mosque. You can buy special compasses which enable you to work out the direction from anywhere in the world. You lay out your musulta (prayer mat). Each rakat is then performed using the following sequence. You raise your hands beside your face and say, 'Allahu Akbar'; you then put your right hand over your left at waist level and recite part of the Koran before raising your hands again as you say, 'Allahu Akbar'. You bow from the hips, placing your hands on your knees saying, 'Glory be to my Lord, the Great'. Straighten up and with your hands beside your face say, 'Allah listens to whoever thanks Him. Our Lord, thanks be to Thee'. Then you prostrate yourself twice with your face and palms to the ground, sitting back between each prostration. When prostrate, you say three times, 'Glory be to my Lord, the Most High'. You then sit back on your heels and say, 'I bear witness that there is no god except Allah'. You turn your head to the right and left after you say your final prayers.

In this set pattern you show your complete humbleness before Almighty God, from whom you expect nothing in return except what

1 Wash hands and between fingers three times.

2 Wash mouth thoroughly three times.

3 Clean teeth with fingertips.

4 Wash and blow nose three times.

5 Wash the whole face three times.

6 Wash up to each elbow three times.

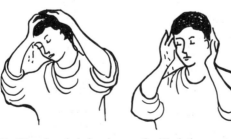

7 Wipe the whole head with water.

8 Wash the ears inside and out.

9 Wash each foot up to the ankle.

The wudu procedure.

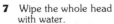

1 Face Mecca; raise hands and say 'Allahu Akbar'.

2 Put right hand over left and recite part of the Koran.

3 Raise hands and say 'Allahu Akbar'.

4 Bow from the hips, placing hands on knees, saying in Arabic, 'Glory be to my Lord, the Great.'

5 Straighten up, raise hands and say, 'Allah listens to whoever thanks Him.'

6 Prostrate yourself twice, nose touching the ground.

7 Straddle your hands and thighs while prostrate and in Arabic say, 'Glory be to my Lord, the Highest.'

8 Sit upright between the two prostrations, with hands on thighs, saying, 'Allahu Akbar'.

9 Turn the head to the right and the left, saying, in the Arabic, 'Peace be on you and Allah's blessings.'

The rakat sequence.

115

you deserve, which in turn is determined by how you have behaved. Du'a (the cry-of-the-heart or voluntary prayer) follows next. You stay kneeling with palms upwards level to your chin and petition God in your own words as well as quoting the Koran. You end by wiping your hands over your face to show your receipt of God's blessing.

83. *What is the purpose of this cleaning rite, wudu, before praying? Describe the rite with illustrations.*

84. *What is the relationship between Allah and the person praying as suggested by the form the Salāt ritual of rakats takes?*

85. *Draw the rakat sequence, explaining each picture.*

86. *What influence is regular prayer several times a day likely to have on Muslims and the maintenance of Islam?*

87. *(a) If one believes it is a man's duty to humbly worship an almighty God, is this best done by having a strict routine to follow?*
(b) Is spontaneous worship more genuine?
(c) Which will have a more lasting effect and be better maintained by the worshipper?

The Third Pillar: Zakat ('purification'). Charity can purify you because giving your possessions to those less fortunate than yourself will make you more generous and friendly. It will help to build up a community sense, free of class distinctions and rivalries.

Alms (sadaqa) shall be used only for the advancement of Allah's cause, for the ransom of captives, debtors, and for the distribution among the poor, the destitute, the wayfarers, those that are

Muslims prostrate in Hyde Park. A mosque has recently been built there.

employed in collecting alms, and those that are converted to the faith. This is a duty enjoined by Allah. He is wise and all knowing. (Surah 9:60)

It is fixed at 2½ per cent or one-fortieth of your savings. However, certain deductions to your income can be made before you calculate what Zakat you must pay. Rent from houses you let, debts, household goods, clothes, car and travel money can be subtracted, for example. You should give Zakat to relatives if they are in need. You can also give it to poor or needy people, but if such people cannot be found you can give Zakat to any organization serving Islam. It is entirely up to you to arrange how to give Zakat. You are put on your honour to do so; after all, if you do not give it you will get what you deserve on the Day of Judgement.

The Fourth Pillar: Saum or Siyam (fasting). You must observe the holy month of Ramadan by fasting. Ramadan is the ninth month of the Islamic year, which consists of 12 *lunar* months, so it comes at different times of our normal (solar) year. Because of this Muslims all over the world get a fair share of different climatic conditions when coping with the strain. Ramadan marks the time when Muhammad received Allah's first revelation of the Koran. You must fast from daybreak until sunset or during the hours when a white thread can be distinguished from a black one. So you must get up before dawn and eat a large breakfast and then another large meal after sunset. Calendars are printed giving local sunrise and sunset times so there can be no error. For example:

Date	London		Birmingham		Sheffield	
	begin	end	begin	end	begin	end
Oct 31	6.34	5.36	6.41	5.32	6.42	5.36
Nov 1	6.35	5.34	6.43	5.34	6.43	5.34
Nov 2	6.37	5.32	6.44	5.36	6.44	5.32

Young children and pregnant women are exempt. If you deliberately break the fast without a good reason, you must give a meal for 60 people or fast 60 further days. Those who are sick or travelling must make up any days they miss later on. No smoking is allowed in the daytime as swallowing any smoke would break the fast; likewise no toothpaste is allowed. You must behave extra well during this self-disciplining month and not talk in a vulgar way or refer to anyone behind their back.

88. *Is a period of fasting a good aid to humbleness? Why do Muslims succeed in keeping Ramadan better than Christians keep their Lent (period before Good Friday)?*

The hajj; above a small part of the pilgrim camp; below the Ka'ba.

118

The Fifth Pillar: Hajj or Hadj (pilgrimage). Hajj literally means 'setting out for a definite purpose' and the place 'set out for' is Mecca. This is designed to purify you from your pride and prejudices and make you realize everyone will be equal at the Day of Judgement. It is hoped that the spirit of companionship you will experience will be carried over into your daily life:

> *Make the pilgrimage and visit the Sacred House for His sake . . . Make the pilgrimage in the appointed months. He that intends to perform it in those months must abstain from sexual intercourse, obscene language, and bitter disputes while on the pilgrimage. Allah is aware of whatever good you do. Provide yourselves well; the best provision is piety.* (Surah 2:196)

You should go once in your life if you can afford it, and each year one to two million camp at Mecca in the 12th month. Men and women wear special clothes to show that they are living in a consecrated state (ihram) of self-denial and total submission to Allah. Sixteen kilometres from Mecca, men must shave their heads and put on two white sheet-like garments, one around the waist and the other over the left shoulder. A woman may go only if accompanied by a male relative, and she wears a covering white garment.

89. *How does wearing special clothes help to fulfil the purpose of Hajj? Clue: Think of colour, class status, nationality.*

As you approach you call out, 'Labbayk' ('I am here [God] at your service'). After camping in the colossal pilgrim camp, the first thing to do is the tawaf (walk three times quickly and four times slowly) round the Ka'ba. This is a cube 15m long, 10m wide and 14m high, and is also known as the Bait-ul-lah, the House of God. It is said to be the first man-made structure built solely to worship one God. It is covered in a black cotton and silk cloth with the Koran embroidered on it. This is renewed annually and pieces of the old cloth are given to distinguished guests. The Black Stone, an oval of 18cm in diameter, mounted in the south-east corner, is traditionally said to have been received by Ishmael, Abraham's son, from the angel Gabriel. It may be an ancient aerolite. It is said to have been white originally to guide pilgrims, but to have turned black due to their sin. Only special visitors are allowed inside the Ka'ba on one day a year.

The next thing you must do is to run 366m seven times between two little hills, Safa and Marwa. This is where Ishmael's mother had once run to and fro looking for water, only to find on return that her dying son had dug his toes in the sand and found water (the Well of

Zamzam). You go on 21km to Mount Arafat, the Mount of Mercy, where you meditate from noon to sunset. You stay overnight in the open at Muzdalifah and then return to Mina, a village east of Mecca, collecting 49 pebbles on the way. At Mina you stone the devil (Jamrat) by throwing them at the three stone pillars where the devil tempted Ishmael to disobey his father. It is believed that Ishmael threw stones then.

After this there is the Eid ul-Adha (Great Festival of Sacrifice) lasting four days. This is a thanksgiving feast in which sheep are sacrificed as Abraham sacrificed a sheep instead of his son (Gen. 22; Surah 37:100–111). Note that Muslims think it was Ishmael not Isaac who was to die (see p. 175).

Finally, you walk round the Ka'ba seven more times. Some dye their beards red after the pilgrimage, and all can call themselves Hajjis (people who have made the pilgrimage). If you cannot afford to go, you give contributions for a substitute to go. He will bring merit to you for making his journey possible.

90. Should Christians be encouraged to make a 'hajj' to Jerusalem once in their lives? If so, would it help them in their belief or way of life?

91. 'You get what you deserve'.
(a) Is this a just and loving way for God to treat you?
(b) What alternative rule could God apply to people's lives?
(c) Does 'You get what you deserve' help to ensure that Muslims take care to follow their faith properly every day of their lives?

92. Draw a picture of the Ka'ba and underneath say where it is to be found and why it is so important to the Muslims.

SIKHISM

Commandments. Guru Nanak taught eleven commandments:

(1) There is only one God. Worship and pray to Him and no other.

(2) Remember God, work hard and help others.

(3) God is pleased with honest work and truthful living.

(4) There is no rich, no poor, no black and no white, before God. It is your actions that make you good or bad.

(5) Men and women are all equal before God.

(6) Love everyone and pray for the good of all.

(7) Be kind to people, animals and birds.

(8) Fear not, frighten not.

(9) Always speak the truth.

(10) Be simple in your food, dress and habits.

(11) God alone can measure His own greatness; what He gives we must treasure.

These are enlarged upon in Sikh holy writings to include other commandments. For example, idol worship is not allowed. Also forbidden is the caste structure, though this may be allowed in practice. Sikhs forbid anything superstitious such as black magic or omens, ancestor worship and the wearing of a sacred thread (see pp. 178–80). These points show the Sikhs' criticism of Hinduism. Sikhs may not cut their hair, partake of alcohol, tobacco or drugs, gamble or steal, or commit adultery.

Burn egoism, selfishness and avarice; remove impurity with the help of God's word; burn attachment, grind it down into ink powder. Wash the mind into clean paper . . . Make love your pen, let your consciousness be the scribe . . . All beings are born from the same light, how can some be good and some bad?

No Sikh is allowed to retire from life to become a hermit or monk. He should meet the demands of family life. He should not criticize others for following their religions sincerely as there is goodness in all religions: 'Words do not the saint or sinner make, action alone is written in the book of fate'.

93. *List any points you can find in the Sikh rules which suggest a particularly modern outlook.*

94. *What examples of (a) tolerance, (b) intolerance of other religions can you find?*

95. *Which are the Sikh rules designed to cope with the usual human weaknesses?*

96. *Do any Sikh rules particularly impress you? Give your reasons.*

Nanak constructed Sikhism from what he saw was best in Hinduism and Islam, ruthlessly sweeping aside what he thought they had got wrong. Like the Hindus, Sikhs believe life on this planet is maya (an illusion, unreal, transient) and the real life will be in the next world. You suffer in this life for two reasons. First, you have either not appreciated what God has created around you or you have forgotten His existence. Secondly, your mind is not under proper control and you allow yourself to keep thinking of worldly pleasures.

So if you want to please God and obtain salvation, you will have to live in brotherhood with other Sikhs and be humble and tolerant. Just believing in God is not enough; you must prove it by your life. You must be prepared to die for your faith if need be. There are two paths open to you: that of Simran, love of humanity; and that of Seva, service to humanity.

You have to realize that the effects of your actions on earth will follow your soul like a shadow. The five main sins you must overcome are lust, anger, greed, pride, and any over-attachment to people or things. 'My adversaries are five, and I am but one. How shall I defend my house, O Soul?'. It is not that you are born evil. In fact you were once good, but evil has overshadowed your basic goodness. However, God's mercy will enable you to find your true self and overcome these problems rather than any good behaviour by yourself doing so. Your good behaviour follows from being saved by God's grace.

Daily worship. You are expected to get up early, wash and meditate on God. You must also recite the 38 verses of the Japji (a Nanak hymn) and the Ardas (prayer recalling the lives of the gurus and those who died for Sikhism): 'beaten . . . shot, cut up or burnt alive with kerosene oil, but did not make any resistance . . . think of their patient faith . . .' The Ardas calls on God to aid them, to unite and humble them:

> May [Sikhism] find a loving place in our hearts and serve to draw our souls towards Thee. Save us, O Father, from lust, wrath, greed, undue attachment and pride . . . Grant . . . the gift of faith, the gift of confidence in Thee . . . grant that we may according to Thy will do what is right. Give us light, give us understanding . . . Forgive us our sins . . . Help us in keeping ourselves pure . . . Through Nanak may Thy Name forever be on the increase . . . Hail Khalsa of the Wonderful Lord who is always victorious.

This prayer performs the role of the Lord's Prayer in Christianity. You may use a cotton mala (rosary) with 108 knots to aid in the meditation (Nam Simran, 'Calling God to mind'), saying 'Waheguru ('Wonderful Lord') at each knot. In the evening you use the Rahiras (Holy Path) prayer. If you have a copy of the Granth, you will have to keep it in a room devoted to it. When praying you can open it anywhere but you must always begin reading at the top left-hand corner. A family facing problems will read the Granth right through non-stop, reading in relays for 48 hours. Such a reading is called Akhand Path.

A three-fold service, physical (tan), mental (man) and material (dhan) is required of you. Physically you must work hard. Your practical training will be sweeping the temple (gurdwara) floor, cleaning the utensils, and so on. Then you must help those in need and defend the weak. 'Useless the hands and the feet if they do not serve humanity'. Mentally you must serve by telling others about God. So you must study the Granth and read it completely every month or so. Praying for others is a mental service too. Materially you must give 10 per cent of your income in charity, bringing it to the gurdwara. It will be used for communal meals, hospitals, the poor, and so on. These three services will enable you to surrender your 'I-hood', yourself, to God's will.

Sikhs do not believe in miracles or animal sacrifices, and they see no merit in fasting. They have no pilgrimage like the Islamic Hajj, but many go to visit the Golden Temple at Amritsar (see pp. 153–4). They will bathe there and file past the Granth which is continually read from dawn until late at night.

97. Sikhs believe all religions began with good intentions and are like different roads leading to the same destination. Do you agree with them now that you have followed these different routes in this chapter?

98. Sikhs welcome people of other religions to their services.
    (a) Do other religions do this?
    (b) Should they do so?
    (c) Why might they not do so?

99. Nanak voiced his criticism of Islam thus: 'The path of the true Yoga is found by dwelling in God while yet living in the midst of the world's temptations. Make mercy your mosque, faith your prayer mat, and righteousness your Koran. Make humility your circumcision, uprightness your fasting and so you will be a Muslim'. Why do you think he said this and what is he trying to say? Do you agree with him?

100. Construct a road to find God by drawing on all you think is best in the various roads you have read about in this chapter. When you have done so, consider whether you have learnt more about (a) God and (b) yourself, your strengths and weaknesses, in doing so.

101. Tabulate the different religions under these headings: (a) Daily set prayers; (b) Ritual washing; (c) Pilgrimage; (d) Fasting; (e) Meditation; (f) Confessions; (g) Penances; (h) Sacrifices; (i) Communal meals.

102. *Tabulate the rules given in this chapter by religions by ticking in the appropriate columns below:*

God	Hindu	Shinto	Taoist	Buddhist	Judaic	Christian	Islamic	Sikh
One God								
Greatness of God								
No idols								
No oath-taking								
Man's duties	**Hindu**	**Shinto**	**Taoist**	**Buddhist**	**Judaic**	**Christian**	**Islamic**	**Sikh**
Working hard								
Do not steal								
Do not covet								
Do not lie								
Do not kill								
Do not harm animals								
Do not drink alcohol								
Honour parents								
Treat all equally								
Love all								

Comment on anything striking or interesting in the results of this table.

103. *Draw up your own set of rules on the assumption that you are a religious leader. Comment at the end on why you have chosen to insert some rules and leave out other possible ones.*
(a) Is 'being good' essential if you are to follow any religion?
(b) How is 'being good' related to God?
(c) Is it obedience or love which (i) does, (ii) should make you serve God by 'being good'?

5.
WHERE AND HOW TO WORSHIP

If we study the structure of places of worship carefully we should be able to find out how they have been designed to serve their religion. Do they point to heaven in the sky? Do they stand out for miles around or merge into the natural background? Do they face a particular direction? Are they designed for worshippers to be mere spectators to a ritual performed by priests, or are they laid out for the congregation to play an active part? Do they make provision for sacrifices, or are they primarily places for preaching sermons? Are they meant to be places for gods to live in? Are they decorated to encourage and aid worship or plain so that worshippers are not distracted? What is the focal point in the building—an altar, a pulpit or a holy book? Remember these questions as you read on.

HINDUISM

The Hindu temple is called a mandir ('place of worship'). It may be of any size but is built to a definite plan so as to face the rising sun. Temples stand within a walled enclosure. As you enter with your back to the sun, the first thing you will meet is a large stone statue of the creature which is said to convey the temple's god around. For example, you may see a lion for Durga to ride or a bull for Shiva. Then you go up some steps to the vimana (central sanctuary) and under the torana (entrance gateway) into the ardhamandapa (porch) before arriving at the mahamandapa or mandapa (the nave). There you can sit on the floor to worship. Beyond is the adytum or garbagriha (the sanctuary or shrine room, also called the cella) where

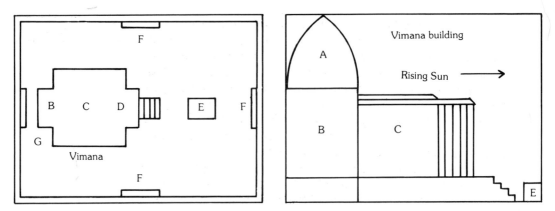

A = Sikhara B = Garbagriha C = Mandapa D = Ardhamandapa E = God's 'vehicle' F = Gopuram G = Pradakshina

Hindu Temple or Mandir. Vertically the temple represents the god's body with the sikhara as head and garbagriha as neck, mandapa as body and gopuram as feet. Write down the uses or meanings of the different parts.

the god's image (linga) is kept. This is a smaller, dark room. It is normally kept shut and only priests may enter there to wash and dress the image, presenting it with flowers, incense, fruit, jewels or other offerings. The image will be dressed in rich garments and have a golden crown on festival days. Above the shrine is the sikhara (pyramid tower) which represents a mountain, always considered a holy place. A pradakshina (processional passage) goes round the garbagriha, and worship may involve walking round and round the shrine. There will also be a large pool for worshippers to descend into for ritual washing. Gopurams (watch-tower gateways) are set in the outer wall and are decorated with scenes from Hindu stories.

Worship starts at dawn when the priests greet the awakening of the god, providing for his washing and refreshment before clothing him ready to receive worshippers. Flowers, fruit and incense will be presented. Music follows to entertain the god and then the worshippers come to offer their bhakti (devotion), by lighting a candle and saying prayers. As they leave, they are given prasad (sacred food) which has been offered to the god earlier in the day. In the evening, food and retiring-to-bed ceremonies are performed by the priests and the image is bathed again.

Congregational acts of worship (puja) consist of three parts. Havan (offering of fire) involves the priest kindling a sacred fire on a portable fire-altar. Wood, camphor and ghee (melted butter) are used. Sections of the Vedas are recited. ('Let us meditate upon the most excellent light of the radiant sun; may he guide our minds'.) The fire represents the mouth of the god devouring the offerings in the smoke. Prayers for purity follow and the priest ceremonially washes himself by touching each part of his body as he says, 'Let my tongue have speaking power, ears have the power of hearing, the nose inhaling power and the eyes seeing power. May the arms and thighs have strength and all the limbs be full of energy'. The worshippers copy him. Arti (the worship of light) involves the use of a flat tray with five candles on it representing the elements (see pp. 132, 134, 162, 184). It is waved in front of the shrine. At the same time, incense and flowers representing the earth are presented, a fan is waved to represent the air, and a conch shell is sounded to stand for ether. Another element, water, is contained in the shell. A spot of red paste is put on the foreheads of the statues of the gods before the arti dish is passed round for people to pass their hands over the flames and then over their heads. This enables them to receive the gods' blessing and power. Prasad is then given out. Finally, the singing of bhajans (hymns) follows. Bells, tambourines, triangles and other instruments will be used and people clap, too. Dancing is another form of worship which may be used. There will be readings from the Gita. The prayer for peace, 'OM, O God, let there be peace, peace, peace', ends the service.

1.   *Draw a plan of a Hindu temple, naming the parts.*

2.   *What does the daily ritual care of the god's image suggest is the Hindu belief about a god's life?*

SHINTOISM

(a) Komainu;

The Shinto shrine is called a jinja (literally 'kami house'). Jinjas are often tiny huts beside a road or a factory or on top of a large building, and they look like little houses. The larger ones are set in the midst of trees, near the sea or on a hill. The aim is to blend them with the landscape. They usually face east (never north, as that is death's side). An avenue of trees leads up to the haiden (hall of worship) which is large and open on all sides to receive worshippers. Along the avenue will be one or more arches called torii (literally 'bird perches'). These have praises to the god on them, usually made of wood but sometimes of stone, bronze or concrete. Worshippers bow and salute them as they pass. Across them are hung shimenawa (sacred twisted rice-straw ropes). Toro (stone lanterns) also mark the route. Komainu (Korean dogs) and karashishi (Chinese lions) guard the

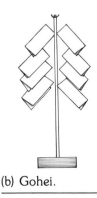

(b) Gohei.

Futaarasan Jinja, Nikko. Draw a sketch of this picture and name
(a) Torii;
(b) Shimenawa;
(c) Toro.

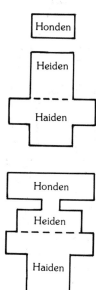

Jinja designs.

god-house. The washing pavilion (temizuya) has a stone basin and wooden dippers for worshippers to rinse their mouths and pour water over their fingers.

In the haiden Shintoists offer gohei, which are small poles with strips of white, gold, silver, red or blue paper, metal or cloth folded into a plait design to the gods. In the heiden (hall of offering) the priests say prayers and make their offerings. The principal shrine is called the honden; it has a small upstairs room where the god lives. Only priests may enter the honden where the mitama-shiro (spirit substitute), a mirror or cloth representing the god, is kept. A mirror symbolizes brightness and purity. The room is otherwise bare except for curtains, branches of the holy sakaki tree, vessels for gifts, and a mat for the priest to sit on. The jinja will also have space for ceremonial dances to be performed, called a kagura-den. Shimenawa ropes mark off every sanctified object or piece of holy ground within the jinja to keep away evil spirits. Pieces of paper hang from these ropes.

The most famous shrine is that to Amaterasu, the sun goddess, at Isé. It is rebuilt every 20 years, the next renewal being due in 1993. In 1973 the eight-year task was completed by 200 000 craftsmen using 13 600 cypress trees and 12 000 bamboo poles at a cost of £7½ million. Renewal is necessary to preserve its purification. It contains sacred symbols sent to earth by the goddess's grandson: namely, a mirror, sword and a jewel. Amaterasu is regarded as the ancestress of the Japanese imperial family. An outer shrine (geku) is dedicated to Inari, the food god. It is set in 200 acres of cedars. This shrine and its torii are painted bright red. Stones and wooden foxes, with keys, or texts, in their mouths, are everywhere, since they act as the god's messengers. The prime minister and cabinet visit Isé once a year and after the formation of a new government.

At the Fushimi-inari shrine to Inari at Kyoto there are 10 000 torii, each 3m high, donated by worshippers hoping to get rich from this agricultural and business god. Worshippers pay for young girls to dance for the god. The Meiji shrine at Tokyo is set among 120 000 trees, and honours the Emperor Meiji (1867–1912).

Since the government ceased to supervise the shrines in 1946, many have opened community centres, with playground facilities. They also offer social welfare help for worshippers if asked.

There are 21 000 priests, of whom 480 are women, in charge of 16 674 jinjas. Most of them are part-timers. Their main function is to worship and serve the kami so as to keep the world on good relations with them. They provide divine protection for people and objects by means of harai purification (see pp. 76–7). They do not preach. They are expected to marry and have children. High priests are called guji and their assistants are negi, while juniors are shuten. Women priests were introduced in World War II, when as priests' wives they often had to care for the jinjas. Priests carry wooden sceptres called shaku, or shaken, which are purely ornamental. Their kari-ginu robes (literally 'hunting robes') vary in colour according to their age and the season of the year. They wear black clogs.

Miko are girl attendants who serve the shrine for five years on leaving school. They work long hours for little pay as dancers, musicians, secretaries and servants. They are usually priests' daughters. They wear white kimonos and vermilion divided skirts and carry cypress fans.

Shinto priest. What is he holding in his hand?

Daily worship (nikku) involves the white-robed priests renewing the sakaki branches, making offerings as they perform their ritual with handclappings to arouse the kami. Otherwise all is quiet as Shintoists believe rituals should be quiet and solemn—in sharp contrast to the performance of lively songs and dances about myths for the lay worshippers in their part of the jinjas.

There is no congregational worship. Individual worshippers stand in front of a shrine, pull a white cord to ring a bell to get the kami's attention, and throw 'homage' coins into a box. They clap their hands (kashiwade) in prayer and bow. They can give offerings too. They can buy charms to drive off evil spirits, or to ensure good harvests or successful business deals. They can shake a box of sticks, pull one out, check its number and collect a printed sheet (o-mikuji) with predictions and warnings on it. If the news is bad, it is customary to knot the paper round a twig to conjure the prediction away. A 1970 survey showed that 66 per cent men and 75 per cent women got a feeling of inner renewal after visiting a shrine.

3. *Draw a plan of a jinja and its avenue, naming the parts.*

4. *Draw (a) a tori, (b) a toro, (c) a komainu.*

5. *Jinjas are deliberately designed to blend with their natural surroundings rather than stand out, and they are modestly constructed of wood. Why do you think Shintoists prefer shrines of this kind?*

6. *What are the value of charms? Do you or your friends carry any? What are they and why do you trust them?*

TAOISM

The Taoist temple, a kuan, is built to a set pattern. A wall keeps evil spirits from the Pai lou (portal of honour) and the marble entrance which opens out into the first courtyard. On both sides are towers or pavilions, one with a bell and the other with a huge drum. In the two opposite corners are two more pavilions with inscribed pillars which stand on turtle or dragon statues. Through a large gateway guarded by gigantic lion statues, you come to another courtyard, followed by several more. Each courtyard is enclosed on its north side by a temple dedicated to a god or holy man. Courtyards also contain huge bronze bowls and incense burners on tripods. Long spirals of incense, looking like bed springs, hang down above the worshippers' heads. Libraries, refectories and dormitories for monks complete the building. A shop will sell joss sticks and paper money and the shopkeeper will tell fortunes and interpret signs.

A Taoist kuan.

The village temple (miao) in Taiwan is a social and cultural as well as a religious centre. It is run by a lay committee who employ priests to perform the rituals. The most famous temple is the Temple of Heaven at Peking, where the emperor used to offer sacrifices. It is different from other kuans and its double red wall encloses 5000 cypresses. It is divided into the Hall of Annual Prayer for Good Harvests, the Hall of the God of the Universe and the Altar of Heaven. The Hall of Prayer has a three-tiered roof of blue tiles; here the emperor spent one night a year in fasting and prayer. The Altar of Heaven is approached by three terraces—for man, earth and heaven. Incense was burnt and an ox sacrificed while the emperor, the 'Son of Heaven', stood in holy ecstasy.

Worship. People go to kuans to burn incense and candles and offer prayers. They bring bananas or a chicken and purchase paper money to burn for ancestors, and joss sticks for their own devotion. They hold the burning sticks in both hands and bow to the altar, and shake the sticks before placing them in an urn. If they want some question about marriage or business answered, for example, they cast divining blocks on the floor. How these fall indicates what they should do—this is an example of divination. Priests also perform divinations, as well as exorcisms. Beggars sleep in the courtyard as it is thought a good thing to die in a god's presence. Temples also serve as schools and relief distribution centres.

On a god's birthday the temple is crowded. Many candles are lit and incense is burnt. Drums, gongs and crackers sound, and the images of the god are carried in palanquins (god-carriages) in procession. There is so much firecracker smoke that a man with a small bellows follows each palanquin.

7. *Draw a plan of a Taoist temple.*

8. *Compare Shinto and Taoist temple construction and the uses made of them.*

BUDDHISM

Buddhist temples vary in design from one country to another. They are usually built to symbolize the Five Elements.

Theravāda temples. In India temples are called stūpas (mounds). They were originally burial chambers, housing bones, hair or clothing of Buddha or his leading followers. Thus they became relic chambers. In Sri Lanka they are called dāgobas (relic chambers). They are bell-shaped and still contain relics of Buddha or his followers, but are otherwise solid. They can be enormous, 70m high for example. The Abhoyagiriya Dāgoba has enough bricks to build a wall 3m high from London to Edinburgh.

In Thailand temples are called chedis or wats (worship centres). There are 23 700 of them, varying in size from single rooms to great monasteries. The people give a tenth of their income to support them so no fund-raising is needed. They are built and maintained by voluntary labour. Their courtyards are covered with sand brought in by locals as a form of merit-making. This ensures they remain above flood level in a land of floods. The main hall faces east as Buddha faced east when he sat under the bodhi tree, and a big bodhi tree grows in the wat. If possible, it is from a cutting of the original tree. Some chedis have huge dome-topped towers, prangs, to the Hindu Shiva.

Burmese temples are called pagodas (relic chambers), and they vary in size. They are white-washed conical buildings. The Golden Pagoda in Rangoon is 61m high, taller than St Paul's Cathedral, London. It is covered with gold leaf and has 25 tons of pure gold

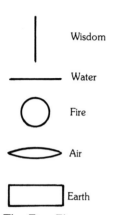

Wisdom

Water

Fire

Air

Earth

The Five Elements.

Theravāda Buddhist places of worship. What is the difference between a stupa and a dagoba? What are the meanings of wat and pagoda?

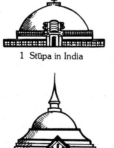

1 Stūpa in India

2 Dāgoba in Sri Lanka

3 Wat in Thailand

4 Pagoda in Burma

statues. It has four main entrances leading to long flights of stairs to chapels, each containing pure gold Buddhas. Large courtyards and small chapels contain countless other Buddhas, many of which are the property of families. The hairs of the Buddha, a sandal and robes of previous Buddhas are kept in a barred basement. In the town of Pagān there are 5000 pagodas.

Theravāda worship. In the temples there is a steady stream of worshippers. In dāgobas flowers, paper lamps and incense are everywhere. Priests sell coloured tiles for people to put on the shrines. Pagodas and wats are surrounded by stalls selling paper umbrellas, flowers, joss sticks, images, rosaries and flat bells. The bells are sounded when gifts are presented. Worshippers bow, kneel and prostrate themselves with the palms of their hands together in front of their foreheads, calling on the name of the Buddha by saying the Three Refuges. Gifts are given to the Three Jewels, namely Buddha, Dharma (the raft, representing teaching of Buddha) and the Sangha (the community of monks). Worshippers throw two horseshoe-shaped pieces of red wood to see which way they will fall and then pull a spill from a wooden box and look at the number on it. The official gives them a printed sheet from a drawer with the same number on it, and this has the answer to the question about the future which they sought—or worshippers may rattle a vase of sticks and pull one out. Alternatively, worshippers may spin the golden wheel of life with its 28 sections and take the paper from the drawer below where it stops.

Worship is individual and not congregational, although great temples like the Temple of the Sacred Tooth of Buddha, Kandy, Sri Lanka, do have daily pūjā, communal worship. Drummers make a deafening noise and trumpets are sounded. Yellow and white flowers are given to the monks who place them on a silver altar containing the tooth. Rice is then consecrated and distributed.

Mahāyāna temples. Chinese pagodas, 9–13 floors high, are often on sites determined by omens. They are not places of regular worship, and are separate from monasteries with their temples (szes). These buildings have halls with alcoves for images with tables of flowers and incense before them. The first hall might contain the Four Lords of Heaven, huge bright colourful images. Maitreya ('Buddha-to-come') holds in one hand a bag of fortune and in the other a rosary, each bead of which represents 1000 years which he spent doing good in previous lives. The Golden Hall will contain the

Pagoda in China.

Buddhist triad ('three precious ones'): Shakya Shakyamuni (a title for Gautama), Amida or O-Mi-T'o-Fu (Lord of the Western Paradise) and Wen-shu (Lord of Knowledge and Meditation).

9.   Draw a stūpa, a dāgoba, a wat and a Chinese pagoda.

The szes are always aligned south to north, and their layout is similar to Taoist ones but with an extra 'Buddha Comes' room in the main courtyard. Monks' quarters are included.

Shukubos (temples) of Zen Buddhism in Japan can be stayed in by interested tourists. The daily schedule is as follows:

4.30 am, rise

5 am, meditation in the hall of worship

7 am, rice-gruel breakfast; clean the building

8 am, meditation

9 am, instruction

10 am, free

12 noon, lunch

1 pm, solitary meditation

2 pm, outdoor work

4 pm, meditation

5.30 pm, evening meal

7 pm, meditation

8 pm, lecture on Buddhism

9 pm, bed.

A symbolic sea of sand is raked daily into forms symbolizing the condition of Man.

In Tibet, pagodas are called chortens (funeral pyres). They are situated in monasteries, beside roads and on hilltops. They may contain a relic or a memorial to a saint. On a plinth representing earth stands a solid dome for water, crowned by a spire for fire, a crescent for air, and a solar disc as space. Two eyes are painted on the base.

10.   Draw a chorten and label the Five Elements on it.

Mahāyāna worship. Worshippers can gain merit by walking round a chorten clockwise and chanting texts. Prayer wheels are everywhere, ranging from small hand ones for use as you walk to huge ones 2m high. The large ones have bells on them. Paper prayer

Chorten in Tibet.

wheels turn slowly over candle flames in the temple. They are inscribed with 'Hail to the jewel of the lotus', and similar texts. Prayer walls and prayer flags are inscribed with texts and pictures of gods.

Buddhist prayer wheels in Nepal.

Monks maintain daily rituals, and people join in by lighting joss sticks, setting the prayer wheels going, and walking round the shrines. Gongs are sounded as they make their offerings. Large rosaries with 108 beads are used by monks and smaller ones by lay people.

11. *Comment on the form of worship which goes on in Buddhist temples. What is the point behind the different things which are done?*

135

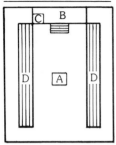

A = Bimah   B = Ark
C = Rabbi's seat
D = Congregation

Synagogue plan.

Synagogues. Jews worship in synagogues ('synagogue' means 'bringing together'). They can be of any shape (for example, oblong, round or octagonal) and seats may face the east or inwards. The holy ark is at the east end, towards Jerusalem. It is a cupboard containing the Torah on a scroll, with a curtain in front (Exod. 26:31–34). Above the Ark are two tablets with the first two words of each of the Ten Commandments on them. At the central point of the service the Torah scroll will be carried in procession to the bimah (reading desk) so that it can be read (Neh. 8:2–8). The scroll is mounted on two wooden rollers with silver heads and bells on the crown which represent God's sovereignty. It is wrapped in velvet with a breastplate to represent the High Priest's breastplate. The Torah is handwritten in Hebrew. As it is taken from the Ark the words, 'This is the Law of

The Torah is carried to the Bimah in Djerba Sem synagogue. Notice the crowns and bells and the men's talliths. What is the mood of the congregation?

Moses set before the Children of Israel . . . It is a tree of life to them

Moses set before the Children of Israel . . . It is a tree of life to them that grasp it', are said. In front of the Ark is the ner tamid (lamp of perpetual light: Exod. 27:20–21) which burns continually to represent the continuity of Jewish tradition and God's presence.

In Orthodox synagogues men and women sit separately and singing is unaccompanied. Services are in Hebrew. In Liberal ones both sexes sit together and an organ accompanies the singing. Tefellin and talliths are not usually worn in Liberal synagogues. Their main service, held in English, is on Friday evenings, and its highlight is a sermon. Reform Jews sometimes have family seating and an organ, but not always. They may have a sermon or a Torah discussion, but their service is mainly in Hebrew.

Worship. The rabbi is the Law expert. He is not a priest but a community teacher, so he will preach but not necessarily lead the service. He should marry and have children as an example to others. The cantor is the musical and ritual expert and he will lead the singing. This is particularly important in Orthodox synagogues as they have no organs. For a service to take place there must be ten adult males present. These represent (among other things) the Ten Commandments, ten plagues, ten days of penitence, and Abraham's ten tests. Worshippers bow on entering and say, 'As for me, in the abundance of thy loving kindness will I come unto thy house'. Men wear hats or cappels (round caps) in reverence, as well as their talliths. The weekly Sabbath (Saturday) service lasts two hours. The siddur (service order) opens with the reading of psalms, before the cantor sings about God's help for the Jews in the past (e.g. deliverance from Egyptian slavery). He then sings God's blessing before the climax is reached with the Shema ('hear') from Deut. 6:4–9, 'Hear, O Israel, the Lord your God, the Lord is One . . .' which is the Jewish statement of belief. The Amidah ('standing') prayer follows with people standing facing the Ark. On the Sabbath this prayer is one of praise, but on weekdays it recalls the Eighteen Blessings on their people, such as knowledge, forgiveness, good crops, punishing the wicked and rebuilding Jerusalem. The doors of the Ark are opened and the Torah is carried from it. Men touch it with their talliths and then kiss them. Members of the congregation are called to the reading of the Torah. They stand beside the reader who points to the place with a special silver or ivory pointer as he reads. The whole Torah will be read through a year of Sabbath services. Further prayers are said before the scrolls are returned to the Ark. At this point the rabbi may preach a sermon. Another Amidah is said and the Kaddish (sanctification) prayer follows, beginning 'Magnified and sanctified be His great Name in the world which He hath created according to His will. May He establish His kingdom during your life. . . '. To this the people reply, 'Let His name be blessed for ever and for all eternity'.

Several rabbis may unite to form a beth din, which is a house of law or court. It licenses kosher butchers after inspecting their premises and issues them with a certificate to display. It also issues divorce documents ('gets') if a marriage really breaks down.

12. *Draw the plan of a synagogue.*

13. *Why is the Torah held in so much reverence?*

14. *A rabbi must marry and have a family; a Roman Catholic priest must stay single. Give arguments for and against both rules, and say why you prefer one of them.*

CHRISTIANITY

Orthodox churches. The plan is basically that of a cross with a dome above the centre. There are no chairs in the nave (congregational area) as the worshippers stand to pray. The choir is out of sight in the transepts (side-arms of the cross). Round the walls and on the iconostasis (screen of wood, stone) are icons, which are paintings of Jesus, the apostles and saints done in bright colours. There are no statues as they might be taken as idols. The icons on the iconostasis may have a message depicted, such as God rescuing Man from sin. In the middle are the royal doors. At certain times during the service the scarlet curtain (symbol of the Jerusalem Temple curtain) is pulled back and the doors opened to show that God has opened the way for Man to be united with Him. Behind the doors is the holy table or throne, a sign of God's presence. Beyond it is the bishop's seat. Only priests may enter this part of the building.

The main service is the liturgy which means 'people's work of thanks to God'. When a worshipper arrives he will buy a candle, and put it before an icon, which he kisses, before crossing himself. The icons will help him to concentrate on his prayers. The choir sing unaccompanied. The first part of the liturgy is the liturgy of the word and it consists of prayers and Bible readings. The climax comes with a priest carrying the Book of the Gospels (stories of Jesus' life) raised

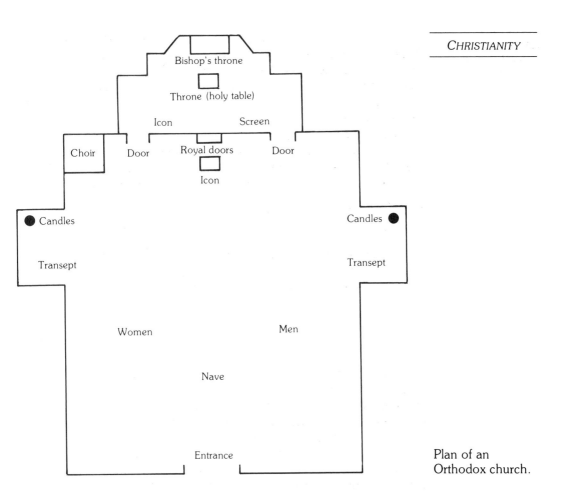

Bishop's throne

Throne (holy table)

Icon　　　　Screen

Choir　　Door　　Royal doors　　Door

Icon

Candles　　　　　　　Candles

Transept　　　　　　　Transept

Women　　　　Men

Nave

Entrance

Plan of an
Orthodox church.

high above his head as he comes through the royal doors to the nave. He then reads passages before returning through the screen. The second part, the liturgy of the faithful, is the preparation of the bread and wine for Communion at the holy table behind the closed royal doors. After the bread and wine are blessed he comes through the doors to give a portion of bread dipped in wine to the communicants.

15. *Draw a plan of the Orthodox church and name the parts.*

16. *Why do you think the blessing of the bread and wine takes place behind the screen?*

17. *Are icons likely to be a better aid to worship and meditation than statues?*

Worship in an Orthodox church. In the photo above the patriarch is facing the congregation. Where is the iconostasis? The photograph below shows Communion.

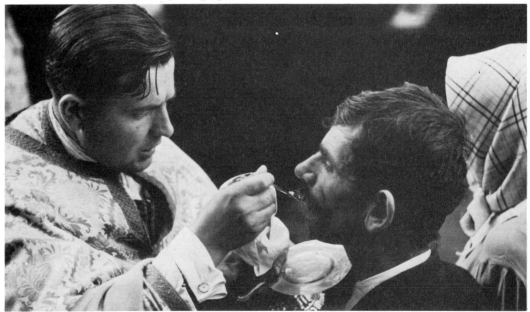

Roman Catholic churches. The church is usually in the shape of a cross or an oblong. At the centre of the east end will be the High Altar with cross and candlesticks on it. The choir stalls will probably be near it and so too will be the lectern, an elaborate stand for the Bible and the pulpit, where the priest stands when he delivers the sermon. An organ will accompany the singing. Round the building will be a number of side chapels, one of which will be dedicated to the Blessed Virgin Mary, Jesus' mother. All priests must say Mass (Communion) daily. Confession cubicles will be placed in convenient places. A font for baptizing new members will stand near the entrance. On the walls will be pictures or carved scenes showing the 14 stages of Jesus' last hours until the crucifixion. Statues of Mary and saints will be surrounded by candles lit by the faithful who have asked their help. A tabernacle (cupboard) behind the altar or in a side chapel will contain the Blessed Sacrament (consecrated bread) to mark Jesus' presence. A light will always be kept burning in front of it.

When a worshipper enters he will cross himself with holy water from a stoup (basin) and genuflect (bend one knee to the floor and bow) towards the altar. He will kneel in prayer. The priest will stand

Two styles of Roman Catholic church:
(a) traditional;
(b) modern 'round' at Clifton, Bristol.

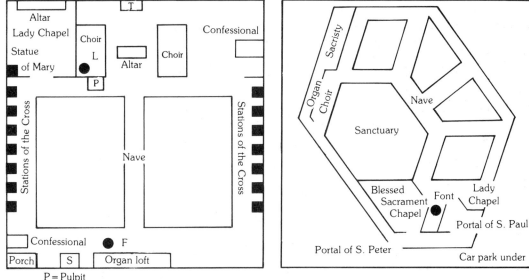

(a) Traditional
(b) Round

P = Pulpit
L = Sanctuary light indicating presence of Blessed Sacrament
S = Stoup containing holy water
F = Font
T = Tabernacle for consecrated bread

141

Priest breaking the
Host while recalling
the events of the
Last Supper.

behind the altar facing the congregation to say mass. All confess their
sins using a set prayer before the priest pardons them. Chants such as
'Glory to God in the highest' are sung and there are readings from the
Old Testament, an Epistle (letter from an apostle to be found in the
New Testament) and the Gospel ('good news' from Jesus' life on
earth). A homily (helpful talk) is given and the Nicene Creed (statement of beliefs) is recited. The offertory (bread, water, wine) is presented at the altar. As the Host (bread or wafer) and the wine are
blessed a bell is rung three times. Catholics believe that the bread and
wine are mystically transformed into the Body and Blood of Christ.
The celebrant (priest) consumes some himself before the host (and
sometime the wine too) is given to those who come forward to the
altar. All Catholics must attend mass on Sundays.

18.   Draw a plan of a cruciform Roman Catholic church.

19.   Why do you think the church has statues to saints and scenes of
      Jesus' crucifixion story? Can you see why some people would
      find this helpful whereas others would not?

In recent years round buildings have been introduced—for
example, the cathedrals in Liverpool and Bristol. These emphasize
the family of Christ gathering around the altar.

Church of England. The church is usually the shape of a cross or
oblong, but some are round, like modern Roman Catholic churches.
Most churches have a stone altar at the east end with choir stalls
between it and the congregation. Newer layouts often involve a
wooden Communion table in the centre, so emphasizing a change of
attitude towards the Communion service from one of humble
offering to one of communal meal. A lectern, pulpit, font and organ
complete the essential parts of the building. There may be one or two
side chapels. The windows may contain stained glass scenes from the
Bible or of worthy Christians. Memorial tablets to the dead may cover
the walls, but these are not the object of worship.

The worshipper kneels for a few moments on entering. There
are three basic services: Communion, Matins (morning service) and
Evensong (evening service). Communal singing and saying prayers
may form a prominent part of all these, with a robed choir giving a
lead. Sometimes matins is replaced by a family service in which
children participate.

The Communion service is in many ways similar to the Catholic
one except that incense and bells are rarely used and the
communicants receive the wine as well as the bread. People come

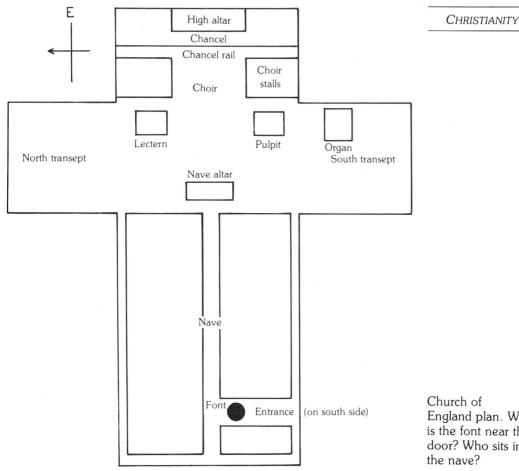

E

High altar

Chancel

Chancel rail

Choir stalls

Choir

Lectern

Pulpit

Organ

North transept

South transept

Nave altar

Nave

Font

Entrance (on south side)

Church of England plan. Why is the font near the door? Who sits in the nave?

forward to kneel at the Communion rail before the altar, where the priest has blessed the bread and wine. When they receive them the priest may say 'The Body of our Lord Jesus Christ' and 'The Blood of our Lord Jesus Christ'. Some members accept the Catholic belief about the bread and the wine, whereas others believe that the service primarily commemorates the Last Supper and no miraculous change occurs. Some take Communion weekly, others less frequently, and a few daily.

In cathedrals (main churches where a bishop is based) the choir sings the services daily and the ritual is more elaborate.

20. *Draw a plan of a Church of England church.*

21. List the things which are not in a Church of England church but which are in a Roman Catholic one. Comment on the list.

22. The communion service is now much less of a 'spectator' service for the congregation and more of a communal one.
(a) Why do you think this change has been made and what advantages are there?
(b) What difference does it make to the relationship of the priest to the people?

Baptist chapel. A chapel's shape will vary, but a large pulpit will dominate one end from which the minister (clergyman) or deacon (lay helper) will conduct the service. A wooden table will have a Bible on it. The baptismal water tank will be in the floor nearby, and it will be uncovered when needed (see pp. 191–3). An unrobed choir will lead the singing to the accompaniment of an organ. The chapel will be part of the whole building which will contain offices, teaching and recreation rooms.

Worshippers sit to pray. Their Lord's Supper (Communion) is usually held fortnightly; other services are devised by the minister and his congregation. During Communion people remain in their seats and each person breaks a piece of bread from the loaf passed round. It is eaten as soon as it is taken, to show that Christ died for individuals. The wine is served in tiny glasses brought round on

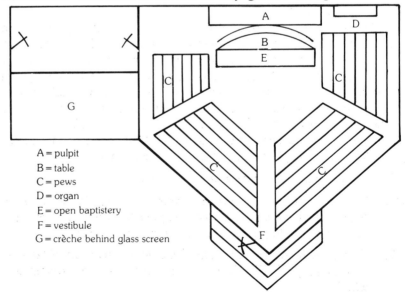

A = pulpit
B = table
C = pews
D = organ
E = open baptistery
F = vestibule
G = crèche behind glass screen

A modern
Baptist chapel
plan. Compare its
layout with that of
a Church of
England church.

slotted trays. When everyone is served they all drink together to show the unity of the church. The glasses are then put into slots in the chair backs for later collection.

23. *Draw a plan of a Baptist chapel.*

24. *List things which are in a Church of England church but not in a Baptist chapel. Comment on the list.*

25. *Why do you think the pulpit dominates the chapel rather than the Communion table?*

26. *In what ways are 'home-made' services (a) better, (b) worse than set ones? Which would you prefer and why?*

Salvation Army citadel. (The word 'citadel' means 'fort'.) The main hall for worship will be part of a building containing offices, teaching and recreation rooms. The hall will be divided into two sections. The upper one, or rostrum, is where the band (of perhaps 30) will sit. In front of this is a reading desk from which the officer can conduct the service. The lower section is for the congregation. The mercy seat or penitent's form (a long bench) will be at the front of the congregation, where anyone can come forward to ask God's mercy or for help. On it will be cards which the penitent can sign to say he or she accepts Christ as Saviour. The choir of songsters with their tambourines will play a prominent role and the corps' flag will be on display (see p. 192).

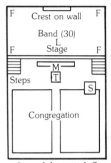

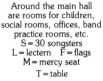

Around the main hall are rooms for children, social rooms, offices, band practice rooms, etc.
S = 30 songsters
L = lectern   F = flags
M = mercy seat
T = table

Salvation Army Citadel plan.

The services are varied and will immediately change in nature and length if anyone is at the mercy seat in need of help. Someone will attend to that person while the rest will stay and pray and sing until the person's needs are met. The services are designed to appeal to the hearts of lost souls as well as to praise God in joyful popular songs. Preaching plays a big role too. Salvationists see themselves as soldiers fighting evil for Christ (1 Tim. 1:18; 2 Tim. 2:3–4; Eph. 6:14–17). Half the services should be held out of doors in a public place to attract people by taking the Gospel to them.

27. *Draw a citadel plan and name its parts.*

28. *List things (a) which are in a citadel but not found in other churches, (b) which you might expect to find in a citadel but which are not in fact there. Comment on your list.*

29. *Compare the different effects of having (a) an organ, (b) a band to lead singing. Which would aid you more in worship and why?*

30. In the Orthodox and Catholic churches the emphasis in the services is on the humble congregation worshipping Almighty God, whereas the Salvation Army makes a point of concentrating on someone kneeling at the mercy seat. Explain why both approaches are right in their ways.

31. Should worship contain joyful popular songs sung to guitars, tambourines, etc? What are the arguments for and against?

32. Should all churches follow the Salvation Army's example of holding regular out-of-door services? In what ways is the Salvation Army better equipped to do this than the other churches?

Modern and traditional Salvation Army music-making and witness. What type of housing is in the background? Why would the corps visit this part of town?

Society of Friends' (Quakers') meeting house. A room with a Bible on the table and chairs gathered round is all that is needed for this 'do-it-yourself' religion! There are no priests, no music, no ritual, no 'usual aids' in the form of pictures or statues. The meeting begins as soon as the first person arrives and sits down to pray and meditate in silence. Peaceful silence pervades the atmosphere and aids the worshippers who have come in from the busy world outside. Because all are there for the same purpose the silence is quite positive in its effect. It gives the worshippers a chance to review the past week and the future in their minds. During the hour someone may read from the Bible or another book which has impressed him, or he may share some experience which has a Christian significance. Perhaps three or four will speak during the hour. Two Friends chosen to be in charge of the meeting will signify its end by shaking hands.

During their meeting Quakers find *Advices and Queries* a help. This is a booklet containing questions such as: 'Do you seek to follow Jesus?', 'Is your religion rooted in personal experience of God?', 'How does it find expression in your life?', 'Do you *try* to make your home a place of friendliness, refreshment and peace, where God becomes more real to all who live there and to those who visit it?'

33.   What do Friends (a) gain, (b) lose by their method of worship compared with that of other Christian churches?

34.   Other churches see the communion service as the main service, yet Quakers have no such sacrament. Why do you think this is?

ISLAM

Mosques. Muslims worship in a mosque ('a place of prostration'). It is usually square with a courtyard at the end. This contains water for ritual washing before prayer. Its outlines of a dome (symbolizing the universe) and four minarets (towers) at the corners is reminiscent of

A large mosque.

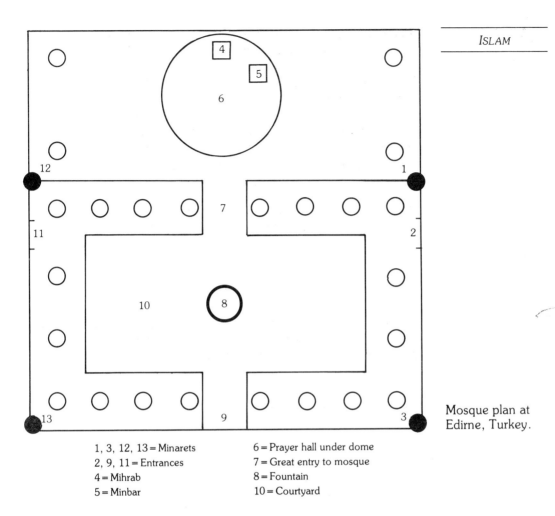

Mosque plan at Edirne, Turkey.

1, 3, 12, 13 = Minarets
2, 9, 11 = Entrances
4 = Mihrab
5 = Minbar

6 = Prayer hall under dome
7 = Great entry to mosque
8 = Fountain
10 = Courtyard

the Arkan (Five Pillars of Faith, see pp. 111–20): Īmān (dome of faith), Salāt (prayer), Zakat (almsgiving), Saum (fasting) and Hajj (Mecca pilgrimage). The number of minarets is not fixed.

The building faces Mecca and the mihrab (niche) in the qibla ('direction') wall of the hall indicates the direction. There are no sculptures or pictures of humans or Allah, but the walls and ceiling may be adorned with tiles or geometrical patterns and lettering in a blaze of colour, particularly green. The minbar (pulpit) is a desk or crowned structure up three steps, from which the Friday khutba (sermon) is given by the khatib (preacher). The leader (imam) chosen by the community performs this function. The khutba is in two parts, the first deals with the problems of today that must be faced; the second gives an explanation of the Koran or religious practices.

Worship. From the top of the minaret the muezzin calls the faithful to prayer five times a day: 'Allahu Akbar . . .'—'God is most great. God is most great. I bear witness that there is no god but God . . .' (see p. 112). The imam leads the prayers. None of the officials are priests as no sacramental duties have to be performed. There is chanting but no other music. There are no seats, but prayer mats are provided on the floor. Muslims must remove their shoes before entering a mosque as a sign of reverence to Allah.

The rakat procedure has already been described on p. 113. All males must be present for Friday midday prayer. Women *may* go to the mosque, especially on these days. Friday is not a rest day like a Sabbath or Sunday as Allah is said never to need a rest. Prayer beads (subha) may be used when reciting the 99 'Beautiful Names' of Allah. A mosque is used as an evening school for Islamic education and as a community centre.

35. *Draw a view of the mosque and name the Arkan parts symbolized by the building.*

36. *Draw a plan and name the parts.*

37. *The emphasis of the worship is on the greatness of God and the sinfulness of humble humans.*
    (a) How does Islamic worship compare with Christian worship?
    (b) What different ideas about God and His relations with mankind are shown by these different types of worship?

SIKHISM

Gurdwaras. Sikhs worship in a Gurdwara, or Gurudwara ('Guru's door'). It is not only a temple but a community and action centre. In fact, any building containing the Granth is a gurdwara. The following description is of a purpose-built one. Above the building is the Nishan Sahib (flag) with two swords (kirpans), a two-edged sword (khanda, indicating one should fight with both spiritual and physical force), and a circle (chakra, showing the oneness of God and Sikhs). The centrepiece is the takht (literally a 'throne'). This is a raised stand for the Granth, which is ceremonially opened beneath a canopy (palki) supported by four poles. The gurdwara is decorated with streamers and fairy lights.

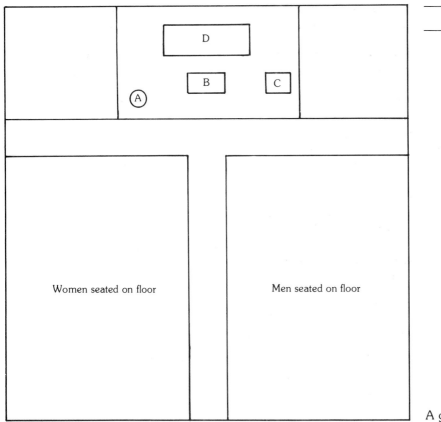

A gurdwara plan.

A = Karah parshad in basin   B = Milk, fruit, etc., offerings   C = Ragis (musicians)
D = Palki (canopy) on takht (platform) below which is the Granth placed on Manji Sahib (stool).
The Granthi (reader) sits behind the waving chauri as he reads.

Worship. Worshippers take their shoes off and bow low on entering
and give their alms money, food or a romalla (silk cloth to cover the
Granth) if they particularly wish to do so. Men wear turbans and
women pull their dupattas (silk scarves) over their heads. No candles,
incense, statues or bells are allowed and no one may bring tobacco or
alcohol inside. The service lasts from one to five hours as people
come and go. The Granth is kept covered as if in bed except when it is
used, then the granthi (reader) carries it out on his head to place it on
the takht.

The sangat (holy congregation) sit cross-legged on the floor,
men on one side and women on the other. A Sikh will sit behind the
Granth, facing the sangat, and wave a chauri (silver sceptre with

The granthi reading the Granth. What are the names for (a) the canopy, (b) the sceptre?

animal hairs) over the Granth as a sign of the book's authority and to keep flies away. Kirtan (hymn-singing) is very important and the music is played on sitars and a tabla or jori (drum). Anyone may conduct the service and men and women are treated equally in this. A sermon is given, followed by unaccompanied singing. Everyone stands and faces the Granth and responds with Waheguru ('Wonderful Lord') to the verses of the Ardas (common prayer). Its three parts are concerned with: (i) remembrance of Nam and the ten gurus; (ii) keeping the Granth's teachings; (iii) asking Nam's blessing on their community and all mankind. For example:

O true King, O loved Father, we have sung Thy sweet hymns, heard Thy life-giving Word . . . May these things find a loving place in our hearts and serve to draw our souls towards Thee. Save us, O Father, from lust, wrath, greed, undue attachment and pride . . . Give us light, give us understanding, so that we may know what pleases Thee . . . Forgive us our sins . . .

Specific prayers for newly-weds, the sick or the dead may be inserted.

The Granth is then read by a man or woman. Sikhs have no priests, as all are equal. At the end a Sikh will stir the parshad (mixture of flour and semolina, butter and sugar) with his kirpan (dagger), and then portions the size of golfballs are given to all to eat to show all are equal and united. It is consecrated by reading the Anand ('The True Name is my support; it is my food and drink . . .'). Parshad is sweet-tasting to stress God's kindness to mankind. Afterwards worshippers join in the langar (free food) served in another room, sitting in pangats (rows). This is designed to bring everyone together and break down any barriers.

Amritsar. The most famous gurdwara is the Golden Temple at Amritsar in the Punjab. Its entire upper part is covered with gold which reflects in the surrounding lake. It has four doors, one on each side to show that it is open to everyone, and to emphasize that it does not point in one direction as mosques do. The Granth is guarded by sentries with kirpans at night and brought in at 5 am in a large silver ark. A trumpeter walks backwards before it blowing on his silver curved horn. It is put away at 10 pm.

38. *Draw the Granth underneath the canopy with the Sikh waving the chauri.*

39. *What does the treatment of the Granth suggest about its importance to Sikhs?*

40. *What is the difference between Christian communion bread and wine and Sikh parshad so far as its significance and meaning are concerned?*

41. *Would all religions benefit from holding langars after services? Find out which other religions do something similar regularly.*

42. *Jews ceremonially bring the Torah to the reading desk as Sikhs bring out the Granth.*
    (a) Why do these religions show such respect for their holy books?

Stirring and distributing the parshad.

153

(b) Should the Bible be ceremonially taken from a special cupboard and carried in procession to the lectern in Christian churches or is it better to have it there the whole time for anyone to read?

The langar.

154

6.
HOLDING FESTIVALS

A festival is an occasion which gives people an opportunity to give special recognition to an event. It can bring the past into the present so that an event can be commemorated by being brought alive again. Jesus' death on the cross is marked by Good Friday while the Jews have their Pentecost to commemorate God's gift of the Ten Commandments, and so on. Most festivals are held annually. Some are solemn because of the sad events they record, while others are joyous occasions. The believer's faith is helped by the stories told and the customs observed.

HINDUISM

Hinduism is much given to festivals and there is space to mention only a few. Every temple has an annual festival to honour its principal god. The main item is the public procession of the image which may be carried on an elephant or in a huge wooden carriage. The image is taken to the river to be bathed.

Holi is the spring festival which lasts three to five days in February or March, at the time of the spring harvest. It is connected with Kama, the god of love, and Krishna. It used to be a fertility festival. People throw coloured water and powder at each other in a riotous way just as cowherds and milkmaids used to do and as Krishna teased the milkmaids. Fortunately it all washes out. Community fires are lit by priests and effigies of demons are burnt.

Krishna Janamashtami (or Krishna Jayanti, or Janamashtami) is the August birthday of Krishna. It begins with a fast the day before and a night vigil. Then at midnight the singing and dancing begin.

Sweet foods are shared around in the temples as gifts to a new-born baby and sometimes an image of Krishna is put in a cradle. The day is kept as a fast but an evening feast concludes it.

Raksha Bandham takes place in August at the full moon. Raksha means 'to protect' and Bandham 'to tie'. Girls tie a rakhi, a red and gold thread, round the wrists of their brothers, or, if they have no brother, round that of a man who becomes their protector. They pray that the rakhi will protect its wearer, who then has to give them a present. It dates back to the story that the god Indra's wife was given a rakhi by Vishnu to tie round her husband's wrist to protect him from the demon-king, Bali.

Ratha Yatra is held in honour of Jagannatha, Lord of the Universe, a title usually applied to Vishnu or Krishna. At the Jagannatha temple three huge images of Krishna and his brother and sister are taken out to be bathed. They are carried in chariots called rathas. Such is the excitement that pilgrims have been known to throw themselves beneath the wheels and get crushed to death. Hence the word juggernaut for a large, menacing lorry.

Navaratri in September or October is a nine-day event for Durga, motherhood goddess. Navaratri means 'nine nights' so the festival takes place in the evenings. Dancing round a Durga shrine is all-important. Newly-weds return to see their parents. It recalls Rama's worship of Durga when he needed help to rescue Sita.

Dashara (or Da Sera or Dussehra or Vijaya Dashami or Festival of Warriors). 'Das' means the tenth day as it follows the end of Navaratri's nine days. On this day Durga's spirit departs from the statue of Durga which has been worshipped for those nine days. The statue is put into the river. If it floats, it is a good sign as it will take away all unhappiness. Originally Dashara was a war festival; now it represents the fight of the hero Rama against the demon Rava or Ravana. The climax is a mighty war-dance with crackers and the explosive disposal of enemy effigies when fiery arrows are shot into the explosives inside them. At New Delhi a 30m high statue of Ravana is the centre of attraction.

Divāli (or Dīpavali or Festival of Lights) occurs in October or November, when the monsoon starts. It is the five-day new year festival, in which Vishnu and his bride, Lakshmi, the goddess of

Dashara, Festival
of the Warriors.
Gigantic figure of
Ravana about to be
burnt at Cawnpore.

prosperity, are welcomed into every house. Alternatively, it is held to
be connected with Rama overcoming Rava. Boys are told to be like
Rama and girls like Sita, Rama's wife. Family vows are renewed.
Husbands and wives remember their duties to each other; likewise
children to their parents, and vice versa. Houses are cleaned, clay oil
lamps lit to welcome Lakshmi, and gifts are exchanged. Dīvālī
means 'cluster of lights'. Everywhere is lit up with lights. Firecrackers
scare away evil spirits. Thus light or good overcomes darkness or evil.
There is a lot of music and dancing. Festival floats carry scenes from
the lives of the gods. Papier-mâché tigers and cows are on sale.
Sweets made of thickened milk and sugar or coconut and sugar are
distributed. Businessmen celebrate by opening new account books
with prayers to Lakshmi for success in the coming year.

Hindu dancing is used to tell stories about the gods. Shiva is
called the Lord of the Dance, and it is claimed that the art originated
among the gods before it was passed down to earth. At one time only
female temple dancers were allowed to perform the dances. Each
movement has a meaning so as to tell the legend. Hand positions

mean 'wind', 'holding a sword', 'a year', and so on. Brahmins must have white faces, female demons wear black robes, and goddesses wear green with pearls. Dancers' faces indicate whether they are afraid, happy or angry. Guitars, cymbals, drums and sitars are played.

1. *What things can you find in common in these festivals?*

SHINTOISM

Matsuri. Each year shrines hold a major Matsuri (worship festival). The purpose may be to bless the crop or the year's fishing or, alternatively, purify the parishioners, or possibly mark a local kami event. The priests will prepare themselves by washing their hair, trimming their nails and dieting. Solemn chanting of prayers (norito) summons the kami before the cooked or uncooked food offerings (shinsen) are made. Shinsen always includes saké and 'happy

Shinto festival. What is in the priest's right hand?

158

presents' of birds, vegetables and fish as these have all been obtained by the grace of the kami. Shinsen rice is grown in a special paddy field and cultivated by hand. Miki (sacred rice wine) is offered too. The ceremony is a grand one and involves the priests passing the offerings from one to another from the shinsen-den (food room) to the heiden. After presentation it is passed back again and eaten by the priests and leading figures at the Naorai. This is a kind of communion meal, which gives the participants the 'prestige' (mi-itsu) of the kami. Much wine is consumed at what can be a jolly meal. Ordinary worshippers are given a sip of rice wine by the priests or miko.

Ceremonial music is played on ancient traditional instruments and sacred (kagura) and classical (bugaku) dances are performed.

Hoko, an ornamental float, weighing 12t, pulled through the streets of Kyoto during the Matsuri commemorating an epidemic in AD 876.

There are 35 dance-dramas which depict the myths of Shintoism. The Lion's Dance (shishi-mai) involves two men impersonating a lion which goes round from door to door at New Year casting out evil.

Sports and processions conclude the Matsuri. Japanese wrestling, archery on horseback and boat races are popular. The horseback archery (yabusame) is used to divine the likelihood of a good harvest from the arrows' angle. Alternatively, a deer's shoulder-blade is heated in a fire and the crack pattern studied. Many other techniques are used. Processions involve taking the kami (shinkyo, or gohei) on a journey in an ornate, gilded palanquin (mikoshi). The mikoshi is carried on the shoulders of young men who consider it a great honour. They zigzag up and down with it shouting, 'Wassho', which the kami is said to enjoy, although a horse follows in case the kami would prefer to ride. The purpose of the procession can be to welcome a kami coming from afar or an occasion for the kami to bless the parish, or to mark some historic event connected with the kami.

Rice-cultivation Matsuri concerned with Inari, the rice kami, occur at different times of the growing season and vary locally too. They can cover water examination, seed selecting, ploughing, weeding, manuring, sowing, etc. The Tao-Asobi-Matsuri (rice-field play festival) at New Year covers the whole rice-growing process. A 'soot and cobweb' (susuharai) to clear evil out is done at New Year too. The god-shelf is renewed to ensure good luck and all bills are paid. Decorations of bamboo and cut-out flowers are everywhere and priests wear blue, purple and scarlet sashes over their white kimonos.

Aki-Matsuri. This autumn festival involves thanking the kami for the harvest. It involves offering fish, vegetables, fruit and saké to the kami.

Kaijin-Matsuri. This honours the sea-kami for the sake of all sailors and their work.

Setsubun. This festival celebrates the change of season, from winter to spring. It is held in February as the main purification matsuri. On that day holly branches and sardine heads are hung outside houses while beans are thrown out to the shout of, 'Come in, good fortune'. During the matsuri ceremony at the shrine, people impersonating devils (oni) attempt to break in only to be driven back by the priests with bows and arrows.

Bon (or Obon). This festival of the dead, in July or August, is designed to console the spirits of the dead. Welcoming fires (mukae-bi) are lit in front of each house and offerings put on the kamidana (god-shelves). Afterwards the 'sending off' fire (okuri-bi) speeds them on their way. Sometimes they are accompanied by tiny boats with lanterns and food aboard. This festival has been influenced by Buddhism to some extent.

2. (a) *Name three reasons for holding a Matsuri.*
   (b) *Summarize the main events of a Matsuri, giving the reasons for the events you describe.*

TAOISM

Chiao Rites of Union (or Cosmic Renewal Festival). The Taoist Masters of the Tao Chiao (Religious Taoism) hold these rites in most Taiwan villages every 3, 5, 12 or 60 years. The event is a very exciting one lasting three to nine days or more. Years of preparation are involved for the purpose of the rite is to restore the balance of Yin and Yang, free souls from hell, cure the sick and help those in need. The local temple will be repaired and the people will do acts of purification and penitence for a month. Kind deeds are done and debts repaid. A host of gods and goddesses are invited including buddhas and bodhisattvas and of course the Jade Emperor. Shrines are set up for them. Ancestors and souls from the underworld are welcome as their coming will release them from bondage.

A Taoist Master and his assistants, wearing elaborate red vestments, will lead the rituals. One assistant represents Yang and another, Yin, and they approach the purified sacred ground from either side of the Master. They sing alternately just as Yang and Yin dominate nature in turn.

On the first day the gods are welcomed and evil spirits driven away. The Master recites lengthy prayers to ensure merit and repentance to release souls from hell. Then the meditation rites begin with Fa-lu (see pp. 81–2). Noisy instruments sound as the Master enters the sacred area through the Gate of Heaven in the north-west corner and his entourage through the Gate of Earth on the south-west side. The Master first unites himself with the Tao by his k'o-i ritual and then uses the supernatural power (Te) to save others. As he starts, the ritual vapours of the five talismen or elements (see p. 184) are burnt: green, red, yellow, white and black. The drum is struck 24 times and he grinds different parts of his jaw on each blow, swallowing his saliva while reciting a spell. Then he kneels to summon out the spirits.

On the third day the Jade Emperor arrives and contact is made with the Three Pure Ones (see p. 15). The Grand Memorial petition naming all the villagers present and their petitions is presented to them. Souls from the underworld are feasted and the Nine Hells Litany of Repentance is said to release all souls from hell. At least 31 ceremonies are included during the festival and noon-day offerings are regularly made. The additional rites of 'climbing the 36 sword ladder', something of a competition due to their sharpness and the ladder's height, may take place, before the gods are thanked and sent home. Each family gets a yellow document to put over the family altar to tell the gods and men for whom the ritual took place that the family was present.

The Goddess Matzu's Birthday has a colourful float procession (see p. 15). Palanquins (god-carriages) are carried by men as firecrackers burst. Each contains an image of Matzu, who honours every home that is passed. The air gets so thick with smoke that a man with bellows follows each palanquin. Near the temple one may see women in trances, and men with weighted brass skewers piercing their backs, but feeling no pain due to their trances. Joss sticks are offered. In effect the Matzu images from village temples are being taken to the main Matzu shrine to be 're-charged' with power for the year ahead.

The other festivals, described below, are primarily Chinese rather than exclusively Taoist.

Hsin Nien is a New-Year festival, a great occasion when all the gods have to report to the Jade Emperor, Yu Huang, the highest god. This means that Tzau Wang, the kitchen god, on everyone's god-shelf must report on the household's last year. A small image of him with a paper horse is burnt symbolically to send him off to the Palace of Heaven. A piece of t'ang kwa (rice sweetmeat) is thrown into the fire so he may make a sweet report. Sometimes sticky candy, opium or wine is put on his lips so that he will not speak clearly. As he will be away for seven days the house is cleaned in his absence.

On the last day of the old year strips of red paper with prayers for peace and prosperity are put round doors to prevent luck leaving.

Everyone stays up all night to await Tzau Wang's return. At 2 am a meal of chu po po (meat dumplings) and nien kao (sticky cake or 'high' made of sticky rice flour, dates and bean flour) is put out. The hope is that each year will be 'higher' than the previous one, that is, more prosperous. His return is marked by a new picture or image of him being placed on the god-shelf, amidst firecrackers and incense.

A sacrifice of a pig, sheep, fish or fowl is made and a cup of blazing wine offered to the god. When the incense has burnt out, the food offering is prepared for the family to eat. On the eighth day the stars are worshipped from 8 to 12 pm, with the table put outside with a picture of the god of the stars on it. T'ang yuan (rice and sugar balls), red candles, incense, yellow paper spirit money and a spirit ladder of yellow paper are put out. The paper is burnt and the family eat the food. Every day the ancestor tablets are worshipped as incense is burnt and food presented. On the 16th day the tablets are returned to their box.

Dragon Boat Festival (or Fifth Month Festival). One of the legends behind this is that a royal official in 459 BC committed suicide by drowning after failing to quell a rebellion. But river folk decided his task had been impossible and he ought to be honoured, so they gave him food for the next life by wrapping rice, sugar and fruit in reeds and throwing them in the river.

Dragons symbolize Yang and a dragon fight in heaven will cause heavy rain. Four heavenly Dragon Kings are under the control of the Jade Emperor. Boats measuring 24–36m by 1·6m, have a dragon on their bows and the rowers throw sticky rice cakes on the water to tempt the fish so as to leave the official's body intact. Then mock battles are held to bring on the rain.

The Festival of Lanterns takes place on the 15th day of the first month. It involves 52m-high paper or cloth dragons with 18 kg heads being carried by 23 men through the streets. The dragons were derived from the Yangtze river alligators. Taoists visualized them with a camel's head, deer's horns, rabbit's eyes, cow's ears, serpent's neck, frog's belly, carp's scales, hawk's talons and tiger's pad palms. The festival is a call for spring rain.

The Hungry Souls Festival (or Ghosts Festival, P'u Tu) falls on the full moon of the seventh month and lasts three days to care for the souls with no descendants to look after them. At the temple a huge effigy of Yen Lo, King of the Underworld, is set up, and facing him Ch'ing Hsu the 'lenient magistrate' flanked by four ghosts who serve

Taoist dragon.

Hungry Ghosts
Festival. Miniature
paper palace.

him. There are images of the Three Pure Ones behind the altar: the
Jade Emperor; Tao Chun, who controls the relations of Yang and
Yin; and Lao-Tse. Incense burns. The 'dark altar' dedicated to the
nine gods who protect mortals from devils and calamities is furnished
with miniature fiends from Hell. A percussion band starts the evening
ceremony. Red-robed priests with black hats and coloured battery-
illuminated pompoms invoke the neglected spirits to come to the
feast.

The second day is a quiet one. For the third day an evening
service is held by the shore for unattended spirits to gather there. An
altar is set up and an image of the King of Hell is positioned with a
pig's head with candles and incense sticks in its skull at its feet.
Children make nine sandcastles for burning paper money on. Bands
play, priests call the spirits to come. Tea and wine are put out and the
paper offerings burnt. The long list of names of those who have paid
for the entertainment for the spirits is read out. The priest slips many
genuine coins, which have been donated, into his wide sleeves.

A final service involves the Lion dancers before the Queen of
Heaven's shrine and then all the effigies are carried to the shore and a
paper junk laden with tea, wine and oil is pushed out to sea.

3.   *How do these festivals compare with the Shinto ones?*

4.   *Briefly describe the Chiao Rites of Union and the Hungry Souls
Festival. What is similar in them?*

BUDDHISM

Theravāda Buddhism has festivals recalling the life of Buddha.

Wesak (or Vesak) commemorates Buddha's birth, enlightenment and entry into nirvana. It is held at the full moon in May and lasts three days. Houses and streets are decorated with flowers and paper lanterns, and presents given to monks and the needy. Colourful processions take place. It marks the beginning of the Buddhist year and is their 'Christmas' event.

The Water Festival in Burma is held at the New Year when water is splashed on everyone as decorated floats pass by and Buddha images are ceremonially bathed. In Laos and Cambodia the monks are splashed by the bystanders as they process. The legend is that a king once had a bet with Brahma and when Brahma lost, his head was cut off in spite of the Buddhist no-taking-of-life rule. The head was said to be hot and had to be cooled with water.

At the end of the rainy season there is another full moon festival marked by the illumination of pagodas and houses signifying the return of Buddha to earth when the gods lit his route for him. It marks the end of a period of retreat during which no festivals or weddings have occurred while Buddha is said to be in heaven preaching to the gods. Robes are given to monks and alms to the poor.

Mahāyāna Buddhists hold a similar festival to Wesak and holy days are observed at the full moon each month. Festivals for the dead called Festivals of Lanterns are like the Chinese Festival of the Hungry Souls. Offerings are made to the dead and lighted candles placed in paper boats to guide their spirits. Higan is a Japanese festival in spring and autumn, when schools offer prayers and gifts to the dead. Mahāyāna Buddhists also recognize the Shinto Bon festival.

5.   What are the main purposes of Buddhist festivals? In what ways are they different from Taoist ones?

JUDAISM

Festivals have been the life-blood of Judaism for centuries and have done much to keep the Chosen People united in the absence of a homeland until Israel was established in 1948. The festivals recall

God's care for the Jews. Feasts always begin at dusk on the preceding day.

Pesach (or Passover, or Feast of Unleavened Bread) begins on 15 Nisan (March/April) and lasts eight days to mark God's 'passing over' the Jews in Egypt sparing their first-born during the plagues (Exod. 11:1–12:39), and their freedom from enslavement in about 1300 BC.

The house is thoroughly cleaned and no trace of leaven is left. Leaven is the raising agent used in bread-making. This is because the Jews ate unleavened bread the night before they left Egypt, having no time to leaven it. During the week Jews use no leaven, yeast or baking powder. For the Orthodox special dishes and cooking utensils, one set for meat and another for milk dishes, which have never come into contact with leaven are used for this one week of the year. Thus a family has four sets of utensils in all, the other two being for the rest of the year.

The night before Pesach fathers search their homes with a candle to see if the leaven has been removed. A ceremonial meal called Seder (Order of Service for Passover Night) takes place. A number of items of food and drink are put out:

- Three matzoth (singular matzah), 'bread of affliction', which look like water biscuits and are flat cakes of unleavened bread.
- One roasted shank bone of lamb (symbol of the lambs eaten in the last meal in Egypt).
- One roasted egg (for the new life and the Passover Temple sacrifice).
- Horseradish (for their bitter slavery in Egypt).
- Parsley (for the herbs used to mark the Jews' doors in Egypt).
- A bowl of salt water (slaves' tears).
- Haroseth (paste of apples, nuts and cinnamon, for the joy and sweetness after slavery and the mortar used when brick making).
- A wine glass for everyone.
- An extra glass of wine called the Cup of Elijah (who will come before the Messiah arrives).

Candles are put on the table which is covered with a white cloth. When all are ready father says the Kiddush prayer and then passes parsley dipped in salt water to everyone. Then he breaks a matzah and hides one half. They begin the reading of the Haggadah (book of

the Passover story). Children may have 'pop-up' picture versions.
The youngest present has to ask four questions about the origin of the festival:

(1) On this night why is there only unleavened bread?

(2) Why are there only bitter herbs?

(3) Why do we dip our herbs?

(4) Why do we eat in a leaning position?

Father reads the Haggadah which gives the answers. The egg is then dipped in salt water as a show of sympathy with the bitter fortunes of the slaves. Wine is drunk in thanksgiving and the Hallel (praise) psalms (Pss. 113–114) are recited. A blessing is said and wine drunk again before hands are washed and the matzoth are eaten as well as the horseradish. The main meal follows. Finally, a search is made for the hidden matzah which is regarded like 'hunt the thimble'. More drinking and singing follows to end with.

Shavuoth (or Pentecost or Weeks Festival) is held seven weeks after the Passover to mark the gift of the Ten Commandments. Pentecost means it is 50 days since the beginning of the Passover. Before the festival synagogues are decorated with flowers to recall the harvest offering taken to the Temple. The Book of Ruth is read as she accepted Judaism so devoutly and it gives an account of harvesting (Lev. 23:9–14).

Rosh Hashanah (or New Year or Festival of the Trumpets) in September or October is marked by the sounding of the shofar (ram's horn). It is both the birthday of the world's or Adam's creation, and the Day of Judgement, as everyone's fate for the coming year is settled then. Readings in the synagogues are Gen. 21–22; 1 Sam. 1–2:10; Jer. 31:2–20. The festival marks the birthdays of Abraham, Isaac and Jacob. Bread (challah) and apples are dipped in honey in the hope that the coming year will be sweet. The following ten days are called the Ten Days of Return, or Ten Penitential Days when Jews consider their failings during the past year and ask for forgiveness (Lev. 23:23–24).

Yom Kippur (or Atonement Day) comes ten days after Rosh Hashanah. It is the holiest day of the year and all fast except the sick and children under 13, as it is a time of repentance (Lev. 16). 'Atonement' means 'at-one-ment with God'. As a sign of purity white coverings are put on the ark and bimah, and the rabbis and others

Blowing the shofar.

Photo opposite
shows the Feast of
Tabernacles.

wear white robes called kittels, which are the shrouds that one day they will be buried in. It is the only day in the year Jews kneel to pray. Members of a family ask forgiveness of one another. In the afternoon the Book of Jonah is read as it tells of God's forgiveness to those who repent. The shofar is sounded again at the end of the day (Lev. 23:26–32).

Sukkoth (or Feast of Tabernacles) for the harvest comes five days after Yom Kippur and lasts eight days. It is a pilgrim feast remembering when Jews took offerings to the Temple (Lev. 23:33–43). It also marks the time when Jews lived in tabernacles (sukkoth) or rough shelters or huts in the wilderness, so sukkoth are built in the garden with branches for roofs so that the stars

can shine through. It is decorated with flowers and fruit and all meals are eaten there. The congregation form a joyous procession round the synagogue seven times, carrying citron fruit and palms, myrtle and willow branches. These are the arba minim, the four parts of the body: citron for the heart, palm for the spine, myrtle for eyes, willow for the lips. Their joining together teaches one that God must be worshipped with all one's being.

Simchath Torah (or Rejoicing of the Law) at the end of Sukkoth marks the completion of the weekly readings of the Torah for the year and the beginning of the re-reading. The Torah scrolls are carried seven times round the synagogue, amidst a lot of clapping, singing and dancing. The reader of the last verses is called the Bridegroom of the Torah and the reader of the first verses is the Bridegroom of the Beginning. Thus the reading never ceases; it is eternal.

Hanukka (or Feast of Lights, or Dedication) lasts eight days in November or December. It marks the time when in 165 BC Judas Maccabeus, the 'Hammerer', led his men to cleanse the Temple after Antiochus Epiphanes had defiled it by setting up idols and forbidding Jews to practise their religion (Apocrypha, 1 Macc. 4:36–59). The menorah eight-branch candlestick is lit in remembrance that Judas lit a lamp with a day's oil in it and it lasted eight days. One candle is lit the first day, two the second, and so on. Hanukka presents are given like 'Christmas' presents.

Purim (or Feast of Esther) in March marks the Persian Queen Esther's foiling of prime minister Haman's plot to destroy the Jews in Persia. The Book of Esther is read in the synagogue. Drums and rattles are banged and whirled whenever Haman's name is mentioned in the story. 'Purim' means 'lots' and refers to Haman casting lots as to which date was best for killing the Jews. Fancy dress parties follow afterwards and liberal drinking is permitted. Giving to the poor is expected.

6. *Read aloud the following verses from Esther and stamp your feet whenever Haman's name is mentioned: Esther 3:1–7, 10–14; 4:1–7, 15–17; 5:1–14; 6:1–14; 7:1–10; 8:1–8, 16–17; 9:5–10; 16–28.*

7. *Make a list of the names, dates and reasons for all the Jewish festivals.*

8. *In what ways do these festivals help to remind Jews of their role in history? Give examples.*

9. *Why are these festivals centred so much on the home and food?*

10. *What things are done to make the events referred to as real as can be? What different ways of expressing (a) sorrow for sins, (b) joy for God's care are used?*

CHRISTIANITY

Christian festivals are essentially centred round the life of Christ and their celebration methods vary a lot among the different churches.

Advent (coming), four Sundays before Christmas, marks the beginning of the Christian year. It celebrates the approach of Jesus' birth and looks forward to his second coming in glory. Thoughts

A school Nativity play.

171

are concentrated on death, judgement, Heaven and Hell. Near Christmas, carol services take place often with nine lessons from the Bible showing how God created Man and cares for him by sending His Son. Nativity plays (on the theme of Jesus' birth) are performed in schools.

Christmas (Christ's mass) is on 25 December, Jesus' birthday. The name refers to the Mass or Communion held on that day. Many Christians go to midnight Communion in candle-lit churches. Manger scenes are set up in churches recording how Jesus was born in a stable. Christmas is traditionally a time when families gather and give each other presents. Children also get presents from Santa Claus, an old man with a white beard who is named after St Nicholas. Special food (turkey and pudding) and decorations (holly, mistletoe and a Christmas tree) all add to a merry occasion.

Epiphany ('showing forth') on 6 January records the showing of the baby Jesus to the Wise Men who were guided by the Star to his birthplace. Jesus is thought of as the Light of the World.

Lent begins 40 days before Easter on Ash Wednesday. It marks Jesus' 40 days in the wilderness (Matt. 4). It is a time when Christians consider their failings of the past year and, by denying themselves some luxuries, try to make a fresh start. In earlier days priest and people covered their heads with ashes in sorrow and repentance. Nowadays crosses in churches are covered with purple veils. The day before Ash Wednesday is Shrove Tuesday, when a feast of pancakes may be eaten before the period of denial begins.

Palm Sunday marks the last week of Lent and the beginning of Holy Week when Jesus entered Jerusalem and faced his trial and death. When he entered the city on a donkey people threw palm leaves before him. In many churches palm crosses are given to everyone, and often processions take place round the church.

Maundy Thursday ('command day') recalls the Thursday of Holy Week, when the Last Supper was instituted. The old tradition is that priests wash the people's feet as Christ told his disciples to do (John 13:2—17). This emphasizes that all must be humble. The Pope washes the feet of his cardinals, and in the Orthodox Church bishops wash priests' feet. In England the sovereign gives Maundy Money (specially minted coins) to the poor.

Good Friday
procession of
witness in
Gloucester.

Good Friday is the Friday of Holy Week when Jesus was crucified, and so it is the most solemn day of the year. Often three-hour services of talks, prayers and hymns on his suffering take place during the period in the middle of the day when Jesus was on the Cross. No communion takes place. In Catholic churches people follow the 14 Stations of the Cross, which means they pray at the scenes round the wall of the church depicting the events. Passion plays on Jesus' trial and death may be enacted. In Orthodox churches the priest carries an icon depicting the dead Christ and lowers it into a stand in the middle of the church and the people stand with candles as at a funeral. Later the icon is carried round outside the church in a 'funeral' procession as the bells toll. In England many Christians of different churches join together in processions behind a full-size wooden cross to hold an open-air service to proclaim their faith to others. Hot cross buns are eaten to mark the event.

Easter Sunday, two days later, is the happiest day of the year as it marks the finding of Jesus' empty tomb. In the Orthodox Church at midnight the people come in procession as the women did who found the tomb of Jesus empty. They circle the church and pause before the closed doors, which represent the stone in front of the tomb. Inside the icon has already been moved to the altar. Outside the people hear the thrice-repeated triumphal shout, 'Christ is risen from the dead. By death He has trampled down death. And to those who are in the grave He has given life'. The people repeat the cry and bells are rung as the doors swing open. People greet each other with 'Christ is risen' and reply, 'Risen indeed!' Easter's date varies from 21 March to 25 April, the first full moon after the spring equinox.

Ascension Day, the Thursday 40 days after Easter, records Jesus' bodily ascension up into heaven after his resurrection. Special Communion services are held in some churches.

Whit Sunday (white Sunday—referring to white baptism robes, or Pentecost) is 50 days after Easter. It marks the gift of the Holy Spirit to the early believers in Jerusalem during the Jewish Pentecostal feast (Acts 2). This used to be a favourite time for baptizing new Christians. The effect of the Holy Spirit coming was such that people present began to speak in 'tongues', that is languages they did not know (Acts 2:4–11). The Pentecostal churches regard it as a mark of evidence that the Spirit has entered a member when he or she speaks 'in tongues' today (see p. 193).

Other festival days in some Christian churches are: Corpus Christi (marking Christ's presence in the Bread); the Assumption of the Virgin Mary into heaven, All Saints' Day and All Souls' Day, as well as saints' days marking particularly outstanding Christians. Some Christian churches dislike the emphasis on numerous festivals and keep solely to the major ones which celebrate Christ's life.

11. List the main festivals and briefly state what they commemorate.

12. Christian festivals are mainly concerned with Jesus' life on earth, while Jewish ones are concerned with the Jews' own past.
    (a) Is this true? Give examples when answering.
    (b) Why do you think this emphasis is made?

ISLAM

The Ramadan Fast is described on p. 117. Eid or Id is the Islamic word for festival, the days of thanksgiving after Ramadan and Hajj.

Id al Fitr (or Eid-Ul-Fitr or Little Bairam or Festival of the Breaking of the Fast) is on the first day of the tenth month of the Islamic year. It marks the end of Ramadan. It is celebrated joyfully and people wear new clothes, visit each other and give presents. Graves are visited by relatives. Charity, amounting to the cost of a meal for the whole family, is given to the poor. Potato pasties (samosas), carrot pudding with salad mixed with yoghourt, and syrupy orange jalebi sweets are eaten.

Id-al-'Adha (or Id-al-Kabir, Eid-ul-Adha, Bairam or the Great Festival of Sacrifice) is the feast of the sacrifice at Mecca during the hajj pilgrimage in the 12th month (see pp. 118–20). It recalls Abraham's willingness to sacrifice Ishmael (Surah 37:100–111; Gen. 22, which names Isaac as the intended victim). A voluntary fast precedes the day of the feast. The Eid prayers are said and a sermon preached, before the sheep, cows or camels are sacrificed. The head of each family slays his own offering or gets a butcher to do it. The animal is placed with its head towards Mecca and killed with one blow by a knife thrust to the throat while the name of God is recited. The flesh is cooked and eaten by the donors with neighbours and the poor have a share too.

Meelad ul-Nabi (or Maulid an-Nabi or Birthday of the Prophet) is on the 12th day of the fourth month. (The original birthday was 20 August AD 570.) Processions, entertainments and poetry readings all recall Muhammad's life, words and sufferings.

Hijrah Day (New Year) marks the beginning of the success and spread of Islam. It recalls the time when Muhammad led his followers away from persecution in Mecca to the welcoming Medina (see pp. 37–8). At Medina they were able to develop their religious community. The festival was first celebrated on 15 July 622. Today greetings are exchanged and stories about Muhammad are related.

13.   *Compare the Great Festival with the Jewish ones ordered in Lev. 6–7.*

SIKHISM

Sikhs have two kinds of festival: (a) melas, meetings or fairs, which reinterpret Hindu festivals; (b) gurpurbs, the birth and death anniversaries of the ten gurus.

Hola Mohalla (the Sikh 'Holi') includes a three-day fair with horse riding and athletics begun by Guru Gobind Singh as a form of military manoeuvres as well as to distinguish it from the Hindu Holi.

Baisakhi on 13 April commemorates the Khalsa's beginning by Gobind in 1699 (see pp. 43–4) and the beginning of harvest and the hot dry summer. It is also held as the anniversary of several battles as feelings often ran high on that day so leading to battles. People wear new clothes and a service of thanksgiving is held at the gurdwara. During the previous 48 hours the Akhand Path (continuous reading) of the Granth will have taken place. Turbans are exchanged as gifts. Animal sales and sporting, music and poetry competitions may be arranged.

Diwali is when Sikhs celebrate the release of Guru Har Gobind (1595–1645) from captivity in 1620. He had been arrested by the Mogul emperor as the Sikhs had not paid a fine and their army was a threat to the emperor. Sikhs came to pray outside the prison where the 16-year-old guru was held until he was released. Thus the festival is seen as one of good triumphing over evil. Lamps are lit, fireworks set off and presents given.

Gurpurbs are the anniversaries of the Gurus. The most important are the birthdays of Gurus Nanak and Gobind Singh and the martyrdoms of Gurus Arjan and Tegh Bahadur. Nanak's birthday celebrations last three days and include a procession in which the Granth is carried followed by singers and players. On the final day the service begins at 4 or 5 am with singing, lectures and poetry reading, and continues until 1 pm. Karah parsad and the langar are served to all (see pp. 153–4). When the Granth is carried in a flower-decked palanquin, five men with drawn swords representing the first five baptized Sikhs escort it. All gurpurbs involve the Akhand Path continuous reading of the Granth.

14.   Why do you think Sikhs have adapted the Hindu festivals?

15.   Why does the reading of the Granth play such a large part in Sikh festivals?

16.   Which religions hold festivals primarily in honour of their gods and which in honour of their human leaders? Give reasons for this difference of emphasis.

17.   (a) Why hold religious festivals?
       (b) Are they a waste of time and money?
       (c) Do they aid a religion? If so, in what ways?

18.   Is there a place for solemn religious festivals as well as joyful ones?

19.   What is the place of (a) music, (b) dancing, (c) plays in religious festivals? Which is likely to make the greatest impression?

20.   Describe two festivals which have light as a theme.

7.
ATTENDING SPECIAL OCCASIONS

In this chapter we shall examine the signing on, coming of age and marriage ceremonies connected with the different religions. Certain rituals may take place to mark the new member with the signs of membership, and some form of cleansing may take place to make the person fit for that membership, and finally vows may be taken too. Marriages may be arranged for the couple or they may make their own match, but in each case rituals will be performed to emphasize their new close relationship and bless their future children.

HINDUISM

Samskāras (ceremonies). A new-born Indian baby is washed and the sacred syllable OM or AUM is written on its tongue with a golden pen dipped in honey. AUM represents the names of the three gods, Vishnu, Shiva and Brahma. This ceremony is the fourth samskāra of sixteen which are performed in connection with a person's life. The first three are to do with conception and the last is performed at death. Each samskāra is held in front of a sacrificial fire to the sound of chanting. The fifth samskāra is performed ten days after birth when the baby is named. Another involves the baby's first haircut at the age of a year.

The most important samskāra is the tenth one, called Upanayana ('drawing near') or Yagyopavit or Janeu, the Sacred Thread Ceremony, which occurs between the ages of seven and 13. This tends to be restricted to boys and girls in the Brahmin class, but can be performed for the second and third classes too (see p. 67).

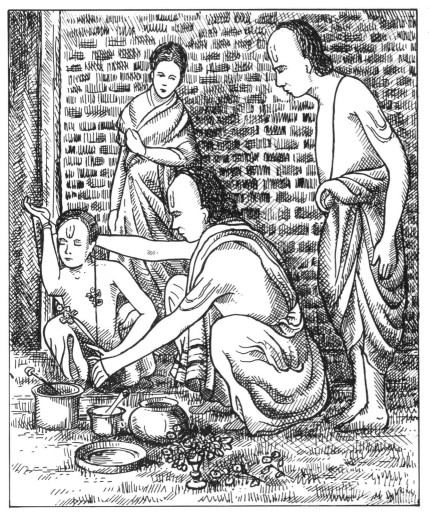

Yagyopavit Sacred Thread Ceremony. What is the thread made of? What is the point of the ceremony? Today the thread is often worn round the waist.

This ceremony consecrates the body and entitles it to receive merit. What happens is like a second, or spiritual, birth and it marks the end of one's education. Hindus consider spiritual birth to be more important than physical birth. They argue that a mother only carries a baby for nine months, whereas the teacher cares for his pupil for many years. The Sacred Thread has three strings made of cotton, hemp or wool and coloured white, red or yellow, referring to the debts one owes to God, parents and ancestors and one's wise teachers. Only after paying these debts is one entitled to salvation. The knot tying the strings of nine twisted strands each, is called the

Brahma granthi (spiritual knot), and it means that whoever knows the Supreme Spirit has paid the debts. The thread is put over the left shoulder and under the right arm and worn for the rest of one's life. Wearing the thread, the child stands in front of a fire to hear the prayers said by its father:

Oh my child this yagyopavit, or sacred thread, is most purified and will lead you to the knowledge of the Absolute. The natural source of the sacred thread is the Lord himself and it is bestowed again and again for eternity. It gives long life and favours thoughts of God. This thread I put round you. By the grace of God, may it give you power and brilliance. AUM, let us meditate on the glorious light of the Creator; May he enlighten your minds.

The child prays that he or she may live a good life and follow the truth. Then the teacher says, 'Oh, my pupil, I accept you as one of my children. From now on your happiness and sorrow will be my happiness, and my sorrow'. A boy's head is shaved to mark the start of his new life as the shaving removes any bad karma (evil from a previous life). He now starts the first of four stages of life, the life of a student (brahmacharin) (see p. 69).

Marriage. Hindus are expected to marry to continue the family and care for the welfare of the dead. Girls may marry at 14 and boys at 18 so far as the religious ceremony is concerned. A country's laws may require 16 for a girl. Marriage is the 13th samskāra. Not only must a Hindu marry a Hindu but the couple must come from the same jati (see pp. 67–8).

The bride will prepare herself carefully for the ceremony and her friends will rub ointment over her skin. Her kājal eye make-up of ghi (or ghee), herbs, camphor and lampblack was originally intended to keep flies away. She will wear a new sari with gold and red bangles and jewellery. In the centre of her forehead she will put a tilaka (red spot) of washable powder to show that she is blessed. All married Hindu women put this spot on. She waits at the temple for the groom to arrive. His face is veiled with threads of beads. When he arrives the two families exchange presents before entering the temple. Wearing garlands of flowers, the couple will stand under a decorated canopy in front of the priest and the holy fire will be lit as a sign of the pure presence of God. The bride's parents give her to her husband by placing her hand in his, and then her brothers pour fried rice on her hands to show they agree. The couple take seven steps (saptapadi) round the fire, making promises to each other at each step. The last time their garments are tied together. The husband says, 'With utmost love to each other may we walk together . . . May we make our minds united, of the same vows and the same thoughts. I am the wind and you are the melody. I am the melody and you are the words'. On the last step they say together:

> *Into my will I take thy heart*
> *Thy mind shall follow mine,*
> *Let the heart of yours be mine*
> *And the heart of mine be yours.*

Flower petals are thrown over them before the guests bring forward their wedding presents. A feast follows and after sunset they look to the Pole Star and pray that their companionship will be life long and as constant as the star is.

A Hindu woman controls the family completely. The husband has no say and does no housework. His wife gives him an allowance. However, the Laws of Manu say she must respect and obey him even if he is unfaithful.

Orthodox Hindus will not consider divorce, although the Hindu Code of the Indian government does allow it. Hinduism does allow polygamy, but Indian law has recently forbidden it. Outside the family organization women are seen as inferior to men. Widows are now allowed to remarry, which was once impossible for them.

1. *Why do Hindus have to marry into the same jati?*

2. *Do you think the wife dominating the household is a good thing? Why?*

SHINTOISM

Shrine visiting. The Hatsu-miyā-maiiri (first shrine visit) or Muja-Maiiri (temple visit) takes place on a boy's 32nd day of life and a girl's 33rd day. They are put under the care of the local ancestor god, Ujigami. The priest chants and claps his hands to arouse the god's attention, and gives the baby a small wooden charm, which is worn round the waist in a little bag. He gives the father a sakaki twig inter-twined with white paper to symbolize purification. Later on, Shinto followers visit their shrine whenever a new stage is reached in their lives, such as adolescence, marriage, getting a job or retirement. It is felt right that respect should be paid to the local god's befriending of oneself. The ages of 7 and 13 for men and women, also 19 and 33 for women and 25 and 42 for men, are considered yaku (unlucky)

Sakaki twig. The flowers are yellowish white and the berries yellowish brown.

181

years, so they will visit the shrine to drive the evil away by prayer and a money gift.

Marriage. The kami accept sexuality and there is no shame attached to it. It is part of human nature, which should be appreciated and fulfilled. Anyone wanting to marry will visit the Ujigami's shrine. The older village style of marriage (mukoiri-kon) involves the couple living at the bride's house for a few years before moving to the husband's. The only rite is the offering of the saké cup (rice wine) by both families to each other. In cities the yomeiri-kon style involves the couple living at the husband's house from the beginning. An arranged marriage may be fixed simply by a miai (an interview to fix the yuino, contract terms) arranged by nakōdo (match-makers, a husband-and-wife team). Sometimes famous people are asked to be nakōdo for the sake of a big announcement party. The nakōdo help the couple in their preparations. Ceremonies vary a lot, but usually the bridegroom in grey and black visits the bride's house with the nakōdo on the wedding day and a saké party is held. Then the bride in a red, gold and white kimono goes to the husband's house for saké with her mother-in-law. The couple will visit the shrine of their Ujigami where they were taken as babies. The priest will wave his purifying wand over them as part of the Harai purification rite (see pp. 76–7). This wand is called a haraigushi and it is made from a sacred tree with white linen or paper attached to it. Love matches are usual but some marriages are arranged. The new couple may take over the running of the household of the husband's parents if they 'retire' from the task. Some temples have special halls for Shinzen-kekkon (weddings) and rent out luxurious bridal gowns.

To divorce a wife, the husband writes a Divorce Letter of three and a half lines. Wives wanting divorce used to have to escape to an enkiridera (temple of cancellation) for three years. Today divorces are granted on grounds of incompatibility.

TAOISM

Protection ceremonies. Children under 16 are protected by the 'Mother' goddess. Three days after birth a ceremony is performed at which red candles are lit and people are careful to say pleasant words in the presence of the hordes of spirits which are believed to be there. The baby is washed and its wrists are tied with red cotton, on which are hung coins and miniature silver toys. They are removed on the

Passing Through
the Door Taoist
ceremony. What
instruments are
played and why?
Why is the sword
needed?

14th day. The idea is to make the baby obedient. Sacred writings
may be tied round its waist or neck for protection. On the 14th day
the baby has its first haircut in front of the Mother shrine and a feast
takes place. Until the age of 16, the rite of 'passing through the door'
is held each year. Priests set up a ceremonial paper arch 2m high and
1m wide, an altar and images of the gods. Gongs and trumpets
sound as the gods are asked to protect the child. The priests hold

swords and bells. Rice is offered as a sacrifice. Then all the family, holding candles, follow the priest, who brandishes his sword against invisible spirits, while going through the arch to the sound of drums. The arch is moved to the four corners of the room and the rite repeated. Each time a small wooden statue to represent the child is made and it is kept until the child is 16 years old. Thus, children pass from a dangerous world into a better one.

At 16 the 'thanking the Mother' ceremony is much the same, the door being the boundary between childhood and adolescence.

3. *What similar things can you find in the ceremonies connected with early life in Hinduism, Shintoism and Taoism?*

4. *(a) What parts of the ceremonies would you call superstitious?*
    (b) What superstitions do people in your home area hold today?
    (c) Are these superstitions connected with religions?

5. *The Taoist baby has a copy of the sacred writings round his waist, the Hindu child wears his sacred thread and Christians often wear crosses, while schoolchildren carry lucky charms at exam time. Do you agree with the claims made for the possession of such charms?*

Marriage is part of Yang and Yin as the joining of these male and female forces produces Tao (the Way) which is one man and one woman together. Sexual intercourse is part of nature, and in marriage two people are bringing Yang and Yin together in harmony as they should. To stay unmarried is unnatural.

Mei-jen (friends, relatives or professionals) are go-betweens who make the preliminary arrangements. All-important are the 'Eight Character' certificates which give the hour, day and year of the couple's births. An astrologer is asked to pronounce on them. Certain years are out of harmony with others, and the couple's elements may not match. The Five Elements are identified with the planets. Water (Mercury) produces Wood (Jupiter), but extinguishes Fire (Mars). Fire produces Earth (Saturn), but melts Metal (Venus). Earth is the source of Metal, but soaks up Water. Thus, for example, a 'Fire' girl would consume a 'Wood' man and their marriage would be unhappy.

Likewise their animal signs may be incompatible. Each year, in a 60-year-cycle, has a combination of one in five elements and one in 12 zodiac animals. 'A white horse will not share a stall with a black cow'. 'The boar and monkey are soon parted'.

The bridegroom's marriage contract is on red dragon-decorated paper and the bride's on green with a phoenix. An auspicious day is chosen. The bride has a ceremonial bath and pays respect to the ancestral tablets before a long farewell with her parents. They do not attend the ceremony. She says she is dying or wants to die and her relatives reassure her in the ritual farewell. Finally, she is carried off in a decorated red sedan chair which contains a mirror to shield her from evil spirits. Cars are often used now. The journey is accompanied with firecrackers to scare off spirits. On her arrival at the house of her parents-in-law, the groom will fire three unheaded arrows under the chair as a further precaution. The chair will be carried over a red charcoal fire. Red is the predominant colour of the day as it symbolizes life and joy. Presents are wrapped in red and the bride wears red.

The couple sit on the wedding bed and the groom raises her veil before they eat and drink together. They bow in front of the tablets of the gods and ancestors before meeting their guests. The presents include a pair of red chopsticks as red is lucky and the word for chopsticks sounds like the phrase for 'quickly a son'. They get pomegranates to symbolize a future birth of sons and apples for peace, as the same word is used for both.

The husband can obtain a divorce by writing down all his wife's faults.

6. *Why do you think a couple's home is at the groom's parental home and not the bride's?*

7. *Give some examples of incompatible (a) elements, (b) zodiac animals.*

BUDDHISM

Act of Homage. You cannot become a Buddhist until you are old enough to think for yourself. The Buddhist life begins with an Act of Homage, in which you say, 'Adoration to Him [Buddha], the Blessed One, the Worthy One, the Fully Enlightened One [one who has seen the Light of Truth]'. You must face a statue of Buddha and think of his teaching about giving up evil, seeking the spirit of truth within you and helping others. Incense is then offered and you say this:

All the evil things which I have committed in past lives were done out of ignorance and I ask to be cleansed of these impurities. They are all due to greed, anger, and ignorance which I have cherished for aeons, and they have been practised through my body, speech and mind. Now, without exception I make full confession of them and repent of them, resolving not to commit them after this until the end of time.

You accept the Three Refuges, which refers to the Three Jewels of Buddhism, by saying, 'I take refuge in the Buddha; I take refuge in the Dharma [Buddhist teaching, see p. 133]; I take refuge in the Sangha [brotherhood of Buddhist monks]'. Finally, you undertake to live by the Five Precepts (guidelines, see pp. 83–4). All Buddhists chant the Three Refuges and Five Precepts daily.

Marriage. Buddhist parents help their children to find suitable partners. No ceremony takes place at a temple as a wedding is seen as a secular, not religious, affair. A group of girls in white recite devotional verses before the couple make their vows. The groom says, 'Towards my wife I undertake to love and respect her, be kind and considerate, be faithful, delegate domestic management, provide gifts to please her'. She replies, 'Towards my husband I undertake to perform my household duties efficiently, be hospitable to my in-laws and friends of my husband, be faithful, protect and invest my earnings, discharge my responsibilities lovingly and conscientiously'.

The couple can go to a monastery after the ceremony to be blessed and hear a sermon on Buddha's teaching on married life. They bow three times to the Buddha and recite the Homage, 'Honour to the Blessed One; the Exalted One; the Fully Enlightened One'. Then they recite the Three Refuges and the Five Precepts. After the monks have recited Buddha's advice, the couple put food in their feeding bowls. The ceremony is called Dāna ('giving').

Divorce and remarriage does occur among Chinese Buddhists but it is very rare. Theravāda Buddhists believe women automatically have bad karma and cannot get to nirvana. Their best hope is to send their sons to be monks as they then obtain credit for them in the next life.

8. *Why might parental help in finding a partner be (a) a help, (b) a hindrance to a happy marriage?*

9. *(a) Would you be satisfied with the promises made by the couple to each other or would you disagree with anything promised?*
   (b) What other points could be included in such promises?

Jewish ceremonies connected with birth and joining the faith are designed to stress that you are becoming members of God's Chosen People. They believe God selected them as the people through whom He would disclose Himself and His plans for all mankind.

Brith Millah (circumcision, a medical operation) is performed on boys on the eighth day after birth. The operation's effect is to make a permanent sign on the boy's skin as a mark of membership. The event is a great family one. When old enough, the first prayer a child learns is the Shema ('Hear'), from Deut. 6:4–9, 'Hear, O Israel, the Lord our God, the Lord is One . . .'. Note its stress on there being but one God. Jews recite it every morning and evening. Mezuzahs containing the Shema are put on the right door posts of all doors in the house to be touched as a reminder.

Bar Mitzvah ('man of duty') is the coming-of-age ceremony held on the Sabbath (Saturday) following the boy's 13th birthday. He prays:

> *Heavenly Father, at this sacred hour of my life, I stand before Thee in the midst of this holy congregation to declare my duty ever to turn to Thee in daily prayer, and to observe the Commandments of Thy Law by which a man may live worthily. I pray humbly and hopefully before Thee to grant me Thy gracious help . . . Implant in me a spirit of sincere devotion to Thy service, that I may hold fast to what is holy and just and good, and resist all evil and sinful temptations. As I grow into full manhood . . . may bodily strength, mental power and moral courage be developed in me, that I may fulfil my duties to Thee . . . as well as . . . to my neighbour . . . Aid my resolve never to separate myself from the [Jewish] Community . . . May the noble example of our ancestors inspire me.*

Then he reads the Torah. He is presented with his tallith ('cloak', prayer shawl; see Num. 15:37–41). It is made of silk or wool and it was once the sign of distinction and learning to wear one. The strands and knots at each corner represent the Torah's 613 regulations. He will wear it on many occasions and when he dies he will be buried in it. He also receives his siddur (prayer book).

Bath Mitzvah is the corresponding girl's ceremony. In the Reform synagogue she will be allowed to read the Torah. Large family feasts follow the ceremony. Before the Bar and Bath Mitzvah one must have at least two years' instruction in Hebrew and the tradition on

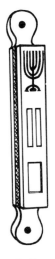

Mezuzah 8cm long. What do the two tablets pictured on it stand for? What is the name of the seven-branched candlestick above them?

several evenings a week from the rabbi (teacher) and possibly have to pass a qualifying exam. Liberal communities also have confirmation services for 15–16-year-olds since they feel that 13 years is too young to really make promises.

10. *The Buddhist Act of Homage and the Jewish Bar and Bath Mitzvah ceremonies stress the need for good behaviour. Do you think this should be an important point to be stressed when joining a religion? Give reasons for your answer.*

11. *(a) Do you consider it reasonable or sensible that someone becoming an adult member of a faith should pass an exam to prove his or her knowledge of that faith?*
    (b) Would this help to strengthen the religious group concerned?

12. *Why do you think boys and girls are sometimes treated differently by some religions?*

Marriage. Jews are keen not to die out as a community. Consequently, all Jews are expected to marry and have families. The Old Testament times made it plain that God expected them to 'be fruitful and multiply' and in those days if a young husband died, his brother was expected to marry his widowed sister-in-law so that she could have children (Deut. 25:5). Men were to marry from the age of 18 and girls from 12. A groom was advised not to join the army or be away from his bride on business for the first year of marriage (Deut. 24:5). Polygamy was finally forbidden in the 11th century AD. Adultery is considered a serious crime.

Marriage is regarded as a holy covenant and is called Kiddushin, meaning 'sanctification'. It is very rare for a Jew to marry a non-Jew as religious life is centred on the home—for example, the kitchen where diet is so important. Yet 30% of British Jews marry outside the faith. The wedding need not take place in the synagogue so that houses or gardens are often used.

The rabbi will officiate and the bride will wear white while the groom will have his cappel on. They stand underneath a chuppah (canopy supported by four pillars) to emphasize the 'royalty' of the occasion as the couple are considered king and queen of the day. It also represents their future home. The groom signs the ketubah (marriage document) which says, 'I faithfully promise that I will be a true husband unto thee. I will honour and cherish thee, I will work for thee; I will protect and support thee'. He and his father will stand under the chuppah and await the bride's arrival as the cantor (prayer

Kiddushin, a Jewish wedding. What is the name for the canopy they stand under and what does it represent?

leader) sings in Hebrew, 'Blessed be the one that cometh in the name of the Lord . . . May He bless the bridegroom and the bride'.

The rabbi then addresses them before they drink wine from a goblet, the cup of joy. The groom puts a gold ring on the first finger of the bride's right hand, saying, 'Behold thou art consecrated unto me by this ring according to the Law of Moses and Israel'. The Ketubah is read over and seven blessings are pronounced and they again drink from the goblet before the groom crushes a glass under his foot to symbolize the destruction of the Jerusalem Temple and hence the sufferings of the Jewish people. Everyone shouts, 'Mazel Tov' ('Good luck').

All Jewish couples are expected to have at least two children to help keep the community going, and a rabbi must set his followers a good example by having his own family. Contraception is permitted provided it does not damage the pleasure of the sexual act. Divorce is allowed and encouraged if life together has become intolerable; however, divorces are rare. The beth din (see p. 138) issues the document (Get). It is said that a love-filled home is a sanctuary, but a loveless one is a sacrilege. The Talmud says a husband can divorce his wife for a burnt supper—but if a burnt supper takes on such great importance, something must be wrong with the marriage! The importance of sons and the sign of divine favour in the form of a large family often encourages couples to stay together. The person wanting a divorce must get the consent of the other. One safeguard against divorce is that it requires the repayment of the dowry, although a wife's bad conduct (e.g. loud cries, cursing the children in her husband's presence, talking with men, going out with her head uncovered) can stop this compulsory requirement.

13. *Buddhists see a wedding as a secular affair, Jews as a religious one. What arguments can be put forward for both views? Which view do you prefer and why?*

14. *Should a religion indicate the minimum number of children parents should have?*

15. *Should a religious leader marry and have children as rabbis are required to do or stay unmarried as Roman Catholic priests must? Give arguments for both viewpoints before giving your verdict.*

16. *How do you think Jews square their practical attitude to divorce with their solemn attitude to the contract of marriage?*

CHRISTIANITY

Baptism (or Christening) is the name given by most Christians to their joining ceremony. In the Church of England babies are brought by their parents to the church for the ceremony. The parents choose relatives or friends to be godparents whose function is to see that the baby is taught the faith. A boy usually has two godfathers and one godmother, and a girl the reverse. Parents, godparents, the baby and a priest gather at a font. This is a large water container, usually made of stone and situated just inside the church door. The position of the

font indicates that the baby is entering the fellowship of the church. The priest uses water to make the sign of the Cross (mark of Christ's death) on the forehead of the baby. He says, 'I baptize you . . . [name] in the name of the Father, Son and Holy Spirit'. Christians believe that this ceremony marks the spiritual birth of the child as it renounces evil and washes away any sin. It also stresses the spiritual equality of all Christians.

Parents and godparents are asked to ensure they carry out their duties properly. In the Roman Catholic ceremony, the priest says to the parents, 'You have asked to have your child baptized. In doing so you are accepting the responsibility of training him/her in the practice of the faith . . . Do you clearly understand what you are undertaking?' To godparents he says, 'Are you ready to help the parents of this child in their duty as Christian parents?' Both groups are challenged point by point on their belief in Christianity.

One Christian church, the Baptist Church, believes that one should not baptize anyone until they are old enough to say they accept Christianity for themselves. They have baby-blessing ceremonies (Dedication of Children).

When a Baptist has reached at least teenage, he or she undergoes 'New Testament Believers' Baptism' after instruction in

Two styles of Baptism. Explain the differences.

the faith. Men wear white shirts and trousers; and women, long white robes. The minister says:

> *In Baptism we are united with Christ through faith, dying with Him unto sin and rising with Him unto newness of life. The washing of our bodies with water is the outward and visible sign of the cleansing of our souls from sin through the sacrifice of our Saviour.*

Wearing fisherman's waders, he then descends into the waist-deep pool set in the floor of the chapel. The person to be baptized enters too, down one of the two sets of steps. 'Do you make profession of repentance toward God and of faith in our Lord Jesus Christ? Do you promise . . . to follow Christ, to serve Him for ever in the followers of His Church?' The minister then puts his right hand over the person's nose and mouth and supporting him with his left hand bends him backwards until submerged. The person leaves the pool by the second set of steps so showing that he is not turning back to the old life.

17. *Draw a picture of Believers' Baptism taking place. Describe what happens.*

The Salvation Army does dedicate babies to God's service, but the real signing on comes at a minimum age of seven, usually not less than 16 years. After instruction the person signs the Articles of War while standing beneath the corps' flag. The flag's red background stands for Christ's blood, its blue for God's purity and its yellow in the middle for the fiery power of the Holy Spirit. The 33 spikes represent Jesus' 33 years on earth; the crown is the crown of life given to those who are saved; the crossed swords are for the fight for God.

Some of the Articles may be summarized as follows:

(1) The Bible is God-given.

(5) Our first parents were created in a state of innocence, but, by their disobedience, they lost their purity and happiness and that in consequence of their fall all men have become sinners, totally depraved and as such are justly exposed to the wrath of God.

(6) Christ suffered to bring forgiveness to mankind; belief in him brings salvation.

(9) We believe that continuance in a state of salvation depends upon the continued obedient faith in Christ.

(11) The soul is immortal and there will be a final judgement resulting in eternal happiness for the righteous and endless punishment for the wicked.

Salvation Army crest. Why do you think it has (a) 'S' round the cross, (b) two swords, (c) a crown?

Pentecostal churches have Believers' Baptism similar to that of the Baptists, but they also expect their members to undergo the experience of Baptism by the Spirit. This experience can come at any time or place when God so decides and a person knows it has occurred if his heart is warmed in the faith. Usually this leads to 'speaking in tongues' (Acts 2:1–21), which can mean speaking in a foreign language or in no recognizable one. Speaking in tongues occurs in Pentecostal services and then someone else interprets the message they believe they have heard the speaker convey from God.

Confirmation is a second ceremony held by churches which allow infant baptism. At this ceremony the grown-up child can confirm the promises made on his behalf by declaring his faith in Christ. Confirmation is based on the belief that the first Christians received the Holy Spirit after Christ had left them (Acts 1:7–8; 2:1–21).

During the special Church of England service the bishop (senior priest) asks those who are being confirmed these questions:
Do you turn to Christ? Do you repent of your sins? Do you renounce evil?
Each must be given a positive answer. The bishop then lays his hands on each believer. By this means, the believer receives the Holy Spirit (Acts 8:17; 9:16) and becomes a full member of the church. The

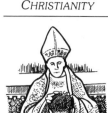

Church of England confirmation. What is the name of (a) the church official performing the ceremony and (b) his hat?

a short guide to church membership

All those who confess Jesus Christ as Lord and Saviour and accept the obligation to serve Him in the life of the Church and the world, are welcome as full members of the Methodist Church.

IN THE CHURCH

A member is committed to Worship, Holy Communion, Fellowship and Service, Prayer and Bible Study, and Responsible Giving.

IN THE WORLD

A member is committed to the working out of his faith in daily life, the offering of personal service in the community, the Christian use of his resources, and the support of the Church in its total world mission.

The kingdom of God is upon you; repent, and believe the Gospel.
St Mark 1:14 (NEB)

Member ....

Minister ....

Methodist Ticket of Membership (both sides). The scallop shell is from the Wesley coat of arms as well as being an ancient symbol of Christian pilgrims. The fish sign is made up of I-CH-TH-US, the Greek word for 'fish', taken as the initial letters of the Greek word for 'Jesus Christ, Son of God, Saviour'.

Church of England usually confirms children during the teenage years, but the Roman Catholic Church may confirm children as young as seven. Sometimes girls being confirmed dress in white, like brides.

Methodists require their members to sign a covenant of belief and intent every year and they carry a Ticket of Membership as proof.

Chrismation. In this ceremony the Orthodox Church confirms babies at the same time as they are baptized. Their baptism involves being immersed in water three times. In Chrismation the priest anoints the forehead, nostrils, mouth, ears and chest, and makes the sign of the Cross with holy oil. Children take Communion with their parents and when old enough are expected to teach, preach and help run the church.

18. *How do the Salvation Army and the Methodists ensure their members stay active Christians? Should all churches have some form of discipline system?*

19. *List the churches which allow full membership (a) before teenage, (b) at teenage or older.*

Marriage. Christianity began as a religion aimed at reforming Judaism. Unlike any other religion, it was firmly against polygamy from the start. Husbands and wives were expected to live as if they were one person (Eph. 5:25–6:4). Basically, divorce was forbidden (Mark 10:2–12), although Matthew's Gospel allowed divorce for fornication (Matt. 19:3–9). Over the centuries the church began to think staying single was more holy than being married. So people wanting to be as holy as possible became monks or nuns. Even today the Roman Catholic Church will not allow its clergy to marry and Orthodox bishops must be single. Among other causes this attitude to marriage arose because Augustine of Hippo argued that mankind's original sin was indulgence in sex. So every sexual act was sinful. In fact, mankind's fall from grace was not due to Adam and Eve having sexual relations as they did not live together until after they were expelled from the Garden of Eden. Their original sin was disobedience to God's command not to eat the tree of knowledge's fruit (Gen. 2:7–4:2). For a very long period many Christians felt every conception was a 'sin' by parents. The 1549 Church of England Prayer Book said marriage was instituted 'to satisfy men's carnal lusts and appetites, like brute beasts that have no understanding'. The baptism service even stated, 'all men are conceived and born in sin' and prayed that 'all carnal affections may die in him'. Gradually it was appreciated that the sexual act was part of God's creation and so something to be encouraged and enjoyed within marriage. The 1980 Alternative Service Book says marriage is for 'comfort and help' that 'in delight and tenderness they may know each other in love, and, through the joy of their bodily union, may strengthen the union of their hearts and lives'. The Baptism service no longer refers to the sin of birth. Other religions do not seem to have found sex such a worrying problem as Christianity has done.

20. (a) *What is your opinion of the three reasons in the Book of Common Prayer for the institution of marriage, namely (i) procreation, (ii) remedy against sin, (iii) mutual help and comfort?*
(b) *Would you put them in the same order or not? What are the main changes made by the Alternative Service Book in 1980?*

Christians are free to marry whom they wish these days although one church may encourage its members to marry someone from the same church. For example, Roman Catholics argue that children of a marriage in which one partner is Catholic must be brought up as Catholics.

Church of England weddings are preceded by three weekly callings of the Banns of Marriage. This involves the priest reading a notice of the forthcoming marriage and calling on anyone who objects to do so. Objections might arise if one of the couple was already married or if they were too closely related already. On the wedding day the groom and the congregation await the entry of the bride dressed in white as a sign of purity. The service begins by the priest explaining the purpose, comforts and joys of marriage before the couple are asked if they will love, comfort, honour and protect each other in sickness and in health 'as long as you both shall live' (Alternative Service Book). At one time the bride had to promise to obey her husband but this vow is now optional. After they have promised themselves to each other, the groom puts a ring on the third finger of the bride's left hand and says:

I give you this ring as a sign of our marriage. With my body I honour you, all that I am I give to you, and all that I have I share with you, within the love of God.

The priest then says, 'That which God has joined together, let not man divide'.

During Orthodox services in Russia crowns are held over the couple, while in Greece garlands are used. They drink wine together to show that they will share the basic necessities of life. Then they make a circular procession symbolizing the fact that their union is intended to last, as a circle has no end.

Quaker weddings begin and end in silent prayer, punctuated by vocal prayers and messages appropriate to the occasion. The couple say to each other, 'Friend, I take my friend [name] to be my husband/wife, promising, through divine assistance, to be unto him/her a loving and faithful wife/husband so long as we both on earth shall live'.

Divorce. The Roman Catholic Church will not allow divorce, but will annul (wipe out) a marriage which has not fulfilled the essential conditions—for example, if it was not properly witnessed or the bride consented out of fear. Separation can also be granted, but this does not relieve the partners of their promises of faithfulness, so neither can marry again while the other lives. The Orthodox Church does allow a bishop to grant divorces in extreme cases of distress. It will also bless a second marriage after divorce, as it sees its role as one of helping rather than condemning people. The Church of England is divided on the whole subject. Some priests will accept divorce as unavoidable at times and charitably remarry divorcees, while others feel that to remarry them would be a mockery of the vows they took in their original marriage.

21. *'That which God has joined together, let not man divide'.*
    (a) Explain, with reasons, why the Church of England is so divided about remarriage in church for divorcees.
    (b) Compare the different standpoints of the Roman Catholic and Orthodox Churches.
    (c) Is there any solution to the dilemma of a solemn 'until death us do part' marriage and the fact that marriages do break down?

22. *The state permits divorce and remarriage while the Christian churches either tend to reject these events or deplore them. If someone is a genuine Christian faced with an unworkable marriage, should he or she primarily follow the law of the land or his or her church's teaching?*

23. *In view of the problems Christians face over divorce and remarriage would the secularization of marriage (i.e. the ending of its religious aspect) solve the problems for (a) active Christians, (b) clergy, or is marriage too basically a religious deed for this to be even considered?*

ISLAM

Initiation. Islam maintains that one is born free of sin, so no baptism is needed. As soon as a baby is born the Adhan ceremony takes place. The baby is washed and the father whispers the Call to Prayer into his/her right ear and then the command to rise and worship into the left ear. Thus the first words the baby hears are the call to worship Allah. A name-giving ceremony (Aqiqa) occurs on the seventh day of the baby's life, when the father names the child after reading passages from the Koran. The baby receives one of Muhammad's names or one of his family's or one of Allah's 99 names with 'Abd' ('servant') added, e.g. Abdullah, servant of God. The baby's head is shaved or washed to take away uncleanliness at birth, then olive oil is put on the head, and money, equal to the weight of hair cut, is given to the poor. Goats or sheep, two for a boy and one for a girl, are sacrificed and the relatives consume two-thirds of the

An Islam initiation ceremony. What is happening?

197

meat and one-third goes to the poor. Circumcision is done in the hospital shortly after birth in some Islamic countries and in others, such as Morocco, it is deferred until the baby is three to four years old. Then the small boy receives a special haircut and the operation is done at home.

Marriage (Aqd Nikah) is arranged by fathers for their children, but the girl has the right to refuse the man chosen for her. The ceremony is a civil one and no Muslim official has to be present. In Morocco the ceremonies last a week. On the first two days the in-laws are introduced to each other in each others' houses; on the third and fourth days similar introductory meetings are made between the couple's friends. The bride and groom promise to do their 'utmost to render their marriage an act of obedience to God, to make it a relationship of mutual love, mercy, peace, faithfulness and co-operation . . .'. Big feasts follow the signing. The bride, wearing an elaborate heavy costume, is carried in a special chair by four women and a ceremonial bedding of the couple takes place.

The groom has to give the bride a marriage gift (mahr) in money, and he cannot claim it back later. Payment may be made over a period of time and the nature of the gift, money, property, etc., will be settled in the marriage contract. The husband has to pay for the housekeeping. His wife does not have to contribute but can use her wealth for whatever she likes.

Muslim men may marry Christian or Jewish women as they believe in the same God. Muslim women do not have this freedom. The Koran permits men up to four wives provided they are treated equally well. The modern interpretation of this is that you should have only one wife as you cannot really treat others exactly alike. 'If you cannot deal equitably and justly with more than one wife, you shall marry only one' (Surah 4:3, 129). Today husbands often promise not to marry a second wife when they first marry.

24. *The Muslim marriage contract contains a variety of points on the insistence of the couple. How does this indicate their equal position? List what things (a) a husband, (b) a wife might regard as (i) reasonable, (ii) unreasonable.*

25. *What are your feelings about parents choosing your partner? Who is likely to know better — you or your parents?*

26. *What conclusions can you draw from the freedom of a Muslim man to marry a Christian or a Jew which is denied to a Muslim woman?*

27.   *Why do you think Muslim men are now less likely to have more than one wife?*

Divorce. Muhammad, in fact, raised the status of women for previously daughters had inherited nothing. He made the marriage service into a firm contract giving them security. Divorce, which requires reasons to be given, is only to occur in the last resort and then the wife must be properly provided for. A divorced mother retains guardianship of the children up to the age of seven. After that, sons tend to live with their father as he is able to provide for them until they are able to earn for themselves.

The divorce procedure of Talāq (repudiation) follows a set pattern, allowing time for reconciliation. A husband can revoke his first two repudiations of his wife, but the third makes the divorce final. The wife can then remarry after four months. Should the husband and wife want to remarry each other they can only do so if the wife has remarried and been divorced from a second husband. All the three repudiations can be given at one time so making a divorce final immediately. The wife can only force a divorce she wants by persuading the court (Shar'ia) that her husband is incurably ill or he has failed to act as a husband. However, she has a right to separation to be followed by a divorce.

SIKHISM

Initiation. The mother takes her baby and the ingredients for karah parshad (a kind of blancmange) to the gurdwara. The cook takes a bath before preparing it and recites prayers as it is cooking. The ingredients are two tablespoonfuls each of flour or semolina, sugar, water and melted butter. The flour or semolina is cooked with the butter for five minutes and then dissolved sugar is added. It is served cold. During the thanksgiving ceremony a little amrit (mixture of sugar and water) is placed on the baby's lips and the Granth is opened at any page and the first letter of the first hymn found will be used as the initial letter of the baby's name, which will be proposed by the Granth reader. Sikh names have meanings, such as Dhanna Singh, 'wealthy', and Ajit Singh, 'invincible'.

Baptism. Sikhs are divided into the Sahaj Dhari (civilian Sikhs) and the Kesh Dhari Singhs (Warrior Sikhs). The Sahaj are true believers but are not prepared to serve as soldiers. Anyone who accepts the teaching of the Granth, forsakes idol worship, takes amrit and believes in the one God (Nam) can be a Sahaj Dhari, but Kesh Sikhs of either sex must undergo baptism (Amrit Sanskar, the drinking of the elixir, or water, of immortality). The Amrit will make one immortal in the sense that death will be nothing but the casting away of one's physical body so as to enable one to enter a higher realm. Water represents purity and humility; the sugar, sweetness and saintliness. Men receive the additional name of Singh ('lion') and girls Kaur ('princess').

This baptism can be done at any age from maturity onwards and you must be instructed beforehand. You stand with folded hands before five Sikhs and beg for admittance. They can refuse it if they think you are not yet fit for the ceremony. Those administering and receiving baptism must bathe and wash their hair first. The five are called Piares ('loved ones') and they wear yellow tunics with blue or red sashes. They represent the first five Sikhs who answered Gobind Singh's call (see pp. 43–4). They read out the rules and duties required before asking those seeking baptism whether they will keep them. This involves the following:

- Accepting the teaching of the Granth and the teachings of the ten gurus (founding wise men).
- Wearing the five K's (see below).
- Abstaining from alcohol and tobacco.
- Not committing adultery.
- Working honestly.
- Putting no trust in magic or charms.
- Accepting other Sikhs as brothers.
- Giving a tenth of personal savings to charity.
- Being ready to sacrifice all for the faith.

Amrit is prepared in a steel bowl, representing the human mind and stirred by a khanda (double-edged dagger), with the five sitting round it, taking it in turn to stir. Those to be baptized cup their hands together to receive the amrit; they consume it five times before more is sprinkled five times on their eyes and hair. They are told, 'From now on your existence as an ordinary individual has ceased and you are members of the Khalsa [brotherhood]. You are to pray to God and God alone, through the scriptures and teachings of the ten Gurus'. They are told to keep the five K's which are Kesh, Kanga, Kara, Kachs and Kirpan.

Kesh means that their hair must be grown long, and in the case of men, beards too, as symbols of devotion to God. A man's beard signifies his strength. Sikhs point out that long hair was customary among Hindu gods, Jesus, Buddha and Muhammad, and refer to Samson's strength lying in his hair (Judg. 16), as well as giving medical evidence that hair is 'a great factory of vital energy. Hair is living tissue and a functioning entity . . . human hair absorbs solar energy and no life can exist without solar rays'. 'Nature does not err, and if the hair were unnecessary it would not have been provided'. They refer to vitamin D in particular. Sikhs must wash their hair every four days.

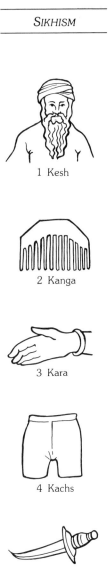

1 Kesh

Kanga is a comb, to keep long hair in place under the turban. It is a symbol of cleanliness. The turban is worn to enclose the bound-up hair, and it is seen as a frontier between faith and unbelief, a symbol of generosity, truthfulness and fearlessness. No Sikh will wear anything less on his head and after a long argument with the law courts in England, a special law (Motor Cycle Crash Helmets—Religious Exemptions—Act 1976) was made letting Sikhs ride motorbikes without crash helmets. Boys wear a rumal (small hand-kerchief) to tie up their hair instead of a turban.

2 Kanga

Kara is a steel bracelet worn on the right wrist, symbolizing Sikh unity. It also symbolizes strength in its shape which gives it structural strength. Mathematically it indicates infinity, as any number (x) divided by 0 equals infinity. So, regardless of a person's size, x, they have strength from their kara. When a Sikh combs his hair in the morning his right hand and so his Kara goes above his head and he says, 'O Almighty God, Wonderful Lord, you are omnipotent, I am nothing, I am puny, I am zero . . . who has no rival? None but God'. Kara is nearly the same as kari (handcuff) and so it shows one is bound as a disciple to the faith.

3 Kara

4 Kachs

Kachs are shorts worn by men and women to give them greater freedom of movement, originally for fighting in battle for their faith.

Kirpan is a short sword, to remind a Sikh of his duty to defend the weak and uphold his faith. Miniature versions are carried today.

5 Kirpan

The ceremony ends with the distribution of karah parshad. If you break your vows, you would have to apologize publicly to the congregation and do whatever penance (tankha) you were given,

The Five K's. What are the English words for each of these?

Sikh wedding.
What will the
couple walk
around while they
are holding the
scarf?

such as saying prayers, cleaning utensils or shoes of the sangat (congregation) or preparing the langar (communal meal).

28. *Draw pictures of the five K's and add a sentence or two under each to explain them.*

Marriage has presented problems to some Sikhs. Nanak's marriage was not a happy one. He and his wife quarrelled and finally separated. Ranjit Singh had four wives and seven mistresses burnt at his funeral to accompany him to the next life.

Sikhs are expected to marry Sikhs and parents have a considerable say as to who is to marry whom. Until recently the couple would not have met until their marriage day. Sikhs point to the number of love marriages which fail in England in contrast to the stability of parentally arranged marriages in their faith.

29. *Is an arranged marriage more likely to succeed than a love match? Give reasons.*

The engagement can be marked by the girl's parents visiting the man's home and presenting him with a kirpan. Sometimes the girl is given a dress, but she may not be present at the engagement parental meeting. The ceremony is called Anand Karaj (Ceremony of Bliss) and it takes place early in the morning. On this day the mother and other females of the groom's family send him off with his father and male relations to the gurdwara. The men then meet the bride's male relatives at the milani (meeting) and give them turbans. The bride wears a red dupatta (scarf), red or pink shalwar (long trousers) and gold-embroidered kameeze (tunic) and a lot of jewellery. The groom's turban will be red or pink. The ceremony can be at the gurdwara, bride's home or in the open air.

They all sit on the floor in front of the Granth. The granthi (male or female officiant) explains the responsibilities and duties of marriage, stressing its holy status and then asks them to bow before the Granth to show they accept. The bride's father puts garlands of flowers round the couple's necks and on the Granth as music and prayers begin. The Granth is then opened at the Lavan (four marriage vows) and he puts one end of a saffron cotton scarf in the groom's hand, passes it over the shoulder and places the other end in the bride's hand. The granthi reads the first verse and this is repeated by the congregation while the couple rise and walk clockwise round the Granth holding the scarf. The same procedure is used for three more verses, each of which tells the couple where true happiness lies, namely in devotion to God. Part of the reading is this:

In the first round, the Lord ordains for you a secular life.
Accept the Guru's word as your scripture
And it will free you from sin . . .
Let your law of life be to meditate on the Name of God . . .
Fortunate are those who hold God in their hearts; they are ever
  serene and happy . . .

The congregation shower them with flower petals as they go round the last time. Finally, all stand for the Ardas (common prayer) and parshad (see p. 199) is then distributed before the marriage feast takes place elsewhere. No contract has to be signed as the ceremony takes place before the Granth.

Husbands call their wives Ardhangi ('better half') as Nanak made it clear that men and women are equal. In fact, he said that Eve, of Garden of Eden fame, was not a temptress but the 'conscience of men'. The Granth states:

It is by women that we are conceived, and from them that we are
  born,
It is with them that we are betrothed and married.

It is the women we befriend and it is the women who keep the race going.
When one woman dies we seek another.
It is with women that we become established in society.
Why should women be called inferior when they give birth to great men?

Nanak made it clear that women could play a leading role in religious services. Widowers and widows may remarry. Divorce and remarriage is allowed, but they are rare.

30. *Compare the position of women in Muslim and Sikh marriages.*

31. *Explain Nanak's comments on Eve in the Garden of Eden.*

32. *Has Nanak given women a status in Sikhism which women do not hold in other religions? What arguments would Nanak produce to defend his pronouncements on women?*

33. *Cleansing, washing, or the use of water, is to be found as a main feature of many 'signing on' ceremonies.*
(a) Why? What does it imply?
(b) Do you think these implications or intentions are sensible ones to make?

34. *(a) What should be the minimum age for someone to become a full member of a faith and why?*
(b) Why do you think some religious groups allow signing on at a very young age?

35. *(a) What should be done about someone who breaks his membership vows?*
(b) Should there be some form of punishment or should this be left to God?

36. *(a) Should a person's appearance, e.g. Sikh's long hair, Jew's circumcision, mark his membership of a faith?*
(b) Why do non-religious groups mark their membership with special hair styles?
(c) Why do you think religious and non-religious groups do such things?

37. *Why do special foods or meals play an important role in the worship of religious life? Give examples.*

38. *(a) What aspects of the joining ceremonies described could be classified as (i) miracles, (ii) superstitions, (iii) supernatural?*
(b) What special elements are essential in such ceremonies?

39. Why are membership ceremonies usually performed by priests or similar people?

40. (a) List religions which allow (i) divorce, (ii) remarriage. List those which do not allow (i) and (ii).
(b) Is a religion which allows (i) and (ii) setting too low a standard or facing up to what can go wrong in married life?
(c) Should a religion be content with demanding only minimum requirements or should it set far higher standards for couples than the law of the land might require?

41. (a) Is a religiously performed marriage more likely to last than a registry office one?
(b) Do religious beliefs help to keep a marriage going?

8.
DYING
AND BEYOND

Man is the only animal who knows he is going to die. Naturally, he wonders why and what can be the purpose of living if death is inevitable. Religions claim there is some form of life after death called eternal life. They disagree as to just what form that life will take, but they are convinced it exists. It provides the opportunity to put right the unfairnesses of earthly life. It is argued that earthly life is not in the end tragic for cripples, the lonely or the poor, as it leads to fulfilment beyond death.

Some religions claim that everything will come to one final climax at the end of time; others do not. If there is life after death a lot of questions arise. Will we remember our life (lives) on earth? Will we be able to recognize relatives and friends? Will we have bodies of some sort? Will we be able to communicate with others? Can bodiless souls recognize and communicate with each other? Will we really exist in any form by which we can be identified? Or will we be so absorbed into the Godhead that we cannot be distinguished from any other person? If our identities vanish, what will we have gained by living a good, religious life? Should we think of gaining anything, or just be satisfied with eliminating our selfishness in the worship of God? What can be the purpose of life on earth?

To begin with you must know what you consist of in this life; otherwise you cannot hope to know what might survive on into the next life. Your 'self' is made up of a combination of genes from your parents. Your 'character' is largely built up from these genes but also from your environment and the way you are brought up. If you ask about your 'soul', difficult questions arise. Did God specially create a soul and insert it into you as a baby? Is an embryo a potential soul? Is a soul reborn in countless bodies by reincarnation? Either way that soul must add something unique to your 'self'. But what?

It is claimed that your moral character is built up by your learning to respond or react to your environment—the situation and people around you. Thus you can become a polite, kind person or a ruthless thug. But the word 'soul' implies you are valuable to God as an individual. Think of the popular phrases, 'You have no soul!', 'It's soul-destroying'. To save someone's soul is to save their unique quality as an individual. So the soul is a person's spiritual and moral personality. Religions feel it essential to stress that a person is more than just 'self'. A person must have a spiritual side too, and that side is called a 'soul'. They argue everyone has a 'soul' whether they like it or not. Hence, in you there is a struggle between your self-centred 'self' and your spiritually-centred 'soul'. If you are to find and reach God your 'soul' must conquer your 'self'.

Western religions (Judaism, Christianity, Islam) argue that you have one earthly lifetime only to achieve this. Eastern ones offer several lives by reincarnation as you cannot possibly fulfil yourself and find God in a single, perhaps very short, life. 'One-life' religions may argue there is an extra stage between death and life in heaven—a purgatory stage where a soul stays until its failings left over from earthly life can be got rid of. When the soul is made perfect it can go on to heaven.

The Western idea of a new soul being created for each baby born can seem very unjust as some are born malformed or in slum areas while others are far more 'lucky'. The Eastern reincarnation idea removes this criticism of God's unfairness as it claims that your previous way of life determines the circumstances of your next birth —a wicked man may be born deformed, for example.

In the main the Eastern religions tend to say that body and soul are distinct, though they are temporarily joined while on earth. This is a drag on the soul, and so it follows that human life is not God's greatest gift to man—it is a curse of nature. Man must free his soul from his body's selfishness. Western religions say man is body and soul together, and death is only their temporary separation. The soul lives on at death and on the Day of Judgement it will be reunited with its body, perhaps in some new spiritual form. Eastern and Western religions disagree as to what a man's construction really is, and hence how he will eventually exist in eternity. Eastern religions see the main aim of life as releasing the soul from the 'selfish' body so that they will never be reunited again. Western religions see earthly life as a preparation for the next life—a soul-making time. Easterners see earthly life as a curse which the soul has to suffer. Eastern man believes he will keep on returning to earth until he has managed to free his soul from his body, i.e. from 'selfishness'.

Other vexing questions are these. Will all people be 'saved' and reach 'Heaven' in the end, or only those who really follow their faith? If all are 'saved', is one really free to reject being 'saved' if one does not want to be? Only those who have died and are in the next life really know the answers. Let us see what the religions teach on the whole subject.

HINDUISM

Funerals. In India the climate makes a prompt funeral (16th samskāra) necessary. If possible, a dying person will be placed on a floating hurdle in the Ganges and the face washed, as this will save numerous rebirths in the future. Then the dead body will be washed and wrapped in a yellow cloth before being put into a coffin or tied to a hurdle. There will be no weeping or wailing, only chanting or silence, as death is welcomed as a release from this life of illusion (maya) to a new and better life.

1. (a) State why Hindus almost welcome death and how this affects their funeral customs.
   (b) Do you think a person should welcome death when it comes?

The body is carried to the riverside steps called ghats. Here it is put on a pyre (pile) of wood for cremation. Ghee (melted butter from which the solid fat has been skimmed off, which keeps well in hot climates) is thrown on the pyre to help the fire burn. Dry pieces of squeezed sugar cane are lit and pushed into the pyre as the priest chants. The bones and ashes are collected the next day and lowered into the Ganges in a cloth in the belief that this will prevent further reincarnation and enable the deceased to go straight to Brahman. Hindus in England are cremated at the local crematorium.

Daily ceremonies are performed for ten days to provide for the naked soul of the deceased with a new spiritual body with which it may pass on to the next life. Rice and milk are offered, for otherwise the soul will remain a ghost to haunt scenes of its past life, irritating relatives. Hindus are anxious to have sons as only they are allowed to perform these rites. On the fourth day relatives and friends revisit the

Cremation on the
River Ganges'
ghats, Benares.
The bodies are
carried on hurdles.

deceased's house and comfort the family, giving them presents while
prayers are said for the departed soul. A final sympathy meeting,
called kriya, is held on the 11th day when the deceased's soul is free
to pass on to a new life.

Part of the Gita is recited at cremations:

Worn out garments are shed by the body,
Worn out bodies are shed by the dweller.
Within the body new bodies are donned by the dweller, like garments.

Suttee (literally 'virtuous woman') is the sacrifice a widow was supposed to make voluntarily by which she was burnt on her husband's funeral pyre. This was to wipe out their sins and ensure them millions of years of bliss together in heaven. A widow who did not do this was meant to shave her head, wear no jewels and remain unmarried. Suttee was officially stopped in the nineteenth century, although it does continue in villages still today.

Reincarnation. A person cannot work out his destiny in one lifetime. It would be quite unfair to give him an eternal punishment because he had made some errors during a few years on earth. It would not fit in with God's love of His created beings. They believe a person's jiva (soul) (which is sexless; sex belongs to the body) was never born and will never die, for it migrates or moves from one body to another. This is called samsara (literally 'that which flows together', hence transmigration). So life is complex, mysterious and ever-changing.

2. (a) *What is your opinion of the Hindu view that one life is too short to find one's atman?*
(b) *Is it helpful to argue that one has numerous lives on earth?*
(c) *Is having only one life less fair?*
(d) *If one's life is affected by a belief in life after death, what differences would it make if one believed one had (i) one life, (ii) numerous lives?*

Starting as a stone a jiva will move to such things as plants and animals quite automatically until it reaches a human being. From then on reincarnation occurs, that is to say it is reborn in people. The new human body a jiva gets into depends on the life it led in its previous human body. The law of karma (works) applies, and this maintains that you get a position in life according to how good or bad you were in the previous life. So karma is a moral or behaviour law and it works because human beings are self-conscious and can know if they are doing right things or not. Your present condition, your happiness and status are directly the product of your previous life. Consequently you are wholly responsible for your present condition and your future. Notice that God does not judge you for your behaviour as the karma law is an automatic one. No god fixes your future; you do so yourself. You decide your own fate. Luck plays no part in life at all. You cannot say you have had good or bad luck in a lottery as whether you win or not has been determined in the past by your karma. You can have dukkha (bad experiences) and sukha (good experiences) in your life. You must not feel that you are a condemned person as it is up to you to decide how you will behave and so what your future will be.

3. (a) Is the law of karma just?
    (b) Why is it easier to say you will get what you deserve in your next life rather than in your present life? When answering this remember that there are good poor people and wicked rich people in the world.
    (c) Will the karma law encourage people to live good lives?
    (d) Would you be content to have your life governed by the karma law?

4. Is the Hindu right in saying luck does not exist? Give examples.

The Laws of Manu list punishments for wrong-doing. The man who kills a priest will be reborn as a dog, ass or bull; a man who steals from a priest will be born a thousand times as a spider or snake. Sometimes it is possible for a jiva to find temporary rest in the heaven of one of the gods before returning to earth. Each god has his own heaven, and, to qualify for such a rest, a jiva must have done a pilgrimage, built a temple or some such good deed. The Upanishads claims that a jiva can spend time in one of the numerous heavens or hells between its incarnations. Yama, god of the dead, dressed in blood-red clothes, and holding a noose, judges jivas by passing them through two fires, in which the righteous will be unharmed but the wicked will suffer.

Although your jiva will go up and down in a zigzag way with transmigration, in the end it will find its atman (real self). Then it will become part of the Godhead and so obtain moksha (release) from the round of transmigration. Until then it can revert to a lower status in life or progress according to its karma. The world is a jiva's gymnasium, its training ground, midway between Heaven and Hell; a mixture of pleasure and pain, good and evil. No social progress, no cleaning up of the world or the bringing of the kingdom of heaven to earth is possible according to Hindus. Notice this contrast with Christianity which is a religion which seeks to improve life on earth. Hindus believe that man cannot convert the world into a paradise. Instead the world will develop his character for him.

5. The Hindu says life on earth is only a temporary business before the real life beyond and the world is only the jiva's gymnasium.
    (a) What is your opinion of this argument?
    (b) Is life on earth designed to mould your character for the afterlife?

211

The law of karma leads on to the classification of humans into strict classes and castes, as we have seen (pp. 67–8). Brahmins are nearest to finding their atmans as they are the top class. A Hindu welcomes death as a step to final union with Brahman. Some say that when the jiva passes into the Godhead it loses every trace of its separateness and so it cannot be identified in any way. Others say that some slight differences remain so that a jiva can be identified.

SHINTOISM

Funerals. Everything connected with death is considered evil but not necessarily a pollution. So, when death occurs, a Shinto shrine is covered with white paper to prevent polluted air affecting it. The Japanese see Shintoism as their religion of the living and Buddhism as the religion of the dead. People do not 'die'; they 'withdraw' and 'rise' to heaven. This means that they will have a Shinto marriage but a Buddhist funeral.

However, there is a Shinto funeral rite, So-sai, for the ten per cent of Shintoists who do prefer it to the Buddhist rite. It is usually held at home and not at a shrine so as not to pollute it. An apron (tafusagi) is put round the body's waist, then a knee-length shirt (hadagi) and a tunic, belt and shoes are added. There are two kinds of coffin (kwan): nekwan, in which the body is lying down; zakwan, when it is in a praying position. To the chanting of the chief mourner the coffin is carried out, while the priest purifies the house by sprinkling salt and using his haraigushi (see pp. 76–7). The service is held inside a curtained enclosure and includes a recital of the person's life. The mourners are purified after the coffin has been buried. Forty-nine days later the Shijūkunichi ceremony installs the Ihai (tablet to the dead) so making the deceased's spirit into an ancestral kami. The Japanese follow the Buddhist custom of grave visiting (Ohakamairi) and carry rice cakes or fruit to show that they treat the dead as living, as kami (see Bon Festival, p. 161).

The soul. Shintoists believe life in this world is more important than any afterlife. As their religion shows little interest in what happens after death, Buddhism has filled the gap (see pp. 219–20). For Shintoists, there is no judgement day to come, souls (tama) are not 'lost' and so do not need 'saving'. Man is called hito, 'human-being-becoming-heavenly'. In other words he is both divine and earthly all his life and so a kami-in-the-making. At death he achieves this new dimension and is called a kami. His soul has two parts: the kuni-tama, which joins his body at conception, and wake-mitama, which arrives at birth. When these two fall out death occurs and the kuni-tama returns to the earth from which it came. The old traditional views claim that the innocent wake-mitama go to Takama-no-hara, the High Plain of Heaven, where the kami live. A year of purification can bring the soul to Toko-yo-no-kuni, the Land of Toko-yo, a place of wealth, pleasure and peace. There is also reference to Yomi, the land where the evil spirit Magatsuhi pollutes the dead using aggressive wasps, centipedes and serpents, but where friendly and helpful mice are also to be found. However, modern Shrine Shintoism does not support these traditional views.

6. (a) *Why do you think ancient religions like Shintoism raised the status of the dead to that of gods?*
    (b) *How might this affect the family of a strong-willed granny who had recently died?*

7. *Shintoism claims life on earth is more important than the after-life.*
    (a) *What is your opinion of this view?*
    (b) *Is it comforting or disturbing?*
    (c) *Is it likely to affect the way you live now?*
    (d) *Do other religions hold the same view or do they put eternal life before earthly life?*

TAOISM

The soul. Typical Chinese funeral rites (Sang Li) are connected with ancestor worship. The wealth and status of the deceased will decide how long and elaborate they are. To understand the rite we must find out what the Chinese belief in the soul's structure is. They say a soul is in two parts: the Hun soul is the higher spiritual soul with Yang qualities, while the P'o one is the earthly soul with Yin qualities. At death the Hun soul takes on a spirit form (Shen) and has to face a dangerous journey into the underworld. It also enters the green and gold tablet as the Shen Chu with the name, age and death date upon it. This is placed in the house and food is put there and paper money burnt from 10 am to 4 pm for 21 days after death. The P'o soul remains at the grave where it must be ritually pacified and sustained with food to make sure it does not emerge as a wicked ghost (kuei). The purpose of the funeral rites is to aid the Hun soul's Shen spirit in

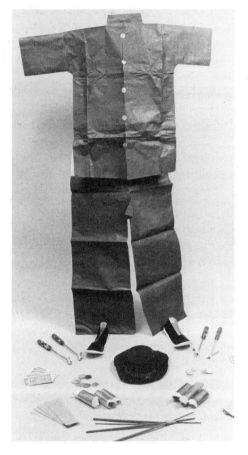

Taoist paper
clothes, money
and joss sticks for
the next world.

its underworld journey and to ensure its safe transference into the tablet.

Funerals. A dying person's grave clothes are prepared to reassure him that he will be properly buried. Just before death he may be carried outside his home so that his soul will not haunt the house by clinging to the bed. Diviners (Yin Yang Sien Seng) work out when the soul will leave the body as a vapour, saying what form it will take, how high it will be, whether it will be black, yellow or white and in what direction it will go. At the appointed hour everyone leaves the dead person's room.

The diviner will advise on the day, time and place for the funeral. Feng Shui (wind-water) determines where it is natural for the burial site to be—usually a south-facing site with a hill to the east so that spring prevails over autumn, yang over yin. The body is washed and clothed and the feet tied together as it is said it jumps about if chastized by evil spirits. A heavy coffin (113 kilos) of white pine lined with silk and bedding is used.

On the eve of the funeral a paper stork is burnt as a messenger to deliver the offerings which are to follow. A life-sized paper car with chauffeur, trunks and slave boys and girls is burnt for the soul's journey. A man will precede the procession scattering cardboard 'money' for evil spirits. Professional teams of priests and mourners put on the Huang-lu Chai, Yellow Register ritual for the dead. This involves percussion and wind instruments and acrobatics. A high-ranking Master and his band of 15 can charge huge sums for the 1½–3-day ceremony, which will open the way to heaven for the soul. They hang pictures of gods near the coffin. Paper gold and silver money is burnt as well as complete sets of miniature paper clothes for the soul. The female clothes set includes tunic, trousers and shoes, together with handbag, mirror, fan, lipstick, earrings, comb, bracelets and a watch (all these small items are just pictured on a sheet of paper; the main clothes are properly made of paper). Joss sticks are burnt too. On the seventh day a two-storey paper and bamboo house with all its furniture, including paper TV, is burnt for the soul's use.

8. *The Chinese burn paper cars, money, clothing and a house to send off a deceased relative. What does this tell us about their view of life after death?*

In Hong Kong, a memorial mass may be said in which both Taoist priests and Buddhist nuns may play a role. Outside the deceased's house a Spirit Road to purgatory will be prepared by means of a long strip of white cloth placed on the table, with the broadest part in the middle, and the ends forming ramps down and up which the soul must pass. Bank notes are pinned at intervals as the soul's travelling expenses as well as food and a model of a large house. The shrine with the spirit tablet to the deceased is placed on the ascending end of the ramp. Relatives then escort the soul slowly along the Spirit Road. Afterwards the tablet is returned to its shrine in the deceased person's bedroom.

An all-night mass will be taken by the shaven-headed nuns who wear special five-pointed birettas. They invite the departed one to attend, listing the person's favourite foods as a temptation. When dawn comes the paper house, ingots and paper clothing are burnt.

Baked meats are eaten by all present. The death room is then thoroughly cleaned.

At the final service of remembrance paper clothing is put in envelopes addressed by the priest to the soul and the dot of a cockscomb's blood is put on the ancestral tablet to change the Chinese character from one for Wang (Prince) to the one for Chu (Lord) so changing the deceased from mortal into immortal.

The family wear sackcloth and let their hair grow unkempt during mourning. The deceased's ancestral tablet is put up in the shrine room after the priest has marked it with blood. The length of the mourning depends on the relationship between the mourners and the deceased. Close relatives should mourn for three years, wearing sackcloth and rush shoes while living in a hut and eating two bowls of gruel a day. The dead are believed to become kuei (ghosts) after three years, and good kuei can be helpful, but bad ones are frightening. So kuei must be honoured. Every day for the first year the family puts food before the tablet as well as before those of the household gods. On the 15th day of the seventh month there is the Ghosts' Feast when food, incense and paper money are burnt as well as a paper boat to take the soul across the river as it is in that month that the door of the unseen regions is opened to the spirits of the dead to walk in.

As tablets of new dead members of a family are put in the shrine room, so the older ones are put in collective ancestral halls in a country setting. The family founder's tablet is on the highest shelf with his descendants below him. All relatives with the same surname use the same hall. In Hong Kong after six years the body is exhumed and if the coffin is still in reasonable condition it is returned to the undertaker for repair and re-use. The jade and jewellery in it revert to the relatives. The bones are put in an urn for placing in a waste spot on a hill. The urns are called chin t'a, golden pagodas.

The journey of the Shen soul is divided into seven periods of seven days each:

First week. It reaches the Demon Barrier Gate and is beset by robbers who demand money, which it pays in spirit money. If the soul has none, it is stripped and beaten. Hence the need to burn paper money bought from the Paper Shop which sells things of paper for spirits. Hell Bank paper money put in large imposing gold embossed envelopes, paper gold ingots and cardboard dollars are all available to burn.

Second week. It is put on the scales of the Weighbridge. Good men's souls are as light as air, while a sinner's are weighed down by evil deeds. The payment for sinning is being sawn asunder or ground to powder. This is only a temporary ordeal as the soul is restored again.

Third week. The soul arrives at Bad Dogs Village. If it is good the dogs will welcome it, but if not it will be torn apart until the blood flows.

Fourth week. The Mirror of Retribution gives the soul a glimpse of its future; a sinner sees his reincarnation as a pig or serpent.

Fifth week. This week allows the soul a last look back at the past life.

Sixth week. The soul is faced with the Inevitable River Bridge made of a single rope 31mm wide and 350m high above the rapids and snakes below. The soul is allowed to straddle the rope to get over. Good souls are allowed to bypass the bridge and cross by the Fairy Bridge.

Seventh week. The soul reaches the Prince of the Wheel's realm to petition for a speeding up of the transmigration process. Free tea is supplied to wipe out memories of good and bad in the past life. Then the Wheel of the Law is whirled round with the soul trapped between its spokes. If it is allowed to leave by the top right corner it will be a noble person; if by the top left, an orphan, lame or blind person; if by the left or right sides, an animal; if by the bottom right, a scale-like creature or shell; if by the bottom left, an insect.

9. *Summarize the stages of the journey a soul takes from the body to purgatory and on to heaven.*

10. *Draw the stages of the journey in a series of pictures.*

Heaven is seen as the place where the ancestors (Pai Tsu) live and from which they control the earth's welfare, so that those on earth should make sacrifices to them. The augury or omen is the connecting language between heaven and earth. Omens can be things affecting the body, such as itchings, stumblings, sneezings, or external signs, like thunder or lightning.

11. *(a) List and explain any omens which have indicated events which did happen, to your knowledge, either to yourself or to someone you know.*
(b) What is your opinion of omens being the connecting language between the dead and the living? Give reasons for your answer.

The Taoists criticize the Sang Li rites. For example, Chuang Tzu (369–286 BC) when asked about his funeral, said, 'Heaven and earth are my inner and outer coffins. The sun, moon and stars are my drapery, and the whole of creation my funeral procession. What more do I want?' When his wife died, a friend found him singing a song and was shocked. Said Chuan:

You misjudge me. When she died I was in despair . . . But soon . . . I told myself that in death no strange new fate befalls me . . . If someone is tired and has gone to lie down, we do not pursue him with hooting and bawling. She whom I have lost has lain down to sleep for a while in the Great Inner Room. To break in upon her rest with the noise of lamentation would but show that I know nothing of nature's Sovereign Law. That is why I ceased to mourn.

Finally, Chuang summed up his confidence in facing death when he wrote:

There is the globe, the foundation of my bodily existence; it wears me out with work and duties, it gives me rest in old age, it gives me peace in death. For the one who supplied me with what I needed in life will also give me what I need in death.

12.   *What do you think of Chuang's views on death and mourning?*

BUDDHISM

Funerals. 'To realize that life ends in death is to escape from the control of death', said Buddha. Buddhist funerals can be very expensive affairs. In 1977 an important grandmother's death, and that of several other relatives who had died sometime earlier, were marked by the employment of a special team of funeral priests costing £20 000. The Taoist-style team included acrobats and in the midst of a varied and colourful programme numerous firecrackers were set off. Usually relatives invite monks to the funeral and the Triple Refuge and the Five Precepts are recited. The relatives offer a white cloth to the monks and ask that the merit they receive from this act may be shared with the deceased. A sermon on Buddha's teaching on death is given and the monks return to give another sermon six days later. The body can be cremated or buried.

Each year villagers process to the graves to cleanse them to the sound of firecrackers. Monks say masses for the dead to help them build up merit for the next life. What happens in the next life is not easy to explain. Buddhists have talked of there being 128 hot hells under the earth, eight cold hells and 84 000 odd ones scattered about the universe for punishment or reward between lives on earth. But such picturesque language can be misleading. Buddha said that man is not made up of a perishable 'body' and an eternal 'soul' (jiva), but of five components, the Five Aggregates, which are:

- skandhas, or skeins, of feeling (vedana),
- awareness of senses (sannā),
- thinking powers (vinnāna),
- physical features (rūpa)
- intentions (sank hara).

All of these are constantly changing. For example, a man's skandhas are very different to the skandhas he had as a baby. As an adult he looks and thinks differently. The skandhas dissolve when a person dies. They are not carried on to the next life. What is carried on into rebirth is the karma, the driving force of desire (tanhā).

Rebirth. Buddha rejected the Hindu version of transmigration of souls as he said eternal souls did not exist. He said one could break the effects of one's karma by giving up one's cravings and so cease the Samsara reincarnation cycle by seeking nirvana. He rejected the Hindu class structure too. It is the things we do and the way we feel that have to be born again and again until we stop doing wrong, wanting things and having selfish feelings. Only then will there be nothing left to be born again. Rebirth is the endless transmission of an impulse, like a billiard ball propelling another it hits while stopping itself!

> All that we are is the result of what we have thought; it is founded on our thoughts, it is made up of our thoughts. If a man speaks or acts with an evil thought, pain follows him as the wheel follows the foot of the ox that draws the wagon . . . If a man speaks or acts with a pure thought happiness follows him, like a shadow that never leaves him!
> (Path of Teaching)

13. (a) In what ways do Hindu and Buddhist teachings on reincarnation differ?
    (b) Which viewpoint do you prefer and why?

Nirvana. No gods, worship or rituals will enable you to stop your rebirths. You have to achieve it on your own. Buddhism depends on self-help, not on god-help. One can become an arhat (enlightened person) and achieve nirvana (literally 'to blow out'; 'to extinguish'). What is 'blown out' is desire. Nirvana is nothingness, neither being, nor non-being; it is oblivion, spiritual freedom, freedom from space and time, from illusion, from passion and from all passing things of this world.

'Nirvana is uncompounded—it is made of nothing at all', said Buddha, as any compounded thing can be dissolved. It is also unborn—otherwise it could die; it is unmade—otherwise it could be destroyed. Only if nirvana is uncompounded, unborn, unmade, outside time and space, unperceived by any of man's senses, can it be really permanent, and eternal. If not it would be limited and endable. Anything that is born, made, touchable, etc., is merely transient or impermanent (anicca). This does not mean that the human spirit has been wiped out but that it has reached its highest destiny, that of being absorbed into nirvana. Like wind it is impossible to see. So Buddha said man had no soul, a condition called anatta ('atta' means 'soul'). By this he meant that man had not got a part of him which lasted separately from the universe for eternity. When Buddha analysed the five skandhas he found nothing behind them which could be called 'I', 'self', 'soul', and so he declared that man has no eternal soul. He claimed the doctrine of anatta does away with the darkness of false beliefs and produces the light of wisdom.

14. *(a) Write a full statement of what nirvana is said to be.*
(b) Do you think the nirvana explanation of life after death makes sense or not? Give your reasons.

Pure Land. Some Buddhists have developed an alternative idea to replace the long struggle to reach nirvana. They argued that there was a nearer goal to hand, Suhkāvati (the Pure Land of the Western Paradise), a colourful heaven of trees, streams, bells and birds, which you can reach by having faith in Amitabha Buddha (Amida in Japanese; O-mi-to in Chinese), King of the Western Paradise. He has vowed to save all who call on his name in faith. He guides weary travellers over the sea of sorrow. This is a Mahāyāna (big raft) viewpoint (see pp. 18–20). Faith, rather than the efforts of following the Eightfold Path, will get you there.

15. *Why should it be easier to reach the Pure Land than to work one's way to nirvana by the Eightfold Path?*

16. *'All that we are is the result of what we have thought'. Do you agree or not? Give examples for and against before deciding.*

Funerals. People hearing of a death say, 'Blessed be the true judge'. The deceased's close relatives make a small tear in their clothing as a sign of mourning. Funerals are arranged promptly, within 24 hours if possible. Arrangements are simple as all are regarded as equal in death. No professional undertakers are involved. The body is dressed in a white shroud (kittel) and tallith with its tassels cut off. It is placed in a plain wooden coffin with no metal extras. There are no flowers or music at the ceremony which consists of a prayer at the synagogue prior to the burial at the cemetery, the House of Eternal Life. The coffin is buried and everyone shovels in some earth. The mourners recite the Kaddish. This praises God and expresses trust in the future coming of the Messiah to set up his kingdom upon earth. Orthodox Jews will not allow cremation as man is created in God's image and so it would be wrong to deliberately destroy a body. 'Dust shall return to dust'.

When the mourners return home they are given a hard-boiled egg as a symbol of life—Jews see death as the doorway to the next life. The family go into mourning (shiva) for up to seven days. The closest relatives must not leave home and they sit on low stools. Neighbours visit to offer consolation and help. One of the best deeds a neighbour can do is to bring the first meal to them. Then for the rest of the year the mourners go without amusements until on the anniversary of the death they light a candle, recite the Kaddish and set up a tombstone. The anniversary is marked each year in the home and synagogue by lighting a candle.

Life after death. Jews believe the soul is immortal, but do not try to say what life after death will be like. At one time they did speak of Sheol, a shadowy underground place where the ghosts of the dead went while waiting for bodily resurrection. It was said to be divided up into sections for the good and the bad, and controlled by God (Num. 16:30–33; Isa. 14:9–10, 15; Job 3:11–19; 7:9–10; 10:21–22; 30:23). Jews used to speak of heaven and hell but not very clearly. 'May he dwell in the bright garden of Eden' was a way one could speak of the dead. Nothing was said about what Hell might be like and they did not guess at any tortures which might go on there. They had enough problems to face on earth.

Day of Judgement. Strict Orthodox Jews still look forward to the coming of the Messiah (*not* Jesus) to set up the messianic kingdom after a period of natural disasters and terrors. He will overcome Israel's enemies and set up his kingdom which will end on the Day of Judgement. Then the dead will come alive again in bodily form to await God's judgement. The Messiah is seen to be a strong, wise leader who will carry out a social revolution based on justice. For Jews, Jesus and later claimants have just not fulfilled the prophecies as they read them, just as Christians ignore Muhammad as a prophet. But nowadays most Jews do not expect an individual Messiah to come, but look forward to the time when the community of Jews will bring in a messianic age of kindliness and justice for all, which will in

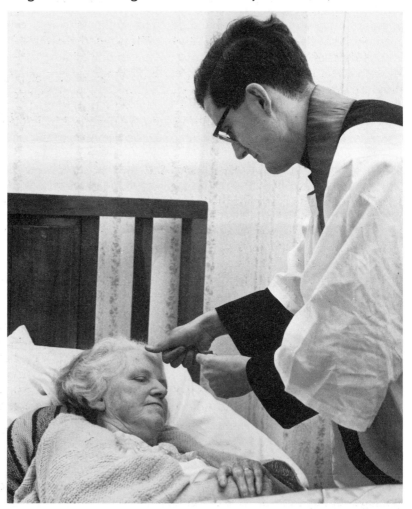

The Christian sacrament of anointing the sick.

turn be the Day of Judgement. Some believe the Messiah's kingdom will be blissful and eternal after the Judgement, while others see it as a worldly, temporary affair pending the coming of the Judgement. Notice the idea that the soul and body stay together in the end (Isa. 34:1−17; 35:1−10). The blind will see, the deaf hear, the cripples will be whole. Essentially you will get what you deserve on that day. Jews point out that the rewards of a good life are open to all, Jew and non-Jew. They have no exclusive right to heaven, and so there is no need for them to press non-Jews to believe in Judaism.

17. *Summarize what Sheol was thought to be from the references given above.*

18. *Summarize the Day of Judgement and its aftermath from the references given above.*

19. *What reasons do you think the majority of Jews would give for abandoning the earlier views about the coming of the Messiah?*

20. *Do you think bodily resurrection is essential for an afterlife? Why?*

CHRISTIANITY

Unction. Roman Catholics help a sick person by giving him the sacrament of Unction or Anointing which is designed to forgive sins and give spiritual strength to the receiver. The ears, eyes, nose, lips and hands of the sick person are anointed. Oil made from green wood gives strength, soothes and relaxes but it is not claimed that it restores health. It is not a kind of faith healing. Orthodox Christians use olive oil.

Funerals. Burial in coffins is now giving way to cremation as not only do the ashes need less space for internment, but the mourners are less upset by seeing the curtains quietly obscure the coffin in the crematorium than they are by seeing the coffin lowered into the grave and covered with earth. Flowers are often displayed. After a Quaker cremation the mourners gather in their meeting house for prayer and members may rise and praise or recall the life of the deceased.

21. *What are (a) the merits, (b) the drawbacks of (i) graveyard burial and (ii) cremation?*

The Church of England Alternative Service Book quotes Bible passages of hope for the future such as:

*I [Jesus] am the resurrection and the life, said the Lord; he that
believes in Me, though he was dead, yet shall he live; and whosoever
liveth and believeth in me shall never die.* (John 11:25–26)

The service concludes with the words 'We now commit his/her body
to the ground, . . . in sure and certain hope of the resurrection to
eternal life, through our Lord Jesus Christ'. There is a victorious, not
sad, nature about the Christian funeral service.

Life after death. The Christian should not fear death but see it as
the gateway to eternal life. Having accepted Christ's death as a
supreme sacrifice for people, he trusts that that sacrifice will pardon
his own sins and secure him a place in Heaven. Roman Catholics
teach that only those who led a really pure life will enter God's
presence immediately. The majority have to undergo a period of
purification called Purgatory, where their chief suffering will be the
loss of their vision of God. But they will no longer be distracted by the
pleasures of the world so their yearning for God will become more
intense. Aided by prayers of the living, the saying of masses and the
help of the saints, their souls will at last be purged of all sin and see
God. The Roman Catholics say that those who die loving evil and
hating God banish themselves from Him for ever. They will suffer
eternally in Hell. One day Christ will come in final judgement and the
dead will rise and the universe be cleansed and changed.

Not all Christians would agree with the Catholics. Creeds often
include the words, 'I look for the resurrection of the dead', but do not

Crematorium
service showing the
coffin disappearing
as the curtains
close.

define what that means. Bible references on the subject are: 1 Cor. 15:20–26, 35–38, 42–44, 53–end; I Thess. 4:13–18. Protestants tend to argue that bodies are mortal and that it is a person's soul which is everlasting. Orthodox churches say bodies will be restored to life again on the last day. In one way Christianity is unique as it proclaims that the end is already here in that God has entered the world in the substance of Jesus, so that the final outcome of history has already occurred (John 1:1–14). The new age in which God's Holy Spirit is available to believers is with us already as Christ has saved us from our sins by his death and resurrection. Those who believe in him have eternal life already. The human race now has a new relationship with God available to it.

22.   State the arguments a Christian would give which convince him he should not fear death.

In another sense the end has not yet come and there have been people who proclaim a second coming of Christ in all his glory which will include the collapse of the universe (Rom. 8; Mark 13:24–27; Rev. 21:1–4). As the Nicene Creed puts it, 'He [Christ] will come again in glory to judge the living and the dead . . . We look for the resurrection of the dead and the life of the world to come'. What form that resurrection will actually take is not clear. However, one thing all are agreed upon, and that is that a person has only one life on earth and that there are no second chances available in future lives here. This gives a sense of urgency to many who preach that one must decide to become a Christian before it is too late. After all one might be knocked down and killed at any time. Christianity, it is claimed, will release you from a fear of death and from a feeling of guilt about your past and give you birth into a new life. Christians believe in the doctrine of Atonement (at-one-ment) by which you can be reconciled to God through Christ's death and resurrection.

23.   Why does it not particularly matter to Christians that they do not know exactly what will happen at the 'resurrection of the dead'?

ISLAM

Funerals. A dead body is washed (a man's by men, a woman's by women), wrapped in three white sheets and carried on a stretcher or coffin into the mosque or burial place. After prayers it is buried in a grave with its right-hand side facing Mecca and the head of the body turned toward Mecca. Muslims believe burial should take place, if possible, on the day of death. Women rarely attend burials. They also believe that the body should have contact with the earth and not be contained in a coffin. In Gloucester in 1976 the local council decided Muslims could be buried without a coffin provided that the body was brought to the cemetery in one and then the coffin, minus the lid, was inverted over the buried body so as to cover it. Mourning lasts for seven days and the grave is visited on the seventh day. After burial it is believed two angels visit the grave and question the deceased about his fitness for the next life and prepare him for the Day of Judgement.

Day of Judgement. Death is only the end of the present life as Muslims believe in eternal life. Allah is seen as the God of the Day of Judgement. It is proclaimed in frightening terms:

> When the sun shall be folded up, and the stars shall fall, and when the mountains shall be set in motion . . . and the seas shall boil . . . then shall every soul know what it hath done. (Surah 81)

> When the earth shakes and quivers and the mountains crumble away and scatter abroad into fine dust, you shall be divided into three multitudes: those on the right (blessed shall be those on the right); those on the left (damned shall be those on the left); and those to the fore (foremost shall be those). Such are they that shall be brought near to their Lord in the gardens of delight . . . They shall recline on jewelled couches face to face, and there shall wait on them immortal youths with bowls and ewers and a cup of purest wine . . . As for those on the left hand . . . they sall dwell amidst scorching winds and boiling water. (Surah 56:4–42)

The turmoil will begin when angels sound the trumpet once; at the second blast all living creatures will die and at the third all will rise from death and await God's judgement when He has heard the angels' reports. Then all will pass over the abyss of Hell by the As-Sirat Bridge which is 'finer than a hair and sharper than a sword's edge'. The righteous will cross into Paradise while the wicked will fall into Hell.

24. *Compare the end of the universe description in the Koran with other religions' theories on the end of the universe.*

25. *Compare the As-Sirat Bridge to the Taoist Inevitable River and Fairy Bridges.*

The arrival in paradise is described thus:

> A state banquet shall they have of fruits; and honoured shall they be in the gardens of delight, upon couches face to face. A cup shall be borne round among them from a fountain. (Surah 37:38)

They will live in mansions waited upon by servants while those in hell will suffer from molten metal, boiling liquids and fire. Only those in heaven will see Allah. Islam is clear cut and positive about the fruits of life on earth. You will get what you deserve.

26. *Why would the Koran's description of paradise delight desert tribesmen?*

SIKHISM

Funerals. When a Sikh dies the body is washed and clothed and the five K's are placed beside it in the coffin (kwan). Cremation follows during which the Sohila (bed-time prayer) is read: 'Strive to seek that for which thou hast come into the world, and through the grace of the Guru, God will dwell in thy heart'. The ashes are thrown into a river or buried. A continuous reading (Akhand Path) of the whole Granth in which all adult relatives take part then goes on for about 48 hours. Alternatively, a Saptah (seven-day) or Dussehra (ten-day) recitation of the Granth is started at the home of the deceased. A deliberate show of grief is forbidden. Memorials are never erected.

Reincarnation. A person is made up of a body and a soul. The body belongs to the Physical Universe where it is born and dies, but the soul belongs to the Spiritual Universe, which is God. This Spiritual Universe is as vast and infinite as the Physical one. Sikhs believe that a person will be reincarnated again and again until his soul is united with God. Man is not basically evil. He was originally good, but evil has overshadowed him. A man's soul, being a minute part of the Eternal Soul, God, has existed from the time of Creation, and until the time it is reabsorbed into Him, it remains separate. The Hindu ideas on reincarnation have been altered by the Sikhs, who stress that all are equal in God's eyes and reject the Hindu class system. A man's soul passes through all stages of existence as with the Hindu transmigration of souls. This is called the evolution of the soul. The purpose of human life is to enable the soul to appreciate its relationship with God, and by living the life of a good Sikh achieve reunification with God. Your deeds follow your soul like a shadow. Your good deeds, as well as God's grace, will enable you to achieve salvation. Your future is not settled; it is up to you. The fate of the wicked is to be condemned to endless reincarnation until they finally repent and deserve God's grace.

Nanak thought only reincarnation could explain why some get

undeserved miseries and others riches in a particular life. The only explanation could be how such people had lived in their previous lives. He thought the Christian and Islamic single birth idea false as it left the unfair suffering or riches some had unexplained.

27. Why do you think Sikhs allow no mourning or memorials?

28. Compare Sikh beliefs with those of the Hindus about reincarnation and man's final destination.

29. How many ways can you think of for the disposal of dead bodies? What are the different religious reasons for these different ways?

30. How many different beliefs are there about what happens to a person after he or she is dead?

31. Some religions state clearly that you get what you deserve in the next or reincarnate life.
(a) Is this fair?
(b) Can anyone ever live a sufficiently good life to enter into God's presence?
(c) Is God's mercy essential if a reconciliation is to be made possible?

32. (a) Is life basically sinful?
(b) Is sin something you inherit from some kind of Original Sin at the beginning of human life?
(c) If not, where does it come from?

33. Is life simply a preparation for eternity, or is it an end in itself?

34. By religions, list in two columns (a) the hopes, (b) the warnings, that religions proclaim on the subject of death and the afterlife.

35. Everlasting life is the continuance of life in time; eternal life is beyond time and space.
(a) Do you agree with this distinction and can you see any other such distinctions between the two lives?
(b) Which religions believe in which?

36. What would you say to a mourner as a (a) Buddhist, (b) Christian, (c) Muslim by way of comfort?

37. (a) Must religions have some theory about life after death if they are to attract and keep followers?
(b) If so, what essential basic problems will a religion have to consider explaining?
(c) Dos it help or hinder a religion to be (i) vague, (ii) very positive, in its theories?

9.
CONCLUSION

What conclusions can we draw? First, it is clear that people's urge to worship has created, and still creates, endless forms of religious activity. A mosaic of beliefs, attitudes and practices has appeared over the centuries. In all ages and in all countries people have sought to solve the mystery of life.

Secondly, a person's religion is usually determined by where and when he or she is born. Anyone born before Jesus' time on earth cannot possibly have been a Christian—just as anyone born in England is very unlikely to be a Shintoist. If there is one truth to be found, it seems there must be several routes to find it.

Thirdly, history with its scientific and technical changes must lead people to finding different answers to their questions. Earthquakes and volcanoes, rain and drought can now be explained scientifically whereas they once obsessed primitive Man with his fear of spirits. Supernatural causes do not have to be sought for, once natural ones are known. Superstitious healing rites can give way to modern medical knowledge and skill too. Contraception offers a new dimension to sexual relations. Psychology has brought a new light to bear on how our minds work.

Thus the changes and developments of history have affected Man's search for truth. Old problems (e.g. earthquakes) have been solved, but new ones (e.g. artificial insemination, mercy-killing) arise. Polygamy of old has been replaced by 'serial polygamy' as a result of divorces and remarriages becoming easier. How should religions believing in life-long marriages react to this? Such questions are open to endless arguments.

Broadly speaking we have found that religions fall into two groups, the Western and the Eastern. If we take the Western ones—Judaism, Christianity and Islam—on their own, we find that they all believe there is only one God and that He has made special revelations or disclosures of the truth to them. The disclosures they have received are similar in some respects and different in others.

Because they believe it is God who has made these disclosures to them they tend to criticize the points on which they disagree more than emphasizing what they have in common. So they dismiss each other's religions as untrue, or only partially true. The Christian argues that the Jews ignore Jesus, while the Muslims say that Christians have ignored Muhammad and the Koran.

Let us look for points they agree on before we examine the disagreements any further. They agree that God sometimes intervenes in the events of history—for example, God helped the Jews to escape from Egyptian slavery; He sent Jesus Christ; He revealed the Koran to Muhammad. Eastern religions would not accept that God acts in quite such ways.

They also agree that God is the Creator and Commander of all and that He created people to manage the earth for Him. It follows that people should serve Him in return. Thus people have an important role to play in God's plan and must obey God's commandments—Jewish, Christian or Muslim. If such commands are kept, then God will judge fairly, show His compassion and be willing to forgive. Jews, Christians and Muslims agree that God acts in this way.

But it is obvious that people have failed to give a good account of their care of the world throughout history (wars, massacres, neglect of the needy, etc.). They are reluctant to face the implications of creating nuclear bombs or allowing abortions to end life, for example. So people are lawless in the sense that they have failed in their responsibilities. Did God miscalculate when He chose to let people run the earth? Muslims and Christians say 'no', but they offer different explanations.

The Muslim answer to mankind's lawlessness is that people have no excuse as the Koran has revealed what they should be doing. Surah 20 says people are weak and forget, but they can be reminded and helped by the routines of regular prayer, fasting, and so on. People can do things by habit and so be 'habituated' into the life God requires of them. Furthermore the government can give a religious lead to the community. In this Muslims are similar to Zionists who talk of a Jewish state, a homeland. Christians may argue that one can defy training by habit, regardless of the fear of severe punishments. Habit training will not cope with a lost sinner, they claim—only the grace of God, the love which suffers alongside the sinner (Christ on the Cross) can do that. They argue that to solve the impasse the spirit God made Himself into flesh in the form of Jesus so as to be able to demonstrate how He wanted people to live. Then He could also demonstrate His love for the sinner by the crucifixion. For the Christian the relationship between God and people is not only one of commanding and obeying: it is also one of loving and being loved.

Thus Islam claims God sent His messenger, Muhammad, with the message of the Koran, while Christianity claims He sent His Son to lay down his life for mankind. Muslims see qualities of love and compassion in Allah, but do not accept the redeeming love theory of Christ on the Cross. Who God is, what mankind's role is and the need for commandments are agreed upon. The disagreement is on what is to be done about people who do not live up to the role required of them. It is not surprising that people's efforts to find the truth should result in disagreements as to how mankind can be brought to fulfil its role.

If we now turn to considering all religions, we find that one basic problem facing them is evil. Where does it come from? Is there an evil god, a devil, behind it? Do we all have evil within us? Buddhists and Christians say that evil is built into the human race. Buddhists claim that life is inevitably bound up in suffering and only the elimination of selfish desire can save one. Christians argue that evil can be overcome and that sin can be forgiven by the believer turning to Christ on the Cross. Shintoists argue that evil is not in-built. A purification ceremony is sufficient to restore a person's goodness. No list of do's and don't's is needed for them.

If we ask the question, 'what is the goal of history?', we will get a different viewpoint to consider. Is history's climax to be a religious or a non-religious one? Karl Marx and his followers expect a marvellous, secular, classless society to emerge. Jews, Christians and Muslims see the goal as the Day of Judgement leading to the life after death. It seems that a person really lives two lives: one here on earth, another in the 'life after death'. For Hindus, life on earth is not real as this world is an illusion (it is not permanent) and the real life will only come after countless attempts to break from this illusion. For any religious person, history acquires a meaning and a purpose when it is related to the truth—when you look beyond the changes and chances of this life to what is to follow. Life on earth by itself is an inadequate answer to the mystery of life as a whole.

Easterners are concerned with the soul's search for immortality, release from this world. Westerners are more concerned to obey God's commands. Easterners do not have a clear idea of God as Creator, Law-giver and Judge, whereas Westerners do. In the West, God commands and man obeys, and a close relationship is built up between God and His obedient servant. In the East it does not really matter if you believe in one god, several or none, as you can still find nirvana or Brahman.

In the search for truth, it is noticeable that Easterners are more willing to learn from the experiences of each other. Buddhas can be found in Taoist temples; the Japanese go to Shinto priests for marriages and the Buddhist priests for funerals. Eastern religions are more likely to appreciate that each religion presents the same truth from a different angle. Life on earth is a burden one must escape from. Buddhism offers salvation by losing oneself in nirvana, in sharp contrast to the humanists' Marxist offer of salvation on the collective farm—a spiritual solution versus a material or earthly one.

So how can we get all these religions into some kind of focus? It will help if we picture a high mountain with God, the truth of all things, sitting on the top. Down below, on all sides, humans are hunting for ways to climb to the top and find out the truth. They are bunched together in religious groups to help each other, for the climb is going to be a difficult one. Some routes will be dangerous, deceptive and misleading, so it will be sensible to follow a guide who speaks our own language. In the wooded foothills each group starts off along a different way, convinced that it is on the right track. Each religion seems to have arguments among its own members, so the Southern Buddhists set off on a different way to the Northern Buddhists, while the Orthodox Jews reject the way the Reform Jews have chosen, to say nothing of the squabbles among different Christian groups such as Roman Catholics, Quakers, Baptists and the Church of England. But as they climb higher they get clear of the woods and find their routes begin to merge. Orthodox Jews find that their strict keeping to the Jewish laws is not really so important as the fact that they and the Reformed Jews, who are not so strict, both believe that God chose the Jews as a special people. The Christian groups realize their arguments about the types of services they hold are less important than the fact that they all believe Jesus is unique as he is the Son of God in their eyes. Without the wood in the way our religious climbers can see so much more clearly what is important to believe in.

As they approach the summit those who have come up one face of the mountain will be able to see those who have come up the other side. They may find they can help each other to climb the last few metres. One thing is certain, and that is that those who arrive at the top will all meet each other. In the end there can only be one truth to find.

In this book we have set off up that mountain from many

different routes to see what happens. We have found a lot of argument over the different starting points, the rules the groups must obey to keep them together, and how the actual climbing is to be tackled. In fact there have even been arguments about what is to be found on the top of the mountain. If there were no arguments this climb of a lifetime would be a dull one indeed.

All this is important to us here and now. Worldwide travel and the migration of refugees and those seeking work has thrown us all together in the twentieth century. The multi-racial, multi-religious society is on our doorstep. We are trying out each other's ways, even if only on the level of curry and sweet-and-sour pork. Some Christians are trying versions of Hindu meditation to help them in their prayers, while Japanese Buddhists are enjoying the singing they find in Christian churches. Clearly a Buddhist is unlikely to replace Buddha with Muhammad, any more than a Christian will abandon Christ for either, but this is not so important as recognizing the good points in each other's religions. Jews make it plain that all religions have their routes to God and that Judaism is simply the best route for themselves.

> The need of the moment is not one religion, but mutual respect and tolerance of the devotees of the different religions . . . The soul of religions is one, but it is encased in the multitude of forms. The latter will persist to the end of time. (Mahatma Gandhi, a distinguished Hindu)

We should not be afraid to compare religions but learn to help each other along the road to truth. We will find a greater appreciation of our own faith if we have something to measure it by. If it cannot answer all our problems then maybe another faith will help to supply them for us. No individual human being can hope to know all.

SAMPLE PUBLIC EXAM QUESTIONS

These questions have been selected from the following exam papers:

GCE O Level
London Paper 560, Section 7, World Religions (L).
Cambridge Paper 2042/4, Men at Worship (C).
AEB Paper 155/1 Paper 1, Syllabus 2, Multi Faith (AEB).

CSE
Yorkshire and Humberside Examination Board Paper 11, Religious Education Theme C (Y).

We are grateful to the various boards for permission to reproduce them.

Chapter 2
1. How did Muhammad reform religion and what were the most important occasions in his life and prophethood? (London, June 1981, question 55)
2. 'There is no God but God (Allah) and Muhammad is the prophet of God'. Show the importance of this statement for understanding the nature of the Muslim religion. (London, June 1980, question 53)
3. Why is Medina famous in Islamic history? (one sentence answer) (Yorkshire and Humberside, 1980, question 6)
4. What are the stories called which Jesus told to illustrate his teaching? Name or identify one of these stories (two sentence answer). (Yorkshire and Humberside, 1980, question 16)
5. What teaching did Jesus of Nazareth give on THREE of the following? (a) The way in which people should treat each other. (b) Love. (c) Giving. (d) Possession. (e) The Importance of Faith. (Yorkshire and Humberside, 1980, question 25)
6. How do Muslims regard Jesus? (Yorkshire and Humberside, 1981, question 1)
7. How did the Qur'an come into existence? (Yorkshire and Humberside, 1981, question 2)

8. Name THREE denominations or branches of the Christian Church. (Yorkshire and Humberside, 1981, question 16)

Chapter 3
1. *Either* (a) Why is the Bhagavad Gita, the Song of the Lord, so highly valued in Hinduism? *Or* (b) Show how the Sikh religion recognizes the importance of the Adi Granth. (London, June 1982, question 62)
2. Why is the Torah the basis of Jewish life and thought? (London, June 1982, question 47)
3. Compare the attitudes of (a) Christians, and (b) Muslims to their scriptures. (London, June 1981, question 61)
4. In *each* of *two* faiths (a) select *one* book of scriptures and describe its origin; (b) state who was responsible for the writing down of the words in their original form; (c) explain the importance of the book you have chosen to worshippers in that faith. (AEB, specimen paper 1984 onwards, question 9)
5. (a) Describe the different kinds of literature found in the central scriptures of *two* different religious traditions. Refer in *each* case to the kinds of material contained in the passage(s) set for study in the syllabus: (b) Explain in *each* case why there is so much variety in (i) style and (ii) content. (AEB, specimen paper 1984 onwards, question 10)
6. In *each* of *two* faiths (a) describe those issues on which the teaching of the scriptures is authoritative; (b) state how the scriptures came to have authority on these issues; (c) explain the value to the faithful of having an authoritative scripture. (AEB, specimen paper 1984 onwards, question 12)
7. (a) How did the Qur'an come into existence? (b) Why have translations of the Qur'an never taken the place of the original Arabic? (c) What are the so-called 'Five Pillars of the Faith' which are to be found in the Qur'an? (Yorkshire and Humberside, 1980, question 21)
8. In which language was the Qur'an originally written? (Yorkshire and Humberside, 1981, question 6)
9. Explain the word 'torah'. (Yorkshire and Humberside, 1981, question 10)
10. (a) 'There is no god but God', the Muslim confirms in his confession of faith. Explain the Muslim's ideas as to the nature of god. (b) 'Muslims are to approach god by the path (shari'ah) of the law'. Give examples to show how the teaching of the Qur'an is reflected in the areas of public and private law. Include the penalties for breaking the law. (Yorkshire and Humberside, 1981, question 21)

Chapter 4
1. Why does Judaism regard the Sabbath as a festival? How is it observed? (London, June 1981, question 50)

2. In personal and social relationships what are the practices and behaviour which are (a) encouraged *and* (b) forbidden by Islam? (London, Jan. 1980, question 56)

3. Outline the main features and ceremonies of the Hajj (pilgrimage) in Islam. Why and for whom are Jerusalem and Amritsar important places of pilgrimage? (Cambridge, June 1982, question 6)

4. Give an account of the different beliefs held by the two groups, Hīnayāna (Theravāda) and Mahāyāna Buddhists. (Cambridge, June 1982, question 4)

5. What is learnt about Buddhist belief from the Four Noble Truths? How is Buddhist belief expressed in religious observance? (Cambridge, June 1981, question 6)

6. Explain the religious importance of (a) fasting in Islam and (b) pilgrimage in *one* religion other than Islam. (Cambridge, June 1981, question 4)

7. Write an essay on 'A Moslem at Prayer'. Include in your answer descriptions of prayer rituals, purification rituals, and the importance of these observances to a Moslem. (Cambridge, June 1979, question 2)

8. Choose *three* of the following and explain the meaning each has for a Hindu: (a) Om (Aum); (b) Moksha; (c) Samsara; (d) Karma; (e) Atman. (Cambridge, June 1979, question 6)

9. In *each* of *two* faiths (a) describe the ritual of private prayer followed daily in the home; (b) explain how much of this prayer is extempore and how much is learnt by heart or read from a book; (c) discuss the role of such prayer in the life of the believer. (AEB, specimen question paper 1984 onwards, question 6)

10. What is the Ka'bah? (one sentence answer) (Yorkshire and Humberside, 1980, question 2)

11. State two of the four basic rules underlying Islamic law. (two sentences) (Yorkshire and Humberside, 1980, question 7)

12. State TWO vices which the Jews seek to avoid. (a) ....
(b) .... (Yorkshire and Humberside, 1980, question 10)

Chapter 5

1. Describe the structure and use of (a) a mosque and (b) a gurdwara. (London, June 1982, question 59)

2. Describe the structure and use of (a) a synagogue, and (b) a mosque, showing points of similarity and difference. (London, June 1981, question 59)

3. Describe the main features of (a) a synagogue and (b) a Christian place of worship. Indicate the importance of these features for the worshippers. You may support your answer with illustrations. (Cambridge, June 1982, question 3)

4. Give an account of the structure and use of (a) a Buddhist place of worship, (b) a gurdwara. You may illustrate your answer with a sketch plan. (Cambridge, June 1981, question 2)
5. In *each* of *two* faiths select a building used for worship and explain (a) how the first buildings of this type developed; (b) what features of the building have a particular influence on the worship that is offered there; (c) whether the building is more suitable for corporate use or for individual prayer. (AEB, specimen paper 1984 onwards, question 1)
6. In *each* of *two* faiths select a building used for worship and explain (a) in which direction it normally faces; (b) which characteristic features distinguish it clearly from other buildings, secular or religious; (c) how important these distinguishing features are in the religious life of the community. (AEB, specimen paper 1984 onwards, question 2)
7. In *each* of *two* faiths select a building used for worship and explain (a) what provision is made for the congregation to sit down during the festivals and services; (b) for what activities they kneel, sit and stand; (c) the symbolism involved in the seating arrangements and in any ritual they perform sitting down. (AEB, specimen paper 1984 onwards, question 3)
8. What is the 'Shema'? (one sentence answer) (Yorkshire and Humberside, 1980, question 8)

Chapter 6
1. Explain the importance and requirements of (a) Pesach and (b) Eid-ul-Adha. (London, June 1982, question 63)
2. Describe and show the importance of (a) Durga Puja, and (b) Diwali. (London, June 1981, question 63)
3. In *each* of *two* faiths (a) describe the main features of worship that occur when a festival is celebrated; (b) select any *one* festival *not* mentioned in question 8 (question 4 below in this book) and describe its origin; (c) explain why this festival is still celebrated today. (AEB, specimen paper 1984 onwards, question 7)
4. Select *two* festivals from the following list: Pesach; Easter; Id ul Adha; Divali; Baisakhi. In *each* case (a) describe the main features of its celebration; (b) recount the story/history that underlies it; (c) explain the religious significance of the festival to those who celebrate it. (AEB, specimen paper 1984 onwards, question 8).
5. Why do the Jews observe the Feast of Weeks? (one sentence answer) (Yorkshire and Humberside, 1980, question 11)
6. What does the Jewish festival of Purim commemorate? (Yorkshire and Humberside, 1981, question 8)
7. What is the significance of the 'bitter herbs' used by the Jews at the Passover? (Yorkshire and Humberside, 1981, question 11)

8. Write about THREE of the following: (a) The Day of Atonement; (b) The 'Shema'; (c) The Feast of Tabernacles; (d) The concept of Holiness. (Yorkshire and Humberside, 1981, question 24)
9. Write about THREE of the following explaining in each case what the Christian believes and commemorates by each festival: (a) Christmas; (b) Good Friday; (c) Easter; (d) Whitsunday. (Yorkshire and Humberside, 1981, question 26)

Chapter 7

1. What marriage ceremonies are used by *either* (a) Jews, *or* (b) Sikhs? What do these ceremonies teach us about the attitude of the religion to marriage? (London, June 1981, question 66)
2. Describe and compare the initiation rites of Christianity (using any denomination) and of *one* other religion you have studied. (London, June 1980, question 62)
3. Describe and compare the initiation rites of (a) Judaism and (b) Buddhism. (Cambridge, June 1982, question 2)
4. Describe and comment on the ceremonies associated with becoming (a) a Christian, (b) a Sikh. (Cambridge, June 1981, question 3)
5. Give the substance of the sentence said by a convert to Islam. (one sentence answer) (Yorkshire and Humberside, 1980, question 1)
6. What does Islam teach about a man having more than one wife? (Yorkshire and Humberside, 1981, question 3)
7. By what ceremony are many people admitted to the Christian Church? (Yorkshire and Humberside, 1981, question 18)

Chapter 8

1. What do Muslims believe about life after death? (London, June 1982, question 58)
2. Describe the Jewish funeral practices and explain the significance of what is done. (London, Jan. 1980, question 48)

Note No other questions seem to have been set recently on the subject of death ceremonies or life after death in spite of the obvious importance of these subjects to religions.

General questions

The Cambridge paper sets a question 1 which cuts across the different subjects contained in these chapters of this book, so that it is necessary to put samples of this question below.
1. Answer all the following questions (a)–(n) as briefly as possible: (a) How does the sabbath begin in a Jewish home? (b) Name two of the sacraments of the Christian Church. (c) State one occasion when the Nicene Creed would be said. (d) Why is The Eightfold Path in Buddhism called The Middle Way? (e) What are 'banns of marriage'?

(f) Name two of the divisions of the Jewish Scriptures. (g) What is a *burning ghat* and what is it used for? (h) Name two of the sects found in Islam. (i) What is the function of (i) the *muezzin*, (ii) the *imam* in a mosque? (j) What is polygamy? Name one religion which allows this practice. (k) What is the purpose of the *langar* in Sikhism? (l) What is particular about the way Muslims bury the dead? (m) What is the importance of *ahimsa* for Hindus? (n) Distinguish between *atman* and *dharma* in Hinduism. (Cambridge, June 1982, question 1)

2. Answer all the following questions (a)–(l) as briefly as possible: (a) Give in one phrase a definition of the word 'worship'. (b) For whom is the Koran sacred scripture? What does 'Koran' mean? (c) Distinguish between sabbath and Sunday. (d) What does 'creed' mean? Name one creed used by Christians. (e) Why do mosques have (i) a fountain, (ii) a *mihrab*? (f) State two things required at the celebration of the Passover meal and indicate why each is used. (g) Why is the Bible divided into the Old and New Testaments? What does 'Testament' mean? (h) What name for God is used by (i) Moslems, (ii) Sikhs? (i) which of the Hindu scriptures is written in the form of 'instruction' for pupils? (j) Name *two* of the avataras of Vishnu. (k) Who compiled the Sikh Holy Book? (l) What do the titles *buddha* and *bodhisattva* mean and to whom is each applied? (Cambridge, June 1981, question 1)

APPENDIX 1
TABLE OF RELIGIONS

Religion	Gods	Foundation date	Founder	Holy books	Numbers today (millions)	Distribution today
Hinduism	Brahman and 360 million others	1500 BC	None in particular	Vedas Upanishads	406	India
Shintoism	Amaterasu and 8 million others	650 BC	None in particular	Kojika	35	Japan
Taoism	Numerous	570 BC	Lao-Tse	Tao Te Ching	30	China, Hong Kong
Buddhism	Not defined	530 BC	Gautama Buddha	Tripitaka Sutras	300	India, Sri Lanka, Thailand, China, Tibet, Japan, etc.
Judaism	God	1250 BC	Moses	Tenakh Torah	12	Israel Worldwide
Christianity	God	AD 1	Jesus Christ	Bible	983	Worldwide
Islam	Allah	AD 600	Muhammad	Koran	850	Turkey, Africa, Iran, Iraq, Pakistan, Indonesia, etc.
Sikhism	Nam	AD 1500	Nanak	Granth	15	India, Britain, East Africa

APPENDIX 3
A NOTE ON CALENDARS

The Gregorian calendar is used in the West and Japan. It is a solar one based on the time it takes for the world to go round the sun.

The Jewish calendar is a lunar one with normally 12 months alternating 30 and 29 days each as a lunar month is actually 29½ days. The year starts on Rosh Hashanah in the autumn.

The Islamic calendar is a lunar one with 12 months alternating 30 and 29 days; a total of 354 days. In a 30 year cycle there are 11 leap years. Each year begins 11–12 days earlier than the previous one, doing a complete cycle in 32½ years. AD 1983 is AH 1404. The first day of the year is called Day of Hijrah.

The Saka calendar of Southern India became the official calendar of India in 1957. It is used alongside the Gregorian calendar. But festival dates may be calculated by other calendars in use in India.

In China, the Gregorian calendar was accepted in 1912, but festival dates are calculated from the old lunar calendar, which begins on the first full moon after the sun has entered into the constellation of Aquarius.

The Religious Education Centre, West London Institute of Higher Education, Isleworth, Middx, TW5 5DU, compiles an up-to-date festivals calendar each year for the Shap Working Party. It is published by the Commission for Racial Equality.

APPENDIX 4
A NOTE ON BIBLE REFERENCES

Bible references are given in the form:

Gen. 1:1

| Abbreviation of book | Chapter number | Verse number |

Abbreviations used are as follows:

Old Testament		*New Testament*	
Gen.	Genesis	Matt.	Matthew
Exod.	Exodus	Mark	Mark
Lev.	Leviticus	Luke	Luke
Num.	Numbers	John	John
Deut.	Deuteronomy	Rom.	Romans
Judg.	Judges	1 Cor.	1 Corinthians
Neh.	Nehemiah	2 Cor.	2 Corinthians
Esther	Esther	Gal.	Galatians
Job	Job	Eph.	Ephesians
Ps.	Psalm	1 Thess.	1 Thessalonians
Pss.	Psalms	1 Tim.	1 Timothy
Prov.	Proverbs	2 Tim.	2 Timothy
Eccles.	Ecclesiastes	1 Pet.	1 Peter
Isa.	Isaiah	Rev.	Revelation
Zech.	Zechariah		

Apocrypha

1 Macc. 1 Maccabees

PICTURE CREDITS

The author and publishers are grateful to the following who provided photographs and gave permission for reproduction:

ATV Licensing Ltd (p. 30)
The *Baptist Times* (p. 191—left)
Barnaby's Picture Library (pp. 97, 116, 128, 135, 158 and 168)
BBC Hulton Picture Library (pp. 17, 98, 136, 141 and 189)
The British Library (pp. 54 and 60—right)
Church Information Office and the United Society for the Propagation of the Gospel (p. 222)
Church Missionary Society and Rev J R Harwood (p. 103)
The *Gloucester Citizen* (p. 173)
Director, Cheltenham Cemetery (p. 224)
Gloucester Photographic Agency and King's School, Gloucester (p. 171)
The *Guardian* (p. 60—left)
Hong Kong Tourist Association (p. 164)
The *Jewish Chronicle* (p. 169)
G K Johnston (p. 214)
Lutterworth Press (pp. 154 and 202)
Ann & Bury Peerless (p. 11)
Popperfoto (pp. 74, 118, 140, 146, 152, 157, 159 and 209)
Religious Society of Friends (p. 102)
Canon C Rhodes (p. 191—right)

We also wish to thank the following who provided illustrations for copying:

Methodist Church Press Service, for their ticket of membership (p. 193)
Percy Thomas Partnership, for their architectural plan of the ground floor of Clifton Cathedral (p. 141)
The Salvation Army, for their 'More than a cuppa' poster (p. 34)

INDEX AND GLOSSARY

(H) = Hindu; (Sh) = Shinto; (T) = Taoist; (B) = Buddhist; (J) = Jewish; (C) = Christian; (I) = Islamic; (S) = Sikh.

annulment (C), wiping out of a marriage, 196

Anointing of the sick (C), sacrament, 222–3

Antiochus Epiphanes (J), revolt leader, 170

Apocrypha (J), a holy book, 58, 170, 244

apostle, see disciple

Apostles' Creed (C), statement of beliefs, see Creed

Adq Nikah (I), wedding ceremony, 198

Aqiqa (I), name-giving ceremony, 197

Arabs, 40

Arafat, Mount, 120

arahat or arhat (B), a person who has reached nirvana, 90, 219

archdeacon (C), Church of England clergyman in charge of an area, 33

Ardas (S), a prayer, 122, 152, 203

ardhamandapa (H), temple porch, 125–6

Ardhangi (S), 'better' half, 203

arhat (B), see arahat

Arjan (S) (1563–1606), a guru, 45, 64, 176

Arjuna Pandava (H), hero of the Bhagavad Gita, 49–50

Ark (J), cupboard for the Torah, 136–8, 167

Arkan (I), see Five Pillars of Wisdom

arti (H), the worship of light, 127

Articles of War (C), Salvation Army's statement of beliefs, 192

asanas (H), body postures, 72

Ascension Day (C), the day Jesus returned to heaven, 31, 62, 174

Ash Wednesday (C), the day on which Lent begins, 172

'asr (I), afternoon prayer, 112

As-Sirat Bridge (I), crossed by the dead above the abyss of hell, 226

Assemblies of God (C), a Christian church formed in 1924, 35

Association of Chinese Buddhists (B), 20

Assumption of the Blessed Virgin Mary (C), her going up into heaven, 174

Assyria, 22–3

Athanasian Creed (C), statement of Christian beliefs, see Creed

atheist, one who believes there is no god, 2

atman (H), one's real self, 8, 47, 48, 69, 73, 211

Atonement Day, day of penitence to secure good relationship with God (J), 167–8; (C), 225

Augustine of Hippo (C), medieval Christian leader, 194

AUM or OM (H), sacred syllable which is said or chanted, 71, 127, 178, 180, 241

Auspicious Alliance Canon Register (T), priest's list of spirits, 15

avatar, avatāra (H), the form in which a god appears, 9–10

ayat (I), a verse of the Koran, 60

Ayatollah Khomeini (I), ruler of Iran, 40

azzan (I), call to prayer, 113, 197

Babylonia, Babylonians, 22

Bad Dogs Village (T), where souls are put to the test, 217

Badr, Battle of (T), 38

Bairam (I), see Id-al-'adha

Baisakhi (S), Khalsa's festival, 176

Bait-ul-hah (I), House of God, 119

Balfour Declaration on Zionism, 1917 (J), 24

Banns of Marriage (C), public announcement of marriage-to-be, 195

Baptism, initiation ceremony (C), 32, 33, 35, 141, 144, 174, 190–5; (S), 64, 199–202

Baptist Church (C), church founded in 1612, 33, 144–5, 191–2

Bar Mitzvah (J), boy's coming of age ceremony, 187

Bath Mitzvah (J), girl's coming of age ceremony, 187–8

Beatitudes (C), sayings of Jesus, 53

Beautiful Names of Allah (I), 39, 63, 150, 197

Becket, Thomas à (C), martyr, 109

Believer's Baptism (C), adult baptism of a believer, 191–3

Belur, centre for Ramakrishna Mission, 11

Benares (H), pilgrimage centre, India, 16, 73, 74, 209

beth din (J), house of law, court, 138, 190

Bethlehem (C), place of Jesus' birth, 27

Bhagavad-Gita (H), 'Song of the Lord', holy book, 49, 71, 127, 209

bhajans (H), hymns, 127

Bhakti Yoga (H), path of love and devotion, 10, 50, 71, 126

Bharatas, Wars of (H), 48

251

Jagannatha (H), Lord of the Universe, a title applied to Vishnu or Krishna, 156

Jamrat (I), stoning of the devil, 120

Janamashtami (H), Krishna's birthday festival, 155–6

Janeu (H), see Sacred Thread

Japan, 11–13, 19, 20, 134, 165, 212, 232, 233, 243

Japji (S), morning prayer, 122

jati (H), birth caste group, 67–8, 180, 212

Jeremiah (J), prophet (active 627–580 BC), 23, 55

Jerusalem, 25, 29, 32, 100, 136, 137, 138, 172, 174, 189

Jesus Christ (C), Son of God, 7, 11, 18, 23, 27–32, 40, 58–62, 73, 100–1, 103, 107, 108, 112, 138, 141–5, 171–4, 191–2, 201, 222, 224–5, 230–1, 232

Jews, see Judaism

jihad (I), holy war, 38, 40

jinja (Sh), kami house in Sanctuary Shinto, 13, 127–30

jiva (H), soul, 210–11

Jnana Kanda (H), a section of the scriptures, 47

Jnana Veda Yoga (H), the Path of Knowledge, 69–70

Job (J, C), a book of the Old Testament, 56

Jodo-shu (B), Pure Land sect, 94

John the Baptist, prophet who baptized Jesus, 27

John, St. (C), Gospel, 58

Jordan, River, 22

Joseph (I), chapter in Koran, 61

Joshua (J), Jewish leader, 55

joss sticks (T), 130–1, 214–15; (B), 133

Judah, Judea (J), kingdom of, 20, 22

Judaism, 7, 20–6, 27, 32, 38, 46, 55–7, 59, 61, 95–100, 110, 136–8, 165–70, 187–90, 194, 207, 221–3, 229–31, 243

Judas Maccabeus (J), cleansed the Temple (165 BC), 170

Judgement Day, see Day of Judgement

juggernaut (H), processional chariot, 156

Jupiter (T), 184

K's, The Five (S), membership symbols, 43, 200–1, 227

Ka'ba (I), centrepoint of Islamic worship, 37, 38, 42, 118–20

kachs (S), shorts, one of the Five K's, 200–1

Kaddish (J), santification prayer, 138, 221

Kagura-den (Sh), ceremonial dance place, 128, 159

Kaijin-Matsuri (Sh), sea-kami festival, 160

Kālī (H), goddess, wife of Shiva, 9, 11

Kali yuga (H), era, 9, 10, 48

kalif (I), successor or leader, 40

Kalimah (I), see Shahāda

Kalu (S), Nanak's father, 41

Kama (H), god of love, 155

kameeze (S), tunic, 203

kami (Sh), gods, 11–13, 75, 76–8, 127–9, 158–60, 181–2, 212–13

kamidana (Sh), god-shelf, 13, 77, 161

kamikaze (Sh), one who dies for State Shintoism, 13

Kandy, Sri Lankan town with Sacred Tooth of Buddha Temple, 133

kanga (S), comb, one of the Five K's, 200–1

kara (S), steel bracelet, one of the Five K's, 200–1

karah parshad (S), sacred food eaten at worship time, 153, 177, 199, 201, 203

karashishi (Sh), Chinese lion statues, 127

kari-ginu (Sh), priest's robes, 129

Karma Kanda (H), a section of scriptures, 47

karma, law of deeds (H), 47, 68, 86, 210–12; (B), 86, 87, 94, 186

Karma Yoga (H), The Path of Works, 71–2

Karuna (B), compassion meditation, 89

kasina (B), object concentrated on in meditation, 88

Kaur (S), title of 'princess' given to girls who join the Warrior Sikhs, 200

Kauravas (H), see Kurus

keisaka (B), wooden stick used to keep Zen monks alert during meditation, 93

kesh (S), long hair, one of the Five K's, 200–1

Kesh Dhari Singhs (S), Warrior Sikhs, 199–203

Kessai (Sh), see Misogi

Ketubah (J), wedding contract, 188

Ketubim (J), The Writings, a section of the Tenakh or Old Testament, 55–6

Khadija (I), Muhammad's wife, 36–8

khalifah (I), viceregent, manager, 110

Khalsa (S), the brotherhood, 43–4, 122, 176, 200

Lourdes (C), pilgrimage centre for sick, 109
low church (C), see evangelical
Lu (T), list of spirits, 81–2
Luke, St. (C), Gospel, 58
Lu-pan (T), carpentry god, 15
Luther, Martin (C), founder of Lutheran Church (1517), 32
Lutheran Church (C), 32

Maccabeus, Judas (J), cleansed the Temple (165 BC), 170
maga (Sh), evil, 76
Magatsuhi (Sh), evil spirits, 76, 213
Magga (B), Fourth Noble Truth, 86–7
maghrib (I), sunset prayer, 113
Mahabharata (H), 'Great Battle of Bharatas', an epic poem, 48–9
mahamandapa (H), temple nave, 125–6
Mahāyāna (B), big raft or vehicle of Northern Buddhism, 18–20, 54, 90–1, 92–4, 133–5, 165, 220
Mahdi (I), the last Imām, ninth century AD, 40
mahr (I), marriage gift, 198
Maitreya (B), the 'Buddha-to-come', 133
mala (S), rosary, 122
Malik, 41–2
man (S), mental service, 123
mandala (H), a volume, 47
mandapa (H), see mahamandapa
mandir (H), place of worship, 125–6
Manji Sahib (S), stool, 151
manna (J), plant lice or gum resin, 98–9
mantra, verse (H), 47; (C), 106
Manu (H), primieval man, 10, 50
Manu, The Laws of (H), see Laws of Manu
Manushi Buddhas (B), man-buddhas, 19
Māra (B), King of Passions, 17, 18
Mark, St. (C), Gospel, 58
marriage (H), 50, 70, 71, 180–1; (Sh), 181–2; (T), 131, 184–5, 186; (J), 96, 137, 138, 188–90; (C), 32, 35, 194–6; (I), 63, 198–9; (S), 64, 202–4
Marwa (I), hill involved in Hajj pilgrimage, 119
Marx, Karl (1818–83), 231, 232
Mary (C), Jesus' mother, Blessed Virgin Mary, 27, 61–2, 107, 109, 141, 174

Mass (C), name for Roman Catholic Communion service, 141–2, 172, 224
Matins (C), morning service, 142
Matsuri (Sh), festival, 158–60
Matthew, St. (C), Gospel, 58, 194
matzoth cakes (J), 166–7
Matzu, or Ma-Chu (T), goddess of fishermen, 15, 162
Maulid-an-Nabi (I), Muhammad's birthday, 175
Maundy Thursday (C), commemoration of day Jesus held the Last Supper, 172
maya, visible things which seem real but are not (H), 69, 96, 121, 208; (S), 121, 231
Maysya (H), Fish God, first incarnation of Vishnu, 9–10
Mazel Tov (J), 'good luck', a greeting, 189
mazzah, or matzoth cakes (J), 166–7
Mecca (I), Islamic holy city, 36, 37–8, 42, 61, 113, 119, 120, 149, 175, 176, 226
Medina, 37–8, 61, 176
meditation (H), 72–3, 76, 126, 233, see also Raja Yoga; (Sh), 76–7; (T), 81–2; (B), 20, 88–90, 91, 93–4, 134; (C), 106–8, 147; (S), 65, 122
meditation hall (B), see semmon dojo
Meelad ul-Nabi (I), see Maulid an-Nabi
meeting house (C), Quaker worship place, 33, 147–8, 223
mei-jen (T), go-betweens who make marriage arrangements, 184
Meiji (Sh), shrine at Tokyo, 129
melas (S), festival meeting, 176
menorah (J), seven- or eight-branch candlestick, 170
Mercury (T), 184
Mercy, Goddess of (T, B), see Kuan Yin
mercy seat, or penitent's form (C), Salvation Army, seat for those in need, 108, 145
Messiah (J), 23, 24, 25, 99–100, 166, 221–3; (C), 23, 28–9, 58–9, 62; (I), 38, 62
Methodists (C), denomination inspired by John Wesley in eighteenth century, 33, 104, 108, 193, 194
Metta Bhāvanā (B), love meditation, 89
mezuzah (J), container for Shema which is hung on door posts, 187
michi (Sh), the way of the kami, 75

miao (T), village temples, 131

Middle Path (B), the Buddhist way to the truth, or way of life, 86

Midrash (J), part of the Talmud, 57

mihrab (I), niche in temple pointing to Mecca, 113, 149

miki (Sh), sacred rice wine, 159

miko (Sh), temple girls, 129

mikoshi (Sh), palanquin, 159, 160

milani (S), wedding meeting, 203

Milinda, King, Greek king who inquired about Buddhism, 53–4

Milinda-Panha (B), Questions to King Milinda, 53–4, 90

Mina (I), place involved in Hajj pilgrimage, 120

minaret (I), mosque's tower, 112, 113, 149–50

minbar (I), pulpit, 149

minister (C), see clergyman

miracles (J), 25; (C), 27

Mirror of Retribution (T), 217

Mishnah (J), legal rulings, 57

Misogi (Sh), water purification rite, 76–7

Missing Persons Bureau (C), run by Salvation Army, 34–5

mitama-shiro (Sh), god-substitute, 128

mitzuots (J), instructions, 24

Mogen David (J), Star of David, 241

Mogul Emperor of India (I), 43, 176

moksha, release from wordly life, from reincarnation, hence salvation (H), 69, 211; (S), 43

momentary gods, 3

monastery (B), see Sangha

monkey god (H), see Hanuman

monks (B), see Sangha

monotheism, belief in a single god, 8

Mool Mantra (S), sacred chant, 64

Morocco, 198

Moses (J), leader (c 1300 BC), 21–2, 55, 61, 95, 137, 189

Moslem, see Muslim

mosque (I), place of worship, 40, 61, 63, 112, 113, 123, 148–50, 225

Mother goddess (T), 182–4

Motor Cycle Crash Helmets (Religious Exemptions) Act, 1976 (S), 201

Mount Arafat (I), involved in Hajj pilgrimage, 120

Mount of Mercy (I), see Mount Arafat

Mount Sinai (J), place where God gave Moses the Ten Commandments, 22, 55, 95

mourning (T), 215–16; (J), 221; (C), 223; (I), 226; (S), 227

Mudita (B), sympathetic or joy meditation, 89

muezzin (I), prayer leader, 113, 150

Muhammad (I) (AD 570–632), Allah's prophet, 7, 36–40, 60–1, 63, 111, 112, 113, 117, 175, 176, 199, 201, 230–1

Muja-Mairi (Sh), temple visit, 181

musalta (I), prayer mat, 113

Muslim (I), 'a surrendered man', follower of Muhammad, see Islam

Muzdalijah (I), 120

Nagasena (B), a monk who explained Buddhism in Milinda-Panha, 53–4

nakōdo (Sh), matchmaker for wedding, 182

Nam (S), 'Name', Sikh word for God, 41–2, 44–5, 122–3, 152–3, 200, 227

Nam Simran (S), 'calling God to mind' meditation, 122

Nanak, Guru (S), (1469–1538) founder of Sikhism, 7, 41–3, 64, 120–3, 176, 202–4, 227–8

Nanakana, village in Pakistan, 41

Naorai (Sh), communion meal, 159

Nara-Sinha (H), Man-Lion God, fourth incarnation of Vishnu, 10

National Association of Shinto Shrines, 13

Nativity play (C), Christmas play about Jesus' birth, 171–2

Navaratri (H), Durga's festival, 156

nave (C), congregational part of a church, 138–9, 141, 143

Nei Tan (T), inner elixir, 81

Nero, Roman emperor, 58, 59

ner tamid (J), lamp of perpetual light, 137

Nevi'im (J), prophet section of the Tanakh, 55–6

New Testament (C), section of the Bible, 32, 58–60, 142, 191, 244

New Year (Sh), 160; (T), 83, 162–3; (B), 165; (J), 167; (I), 175–6

Nicene Creed (C), statement of Christian beliefs, 142, 225

Night of Power (I), see Lailat-al-Qadr, 37

Pesach, or Passover (J), festival of unleavened bread, 166–7

Peter, St. (C), Jesus' disciple, 59

Pharaoh of Egypt, 21, 22

Philosophical Taoism, see Tao Chia

phylactery (J), small scripture container, 97–8

Piares (S), 'loved ones', 200

Pilate, Roman governor of Jerusalem in Christ's time, 29

pilgrimages (H), 73–5, 156; (Sh), 78; (J), 100, 168; (C), 109; (I), 63, 118–20, 149; (S), 65, 123

plagues (J), 22, 137, 166

P'o (T), earthly soul, 213

Pochama (H), God of Smallpox, 10

polygamy, multiple marriage, 229; (H), 181; (J), 188; (C), 194; (I), 32, 198

polytheism, belief in many gods, 7–8

Pope (C), head of the Roman Catholic Church, 32, 109, 172

pradakshina (H), processional passage of temple, 75, 126

pranayama (H), controlled breathing, 72

prasad (H), sacred food, 126–7

pratyahara (H), 'being alone', fifth step of Raja Yoga, 73

prayer (H), 71–2, 126–7; (Sh), 77–8, 129, 130; (T), 131; (B), 88–90, 93, 132–5; (J), 97–9, 137–8, 141, 168; (C), 106–8, 138–40, 142–7; (I), 112–16, 150; (S), 122–3, 151–3; see also meditation

Prayer Books (C), Church of England, 194, 195, 223–4

prayer flags (B), 135

prayer-mat (I), musalta, 113, 150

prayer wheels (B), 134–5

Presbyterian Church (C), 33

preserver god (H), see Vishnu

priest (Sh), 76–7, 128–9, 158–61, 182, 212, 232; (T), 81–3, 161–2, 164, 183–4, 214; (B), 133; (J), 131, 136; (C), 32–3, 107, 138, 140, 141, 142, 143, 172, 174, 190–1, 194, 196; see also clergyman, brahmin

Prince of the Wheel (T), 217

Promised Land of the Jews, 22

prophet (J), wise man, 22–3, 27, 62, 112; (I); see also Muhammad

Prophets (J, C), section of the Tenakh or Old Testament, 55–6

prostration (I), a position during prayer emphasizing submission, 113, 115

Protestant churches (C), those rejecting papal rule, 32–5, 58, 225

Psalms (J, C), book of songs in Tenakh or Old Testament, 55, 137, 142, 167

P'u-shien (B), a bodhisattva, 19

P'u Tu (T), Ghosts' Festival, 163

pūjā (H), an act of worship, shrine room or god-shelf, 71, 72, 126–7; (B), communal worship, 133

pulpit, place where preacher delivers a sermon (C), 141–4; (I), 149

Punjab, 45, 64, 153

Puranas (H), 'Old Writings' popularizing the Vedas, 50

Pure Land of the Western Paradise (B), a Buddhist sect, 94, 220

Purgatory, stage between earthly life and heavenly life (T), 215; (C), 224

purification rituals (Sh), 76–7, 129, 160, 212, 231; (T), 83

Purim (J), Feast of Esther who saved the Jews in Persia, 170

pyre (H), wood pile for funeral, 208–10

Qibla (I), the 'direction' wall of a mosque on side facing Mecca, 113, 149

Quakers (C), see Society of Friends

Qur'an (I), see Koran

rabbi (J), learned man, leader, 57, 136–8, 167–8, 188–90

ragas (S), tunes, 64

ragis (S), musicians, 151

Rahiras (S), Holy Path prayer, 122

rain control (T), 163

Raja Yoga (H), Path of Psychological Exercises, 72–3

rakat (I), prayer sequence, 112–16, 150

rakhi (H), red-gold protection thread, 156

Raksha Bandham (H), protection festival, 156

Rama (H), Brahman's son, 10

Rama-candra (H), seventh incarnation of Vishnu, 10, 11, 48, 73, 156–7

songsters (C), Salvation Army female choir with tambourines, 145

So-sai (Sh), funeral rite, 212

Soubrious, Bernadette (C), she saw Virgin Mary at Lourdes (1858), 109

soul, 206–7; (H), 8, 47, 210–11, see also Jiva, Atman; (Sh), 212–13; (B), 85, 213–17, 219, 220, 221–3; (C), 107–8, 224–5; (S), 227; see also spirits of the dead

Southern Buddhism, see Theravāda Buddhism

Spirit Cloud Sect (T), a Tao Chiao sect, 15

spirits of the dead (H), 210–11; (Sh), 212–13; (T), 213–16; (B), 219; (J), 221–3; see also ancestors, soul

Spirit Road (T), ritual road for the soul to purgatory, 215–17

Sri Lanka, 10, 18, 20, 48, 132, 133, 165

Sruti, Shruti (H), 'hearings', a group of holy books, 46–8

Star of David (J), 241

State Shinto, Kokka, or Sanctuary Shinto, ended in 1946, 13

Stations of the Cross (C), 14 stages of Jesus' last hours before crucifixion, 141, 173

stoning the devil (I), part of the Hajj pilgrimage, 120

stoup (C), basin containing holy water, 141

stūpa (B), relic chamber, temple, 132

subha (I), rosary for counting Allah's names, 39, 150

Sudras (H), unskilled class, 67

suffering (B), see Dukkha

Suffering Servant (C), term for Jesus, 29

Sufis (I), 'wearers of undyed wool', mystical sect, 40

Suhkāvati (B), see Pure Land of Western Paradise

sukha (H), good experiences, 210–11

Sukhākara (B), see Pure Land of Western Paradise

sukkah (J), rough shelters, tabernacles, 168–70

Sukkoth (J), Feast of Tabernacles, harvest time, 168–70

Sunday (C), holy day as Jesus rose from dead on a Sunday, 142

Sun goddess (Sh), see Amaterasu

Sunnah (I), rules of life, 63, 111

Sunni (I), largest Islamic sect, 40, 64

Surahs (I), chapters of the Koran, 37–8, 60

Susanoo (Sh), storm god, 12

Sūtras (B), 'threads', collection of rules or sayings, 54

Sūtras Yoga (H), yoga exercises, written AD 100–200, 50

Sutta Pitaka (B), Teaching Basket, one of the Tripitaka books, 52–3

suttee (H), widow's death on husband's funeral pyre, 210

synagogue (J), place of worship, 23, 56, 136–8, 167, 170, 187, 221

Synod (C), governing body of the Church of England, 33

Synoptic Gospels (C), Matthew, Mark, Luke and John, 58

sze (B), temple in China, 133, 134

tabernacle (J), shelter built for Sukkot, 168–70

Tabernacle (C), cupboard for the Blessed Sacrament, 141

Tabernacles, Feast of (J), Sukkot, 168–70

Tai Chi (T), the pattern of Yin and Yang, 78

Taiwan, 15, 20, 131, 161

takht (S), 'throne', the stand for the Granth, 150–2

Talāq (I), repudiation for divorce, 199

talisman (T), 162

tallith (J), prayer shawl, 98, 136, 137, 187, 211

Talmud (J), 'traditions', holy book which explains the Torah, 57, 190

Talwandi, 41

Tama (Sh), soul, 212–13

tan (S), physical service, 123

tanhā (B), craving for things, 85–6, 219

tankha (S), penance, 201–2

Tantra (H), 'Rule System', books on Shaktism, 50

Tao (T), 'The Way', 14, 51–2, 78, 79, 80, 81, 161, 184

Tao Chia (T), Philosophical Taoism, 15, 79–81, 83

Tao Chiao (T), Religious Taoism, 15, 52, 79, 81–3, 161–2

Tao-Te Ching (T), The Way and Its Power, holy book written 350–300 BC, 14, 51–2, 80

Tao Chun (T), controller of Yin and Yang, 15, 164; see also Three Pure Ones

Tao Tsang (T), collection of books made in 1436, 15, 52

Taoism, 7, 14–16, 51–2, 78–83, 130–1, 161–4, 182–5, 213–18, 232

Taoist Master (T), priest, 81–3, 161–2, 215

tawaf (I), pilgrim's walk round the Ka'ba, 119

Te (Power) of the Tao (Way) (T), 14, 81–3, 161

tefillin (J), small scripture container, 97–8, 137

Tegh Bahadur (S), ninth guru (1621–75), 64, 176

Tel Aviv, 24

Temizu (Sh), a purifying wash, 77, 128

temples, Chapters 5, 6; see also (H), Mandir; (Sh), jinjas, kyokai; (T), kuans, miao; (B), chedis, chorten, dāgoba, pagodas, shukubos, stūpa, szes; wats; (J), synagogue, Jerusalem temple; (C), cathedral, chapel, church, citadel, meeting house; (I), mosque; (S), gurdwara

Temple at Jerusalem (J), 23, 57, 100, 138, 166–7, 168, 170, 189

Temple of Heaven, Peking (T), 131

Temple of the Sacred Tooth of Buddha, Kandy, Sri Lanka, 133

Tenakh (J), holy book containing Torah, Prophets and Writings, 55–7

Ten Commandments (J, C), 22, 55, 61, 95–6, 100, 111, 136, 137, 167

Ten Days of Return (J), Ten Penitential Days, annual penance period, 137, 166

Ten Penitential Days, see Ten Days of Return

Tenri-kyo (Sh), Divine Wisdom sect, 75–6

Thailand, 18, 20, 91, 132

Theravāda Buddhism, Way of the Elders or Southern Buddhism, 18–20, 52, 54, 132–3, 165, 186

Three Baskets (B), Tripitaka, scriptures of Theravāda Buddhists, 52–3

Three-Body Doctrine (B), 19

Three Jewels (B), Buddha, Dharma and Sangha, 133; see also Three Refuges

Three Precious Ones (B), 134

Three Pure Ones (T), San Ch'ing, the Lords of Heaven, Earth and Man, 15, 162; see also Jade Emperor, Tao Chun, Lao Tse

Three or Triple Refuges (B), referring to the Three Jewels, 133, 186, 218

Three Treasures (T), 51, 80

Thunder Magic (T), 82–3

thunderblocks (T), vajra, used to summon the thunder power, 83

Tibet, 19, 20, 92, 134

Ticket of Membership (C), Methodists' commitment card, 193

tilaka (H), red spot on forehead indicating blessedness, 180

Tokyo, 129

Tok-yo-no-kuni (Sh), Land of Tokyo, 213

tongues, speaking in (C), Holy Spirit speaking through a person, 35, 174, 193

Torah (J), The Law, section of the Tenakh holy book, 24, 25, 55–7, 61, 99, 136, 137, 170, 187

torana (H), entrance gateway to temple, 125

torii (Sh), 'bird perches', arches at approach of temple, 78, 127–9, 241

toro (Sh), stone lanterns at approach of temple, 127–8

tortoise god (H), see Kurma

transepts (C), the 'arms' of a church, 138–9, 143

transmigration of souls, see rebirth

treyfah (J), forbidden foods, 99

Triad (H), three gods, Brahma, Shiva, Vishnu, 9, 71

Trinity (C), 'three-in-one', referring to God the Father, Son and Holy Spirit, 31, 62, 107

Tripitaka (B), Three Baskets, scriptures of Theravāda Buddhists, 52–3, 54

Triple Refuges (B), see Three Refuges

Trumpets Festival (J), see Rosh Hashanah, New Year festival

turban (S), 151, 176, 201, 203

T'u Ti Kung (T), earth god, 15

Twelve Tribes of Israel (J), 22, 28

Tzau Wang (T), kitchen god, 15, 83, 162–3

Uhud, battle of (I) (AD 625), 38

Ujigami (Sh), god of ancestors, 12, 181–2

Unction, Sacrament of (C), to aid the extremely ill, 222–3

Underworld, King of (T), Yen Lo, 163–4

United Reformed Church (C), formed in 1972, 33

Universe, Lord of (H), Japannatha, 156

Unleavened Bread, Feast of (J), Pesach or Passover, 166–7

untouchables (H), see pariahs

Upanayana (H), 'Drawing near' rite of the Sacred Thread, 178–80

Upanishads (H), a Sruti sacred book, 'Sit down near', 9, 47, 69, 211

Upekkhā (B), balanced mind meditation, 89

Vaishnavism (H), sect supporting Vishnu, 10

vaisyas (H), farmer, merchant, official class, 67

vajra (T), thunderblocks, used to summon thunder power, 83

Valmiki (H), wiseman (c 300 BC), 48

Vāmana (H), dwarf god, fifth incarnation of Vishnu, 10

Vana Prastha (H), retirement stage of Jnana Veda Yoga, 70

Varāha (H), boar god, third incarnation of Vishnu, 10

varna (H), occupational classes, 67, 212, 220, 227

Varuna (H), god of space, 10

Vatican (C), Pope's palace and administration centre of Roman Catholic Church, 32

vedana (B), feelings skandhas, 219

Vedanta (H), alternative name for Upanishads, which see

Vedanta Hindus (H), 8, 11, 16

Vedantism (H), Knowledge of God, a better name than Hinduism, 8, 11

Vedas (H), 'Divine knowledge', one of the Sruti holy books, 47, 50, 68, 126

Venus (T), 184

Vesak (B), Wesak, Buddha's Birthday Festival, 165

vicar (C), priest in charge of a parish, 33

Vijaya Dashami (H), Da Sera, Festival of Warriors, Durga's festival, 156–7

vijra (T), see vajra

vimana (H), temple's central sanctuary, 125–6

Vinaya Pitaka (B), Discipline Basket, one of the Tripitaka books, 52

vinnāna (B), thinking power skandhas, 219

Vipaassana (B), insight meditation, 89–90

Virgin Mary (C), Jesus' mother, see Mary

Vishnu, Preserver God (H), 9–10, 16, 48, 71, 156, 178; (B), 16

Vrindaban (H), pilgrimage centre, 74

Waheguru (S), 'Wonderful Lord' prayer, 122, 152

Wailing, or Western Wall of the Jerusalem Temple (J), 100

Wai Tan (T), external elixir, 81

Wales, 33

Warriors, Festival of (H), see Vijaya Dashami

wat (B), worship centre, 132, 133

water, cleansing agent (H), 74, 208; (Sh), 76–7, 158; (T), 185; (C), 190–4; (I), 113–14, 148–9, 197, 225; (S), 199, 201, 227

Water Festival (B), 165

Way of the Elders (B), see Theravāda Buddhism

Way of Virtue (B), see Dhammapada

Weeks Festival (J), Shavuoth or Pentecost, 167

Wen-shu (B), Lord of Knowledge and Meditation, 134

Wesak (B), Vesak, Buddha's Birthday Festival, 165

Wesley, John and Charles (C), founders of Methodism, 4, 33, 104, 108, 193

West Indian New Testament Church of God (C), 35

Western Paradise, Pure Land of (B), 19, 94, 134, 220; see also Amida

Westminster Confession (C), statement of belief (1648), 26

Wheel of the Law (T), 217; (B), 87, 241; see also Dharma-chakra

whirling dervishes (I), Sufi sect, 40

Whit Sunday (C), festival marking gift of Holy Spirit, 174

wisdom, god of (H), see Ganesha

Wise Men (C), men guided by a star to Jesus' birthplace, 172

World Council of Churches (C), 35

worship, see prayer

wrestling (Sh), 160

Writings (J, C), part of the Tenakh or Old Testament, 55–6

wudu (I), act of cleansing before prayer, 113–14, 148

Wu-wei (T), the non-effort way, 80–1

Yad Vashem (J), 'A Place and a Name', the Holocaust Memorial, 100

Yagyopavit (H), Sacred Thread samskāra, Janeu, 178–80